AF487187

Praise for *American Salvation*

"Gregg Coodley's painstakingly researched historical book *American Salvation: How Immigrants Made America Great* focuses on the contributions that immigrants made to the US... This book deftly and uniquely addresses a subject that has been the center of intense political and social discourse... This book is filled with invaluable, thought-provoking, and paradigm-challenging material that challenges conventional wisdom... Among the best historical writings now in print, it is notable for its meticulous attention to the background from which America emerged. It is a read that makes use of well-chosen words, simple language, perceptive conclusions, and a basis of thoughtful analysis. *American Salvation: How Immigrants Made America Great* transforms fear into hope and emphasizes the crucial part that every one of us plays in determining our common destiny."

Ephantus Muriuki, *Feathered Quill*

"Coodley's book looks at how important immigrants have been for America and its history...(it) is thought-provoking and well-written. It should be required reading for every citizen who votes, especially people who are interested in history and politics.
"RECOMMENDED by the *US Review.*"

The US Review of Books

"*American Salvation,* by Gregg Coodley, offers a fascinating exploration of the critical role immigrants have played in shaping the United States...(it) is a valuable read for anyone interested in the history of immigration in America... Coodley's thorough research and balanced approach make it a compelling and informative text... the book is well worth your time."

Literary Titan

"*American Salvation* is both a history of the grand currents and rip-tides of changing US immigrant policy and a more intimate narrative of individual immigrants who have enriched and renewed this country. The book surveys the powerful role immigrants have played in US industry, entertainment, science, politics and technology, fortifying the case that...the vitality and resourcefulness of immigrants is clearly what made America great."

William McRae, author, *Moon Oregon*

"This in depth work examines the pivotal role of immigrants in shaping the United States...Gregg Coodley put a lot of research and enthusiasm into crafting an enlightening journey through the tapestry of immigrant experiences in America...The narrative style is clean, confident and as concise as you'd want a good historical account to be, but there's a warmth and positivity that runs subtly below the surface for an inclusive and enthusiastic overall feel... *American Salvation* is a recommended read for anyone interested in American social history and its relevance to the here and now."

K.C. Finn, *Readers Favorite*

"*American Salvation*...stands out with its unique approach of intricately weaving together the stories of various immigrants... Gregg Coodley's vivid prose and meticulous historical research [in] this book promises an enlightening and thought-provoking exploration of a pivotal era in American history. The research in this one book is outstanding. Being a history buff, I was enchanted by all this book reveals."

Suzie Housley, *Midwest Book Review*

Praise for *Patients in Peril*

Literary Titan "Five Stars"—Winner, *Literary Titan* Gold Medal Award for Best Books by Small Presses in 2023

"Coodley writes an easily readable text for almost anyone. This book belongs on the required reading list for college."

United States Review of Books

"His revelations are terrifying and compelling... Highly recommended."

Readers' Favorite

"Ideally, *Patients in Peril* will be assigned reading to medical students and would-be health professionals."

Midwest Book Review

"*Patients in Peril: The Demise of Primary Care in America*, should be given serious attention and his ideas widely propagated."

Feathered Quill

Praise for *Taming Infection*

"An engrossing history of infectious diseases' toll on humanity."

Independent Book Review

"A wide-ranging history that should appeal to a broad audience."

Midwest Book Review

"A scholarly guide that concerns and should be accessed by all Americans."

Feathered Quill

Praise for *The Green Years*

"*The Green Years* is vivid, thoroughly researched and authentic ... absorbing and full of insights."

Michael McCloskey, former Executive Director, Sierra Club

"*The Green Years* is the most comprehensive history of environmentalism's legislative achievements during its most fruitful period."

Robert D. Lifset, author of *Power on the Hudson: Storm King Mountain and the Emergence of Modern American Environmentalism*

Praise for *The Good Monarchs*

"Insightful" in its examination of "the life and times of 18 rulers whose reigns extend from the mists of history to the 21st Century."

Midwest Book Review

Praise for *The Magnificent Losers*

"Impressively well researched, written, organized, and presented ... A uniquely informative approach to history, *The Magnificent Losers* is an inherently fascinating read that is as thoughtful and thought-provoking as it is inspired and inspiring."

Midwest Book Review

AMERICAN SALVATION

HOW IMMIGRANTS MADE AMERICA GREAT

GREGG COODLEY

atmosphere press

Dedicated to my grandparents:
Oscar Coodley, Rae Korot, and David Sirkin,
who were immigrants, and Betty Goblinger,
who was the daughter of immigrants.

ACKNOWLEDGMENTS

I appreciate the help of so many who helped me complete this book.

I don't know what I would do without the assistance of the Multnomah County librarians. I am particularly grateful to the librarians in my local Hillsdale branch and the Inter-Library Loan Program. They are all always a pleasure to work with.

The staff of Atmosphere Press have been invaluable during the production process of the work. I want to especially mention Kyle McCord, Albert Liau, Alex Kale, Ronaldo Alves, Cassandra Felten, Cameron Finch, and Hayla Alawi.

I appreciate the feedback of my agent, Susan Schulman.

I appreciate my sister Cheryl, who read the manuscript and made a variety of helpful suggestions. I also want to thank my sister Lauren for her wisdom and advice at many stages in the process. I also appreciate the reference materials that Lauren was able to give me that originated in the courses she had taught.

I have been fortunate to have many wonderful colleagues at work. Their ancestors came from many nations. I wanted to single out two co-workers who are immigrants and friends, Meei Choong and Fatima Awada, whose lives have inspired me.

I always appreciate the encouragement and love from my children, Sam, Scout, Sarah, David, and Mimi. My brothers-in-law, Michael and Jon Levine, have also been wonderfully supportive.

Most of all, I thank my wife, Karen, for her support, tolerance, and encouragement. She is the best part of my life.

TABLE OF CONTENTS

"America is open to receive not only the opulent and respectable stranger, but the oppressed and persecuted of all nations and religions, who we shall welcome ..."

George Washington

"When the stranger resides with you in your land, you shall not wrong him. The stranger who resides with you shall be to you as one of your citizens; you shall love him as yourself, for you were strangers in the land of Egypt."

Leviticus 19.28

"Receive the fugitive and prepare in time an asylum for mankind."

Thomas Paine

"Immigration also gives America a quality rare for a rich country—hunger and energy ... America has found a way to keep itself constantly revitalized by streams of people who are looking to make a new life in a new world."

Fareed Zakaria

"Thanks to each wave of new arrivals to this land of opportunity, we're a nation forever young, forever bursting with energy and new ideas, and always on the cutting edge, always leading the world to the next frontier. This quality is vital to our future as a nation. If we ever closed the door to new Americans, our leadership in the world would soon be lost."

Ronald Reagan

INTRODUCTION

Immigrants are America's greatest strength, the single biggest factor that has made the United States a superpower. Most of the great nations of the world developed in a single location, often with a relatively homogenous population. Russia, China, Japan, India, and, notwithstanding recent immigration, most of the European nations are largely homogenous societies. They may have expanded, in some cases through conquest and assimilation of minorities, but the core populations have remained largely unchanged for centuries.

The United States is one of the few nations made up principally or completely of immigrants. In a way, all inhabitants of the United States are immigrants, with the Native Americans leading the way thousands of years before the rest. It is our great shame that a large part of earlier American population were involuntary immigrants, African slaves taken against their will to our shores. They were preceded and followed by voluntary immigrants from across the globe. Between 1607 and 1958, over 42 million people immigrated to the United States, the largest migration of people in recorded history[1].

An estimated thirty million would come from Europe. Since the 1960s, most immigrants have come from other parts of the world.

Among the European immigrants to America, one striking feature is the diversity of the sources of immigration. In contrast, most immigrants to Canada and Australia came from the British Isles, while immigration to Argentina was dominated by Spanish and Italians[2].

Americans are not a single monolithic group with periodic dollops of different immigrants added in. As economist Thomas Sowell pointed out, "The massive ethnic communities that make up the mosaic of American society cannot be adequately described as 'minorities.' There is no majority. The largest single identifiable ethnic strain are people of British ancestry—who make up just 15% of the American population" [3].

Immigrants tend to be young. An estimated 40% of Irish immigrants in the late nineteenth and twentieth centuries were between 20 and 24 [4].

Another common feature of immigration is that, often, families did not all arrive at once. Frequently, one or two people would arrive first and, having achieved a certain stability, then bring in their other family members. Such "chain migration" is nothing new.

Historically, immigrants were more often men, with perhaps the greatest gender disparities found among Chinese and Japanese immigrants in the nineteenth century. In 1900, the 24,326 Japanese immigrants in the United States included only 985 women [5].

Immigration is not just one-way. A proportion of immigrants would leave America to return to their home countries, with the lowest percentage of those leaving occurring among Irish and Jewish immigrants, probably reflecting the conditions from which they had left [6]. Remigration tended to be higher during difficult times in the United States. During the early Great Depression, the years 1932–36 saw over twice as many leaving as those arriving [7]. This figure was skewed by the strict immigration limits that were instituted in 1924.

The problems of American society are not hidden. We suffer an appalling annual toll of deaths from guns and drugs. Despite valiant efforts, inequality is too much a feature of our society. Too many are homeless or lack medical insurance. The United States seems wracked by ideological conflict and distrust.

Yet despite all this, vast numbers of non-Americans want to immigrate to the United States. There are no similar numbers wanting to immigrate to Russia, China, Japan, or India.

This is our great strength, for immigrants have repeatedly bolstered our nation.

Sowell noted, "Among the world's leading scientific, political, and economic figures today are Americans whose immigrant ancestors were once dismissed as 'the beaten men of beaten races.' Nothing has so vindicated the untapped potential of ordinary people as the American experience" [8].

Opponents of immigration have argued that each new group of immigrants is too different to become Americans. The reality is always different. Journalist Sanford Ungar wrote, "In most cases, however, the dream of America that we have sold to the immigrants—the dream of economic success—and financial independence, the concept of participating in a civil society and gaining some control over one's destiny without fear of arbitrary power—still takes effect. The newcomers are not all enduringly or unanimously happy with the lives they carve out in America, and their presence may at first seem threatening to those who have been here longer. Yet, however distinct they may try to remain, they soon come to consider themselves Americans" [9].

Yet there are those who, for reasons of ignorance, misunderstanding, honest difference of opinion, or bigotry, demonize immigrants and seek to limit or halt immigration. To do so would be the equivalent of shooting ourselves in the head.

This book will attempt to demonstrate a few of the many ways in which immigration has been the salvation of the United States. The American Revolution might have been lost except for immigrants. The South, with its advantage of interior lines and needing only to defend its own territories, should have won the Civil War and broken the nation in two. Immigrants were a key factor in the Union victory in the War, as were those involuntary immigrants, the slaves.

Many of the great captains of American industry were immigrants. So were many of the leaders of organized labor who fought to improve the conditions of working people.

Much of what we know as typically American are the creations of immigrants. Without them, we would not have had Hollywood and the movies or the Manhattan Project and the atomic bomb. Nor would we have kindergartens, Christmas trees, bagels, pizza, hamburgers, or symphonies. Much of the tech giants of Silicon Valley were created in part by immigrants.

The American leadership in science and medicine is in large part due to immigrants. When we take satisfaction from Americans winning Nobel Prizes, we should understand how many are immigrants to our shores.

Sowell wrote, "The assimilation of American ethnic groups has not been a one-way street. Much of the vernacular, food, music, and other cultural characteristics of the American society today were once ethnic peculiarities but are now part of the common heritage" [10].

In each chapter, I review the contributions of immigrants. By necessity, in almost every chapter, I leave out other immigrants who played major roles, lest the book become an excessively lengthy and unreadable tome. Thus, the chapter on the American Revolution leaves out Charles Lee and Horatio Gates, two leaders whose early successes would be eclipsed by later disasters. I have omitted scientists such as Reginald Fessenden and successful business innovators such as Adam Gimbel and Meyer Guggenheim, mainly to spare the reader an overwhelming number of immigrant contributors to the United States.

I also opted to omit the children of immigrants, for then the book would have required many volumes to do justice to all those who were crucial to American success. The book, for the same reasons, doesn't credit enough the contributions of the Native Americans (the original immigrants) or Black Americans brought here against their will. The book cannot simply be a catalog of every American who contributed, but is rather narrowly focused on describing the contributions of immigrants in defense of the case that immigrants are one of America's greatest strengths. Thus, the book will focus on those who voluntarily immigrated to the United States from just before the American Revolution up to 2024.

Immigrants have historically done the jobs that no one else wanted to do, from growing our food to transporting our people to filling all the other gaps in the workforce.

While Emma Lazarus described those wanting to immigrate as "the tired, the poor," immigrants are more often among the best people of each nation. Ungar commented, "Most of these new immigrants, of course, like those who came before them, are self-selected. Legal or not, they tend to be the adventurers, the risk takers, the strong of mind and body who can cope with being uprooted and landing in a totally new environment" [11]. Those who brave the trip across the ocean or through the desert are among the strongest and most courageous of each nation. America is really often getting the best of each nation.

Many of the great nations of the world face the demographic trap of declining populations. Thus far, immigration is the one thing that has spared the United States this problem, when there are too few workers to support an aging population.

Many have fears that the nation will be overrun with immigrants. Yet the percentage of those born abroad, at about 14% of the population, is similar to those in the census from 1860, where the percentage of foreign-born was between 13–15% [12].

Despite the benefits of immigration, surveys of Americans, starting in the 1930s, show persistent hostility toward immigration, with majorities in every survey favoring less immigration. Sociologists Rita Simon and Susan Alexander concluded, "The prospect of higher immigration is not, and never has been, a popular issue with the American public" [13].

Ungar wrote, "There is something profoundly contradictory—some would say hypocritical—about the fact that public sentiment runs so strongly against immigration in a wealthy country built by immigrants. Indeed, few of today's Americans would themselves enjoy the privileges associated with American citizenship if there had not been a liberal immigration policy at some earlier stage of the country's development" [14].

The aim of this book is to demonstrate how helpful, and crucial, immigration has been for the success of the American experiment. Blocking immigration causes harm that we do not even know about. How many Teslas and Einsteins have we unwittingly kept out? At the end of the book, we will explore what might have happened had the United States closed itself to mass immigration.

Immigration brings multiple concrete benefits to the United States, bolstering our economy, our military, our science, and our culture. Even for purely selfish reasons, we should embrace immigration for its myriad benefits.

Yet beyond this, we should embrace it, for the world needs a refuge, a place to serve as a beacon of hope to oppressed or starving people when all hope has been lost. In World War Two, Britain was the last hope of Europeans whose nations had been conquered by the Nazis [15]. America should accept with pride the role of the last best hope of people across the globe, the one refuge where the persecuted can always find safety. We could have a worse national objective.

---

1 John F. Kennedy. *A Nation of Immigrants*, Harper Perennial, New York, 2008 (first published by Harper, 1964), 2.

2 Roger Daniels. *Coming to America: A History of Immigration and Ethnicity in American Life*, second edition, Harper Perennial, New York, 2002, 24.

3 Thomas Sowell. *Ethnic America*, Basic Books, New York, 1981, 4.

4 Milton Meltzer. *Bound for America: The Story of the European Immigrants*, Benchmark Books, New York, 2002, 17–18.

5 Emma Gee. "Issei: The First Women," *Civil Rights Digest*, Spring, 1974.

6 Daniels, 21.

7 Daniels, 21.

8 Sowell, 14.

9 Sanford J. Ungar. *Fresh Blood: The New American Immigrants*, University of Illinois Press, Urbana, 1998, 20.

10 Sowell, 14.

11 Ungar, 23.

12 Tim Kaine. *The Immigrant Superpower: How Brains, Brawn and Bravery Make America Stronger*, Oxford University Press, New York, 2022, 59.

13 Ungar, 109.

14 Ungar, 110.

15 Lynne Olson. *Last Hope Island.* Random House, New York, 2017, xvii.

Thomas Paine

Thaddeus Kosciuszko

CHAPTER 1

The American Revolution

When the American Revolution broke out, all of the population of the thirteen colonies, save the Native Americans, were either born elsewhere or were descendants of those who had arrived in the prior 168 years. Yet most of the population increase from settlement to independence came from births in America rather than immigration. Census figures in 1790 showed that six out of every seven Whites originated in the British Isles, with those from continental Europe being concentrated in the middle colonies. For example, a third of the population of Pennsylvania were Germans, and a sixth of New Yorkers were Dutch[1]. Census figures in 1790 would reveal some 3.1 million Whites and 750,000 Blacks. Since many of the White immigrants had come as indentured servants, the percentage of those immigrating freely was smaller than is usually imagined[2].

Historians have noted five distinctively different flows of immigration from Britain prior to the Revolution. Historian Michael Barone noted that New England was principally settled by some 21,000 people, principally from East Anglia, who mostly arrived in the 1630s, with little migration in or out for the next 150 years. In the 1640s–1650s, some 30,000 settlers, primarily from the more pro-Royalist western part of England, ended up in Virginia and Maryland. In the 1680s, some 40,000, with a large percentage of Quakers, primarily from the Midlands and Northern England, settled in Pennsylvania,

New Jersey, and Delaware. Another smaller group would settle in the Carolinas and Georgia. By the middle of the eighteenth century, this population had increased due to high birth rates and abundant food to some 1.2 million people, which included a large number of slaves, primarily in the southern colonies[3].

The final surge of British immigrants prior to the Revolution came from 1763–75, in the years between the ousting of France from North America and the outbreak of the American Revolution. These immigrants, described as Scots-Irish, came from lowland Scotland and from Scots who had settled in Ulster in Northern Ireland. Some 125,000 of these had immigrated to America from 1713–63 and another 125,000 from 1763–75. They largely consisted of whole families and people with enough resources to make the voyage[4].

The Scots-Irish settled primarily along the western frontier, where there was plentiful land. The 125,000 who came in 1763–75 were equal to about 10% of the entire population of the colonies. In the Revolution, they tended to support the revolutionary cause. British government attempts to limit westward migration may have played a role in this[5].

Aside from these recent immigrants, most of the participants during the Revolution had been born here. Yet many new immigrants made signal contributions to the American fight for independence in myriad areas.

The greatest contribution came from one of the unlikeliest of men. Thomas Paine had worked in a variety of trades in his native England without notable success in any. He arrived in America barely a year before the fighting started. Yet among all the gifted orators and writers among America's founding fathers, his words would do the most to make independence a reality. Benjamin Franklin would later tell him, "You, Thomas Paine, are more responsible than any other living person on this continent for the creation of what are called the United States of America"[6].

Paine was born January 29, 1737, in Thetford, a small town

in the English county of Norfolk. His parents put him into school at age seven but took him out at age twelve to become an apprentice in his father's corset-making shop. Within a few years, he moved to London, where he lived amidst the slums, every day passing hundreds of "ragged and hungry children, and persons of seventy and eighty years old, begging in the streets" [7]. Paine later wrote, "The contrast of affluence and wretchedness continually meeting and offending the eye is like dead and living bodies chained together" [8]. From 1757–74, Paine's fortunes waxed and waned before hitting bottom in April 1774. He worked as a corset maker, served on a privateer, was an exciseman, was a schoolteacher, ran a tobacco shop, and married twice, with one marriage ending with his wife's death in pregnancy and another failing for unknown reasons. During his better periods, Paine wrote and debated issues with members of the Hellfire Club. He wrote a pamphlet titled "The Case of the Officers of Excise," arguing that corruption was due to low wages[9].

Destitute and without prospects, Paine moved back to London, where a friend introduced him to Benjamin Franklin, who was serving as the envoy of the Pennsylvania Legislature to the British government. Franklin urged Paine to move to America. In October 1774, Paine sailed to America carrying a letter of recommendation from Franklin. Paine almost died from typhus during the voyage but survived to arrive on November 30 in Philadelphia, whose 30,000 people made it the largest city in the colonies.

Paine became editor of the *Pennsylvania Magazine*. Here, Paine attacked slavery, then legal in every colony, writing, "Too many nations enslaved prisoners they took in war ... But to go to nations whom there is no war ... purely to catch inoffensive people like beasts for slaves, is [the] height of outrage ... one may, with a much reason and decency, plead for murder, robbery, lewdness, and barbarity, as for this practice" [10].

At the start of 1776, it was not at all clear that even those fighting against the British really desired independence. The colonists frequently blamed the misdeeds of the British government on Parliament while retaining a certain affection for King George III.

Dr. Benjamin Rush, who favored independence, persuaded Paine to write a pamphlet outlining the case for independence.

In January 1776, Paine anonymously published under the rubric "Written by an Englishman," a short book (or long pamphlet) called *Common Sense*. Within three months, demand was so high that 120,000 copies had been printed; within a few months, as many as 500,000 may have been published[11]. This was an enormous number considering that the total population of the Thirteen Colonies was about 2.5 million, meaning that there was a copy printed for every five Americans. No other book save the Bible has been published in such numbers relative to the population. Paine donated his earnings to buy clothing for the American troops.

In *Common Sense*, Paine eloquently made a case for independence. He showed the absurdity of respect for royalty, writing of kings, "the first of them [was] nothing better than the principal ruffian of some restless gang" [12]. Rejecting the claim that the British government was the best in the world, Paine pointed out that it was founded on "the base remains of two ancient tyrannies [monarchy and aristocracy]" [13].

Instead, Paine argued that America must become a haven for freedom, stating, "Ye that love mankind! Ye that dare oppose not only the tyranny, but the tyrant, stand forth! Every Freedom hath been hunted round the globe. Asia and Africa have long expelled her. Europe regards her as a stranger, and England has given her warning to depart. O! receive the fugitive and prepare in time an asylum for mankind" [14].

Paine also argued that America would be more likely to receive assistance from other European powers if it declared independence. He also argued that they would be eager to trade with the new nation with its rich resources as long as "eating is the custom in Europe" [15].

Arguing that "Independence is the only BOND that can tye and keep us together," Paine also proclaimed, "We have it in our power to begin the world over again ... the birth-day of a new world is at hand" [16].

No other writing or speech was to do so much to motivate the Continental Congress to declare independence in July 1776. George Washington praised it as "sound doctrine and unanswerable reasoning," while Thomas Jefferson called it "the simple voice of nature and reason" [17].

Although little remembered today, British restriction of immigration to the Colonies was one of many reasons that drove the colonists to eventually opt for independence. It was an important enough issue to be included in the Declaration of Independence, which attacked the King of Britain, stating, "He has endeavoured to prevent the population of these States; for that reason, obstructing the Laws for the Naturalization of Foreigners; refusing to pass others to encourage their migrations hither, and raising the conditions of new Appropriations of Lands" [18].

Paine's views were far in advance of his time, opposing slavery, dueling, animal cruelty, and oppression of women[19]. Paine appealed openly to the ordinary citizens with the intent "to make those who can scarcely read understand" [20].

Yet Paine's contributions were not finished. 1776 saw a string of American military defeats, leading many to predict that the call for independence would die stillborn. The Continental Army had been driven out of New York in defeat. It was in these grim days that Paine, now serving as aide-de-camp to General Nathanael Greene, published the first installment of *The Crisis* on December 19. It would be read to the American soldiers on December 23 in words that are known to many who do not know their source. Paine wrote, "These are the times that try men's souls. The summer soldier and the sunshine patriot will, in the crisis, shrink from the service of their country, but he that stands it now deserves the love and thanks of man and woman" [21]. Two days later, Washington launched a surprise attack across the Delaware River, winning a decisive victory in Trenton. New recruits joined the Continental Army. Paine would write 13 essays in the series *The Crisis* from 1776–1783, all aimed at bolstering American morale.

Paine also shrewdly assessed the state of the war, writing a public letter to the British Commander, General Howe, in early 1777, where he wrote, "In all the wars which you have formerly been concerned, you had only armies to contend with. In this case, you have both an army and a country to combat" [22].

Other immigrants would also make vital contributions to the Americans' eventual victory.

Peter Francisco first appeared in the historical record when, at only five years old, he was mysteriously unloaded by a ship in Virginia. Believed to be of Portuguese origin, Francisco became an indentured servant to Judge Anthony Winston, an uncle of Patrick Henry. By age 15, Francisco was six feet six inches tall when Winston took him to hear Henry's famous oration that ended, "Give me liberty or give me death" [23].

Winston made Francisco wait a year until he turned sixteen before allowing him to enlist in the 10th Virginia Regiment. Francisco fought in the Battle of Brandywine, where he was wounded. He recovered in time to fight in the Battle of Germantown and the siege of Fort Mifflin. He received further wounds at the Battle of Monmouth and the capture of the British fort atop Stony Point. Commenting on Francisco continuing to fight despite being bayoneted, Captain William Evans commented that Francisco's "name was reiterated throughout the whole army" [24].

Francisco achieved his greatest fame at the disastrous American defeat at Camden. There, he tried to rally the fleeing American soldiers. Unsuccessful at that, he managed to free his regiment's colonel, who had been captured by the British.

Finally, Francisco was reported to have picked up and carried an 1100-pound cannon away to prevent it from being captured by the British[25].

Having joined the cavalry, Francisco fought at the Battle of Guilford Court House, where he singlehandedly killed 11 British soldiers before suffering his fourth wound. He then became a scout for the army. Francisco was resting outside Ward's Tavern in Virginia when nine British cavalrymen rode in. Before the battle was over, Francisco killed one, wounded another, and forced the other seven to flee on foot, having captured their horses. Francisco was nicknamed the "Giant of Virginia" and the "Hercules of the Revolution." George Washington commented, "Without him, we would have lost two crucial battles, perhaps the war, and with it our freedom. He was truly a one-man army" [26].

Haym Salomon was originally from Poland. Like many others, he fled, protesting Russian control. Before he reached America, he traveled widely in Europe, learning English, French, Italian, German, and Russian, in addition to his native Polish[27]. Upon arriving in New York, he joined the Jewish synagogue and became a merchant. Salomon, along with other young members of the synagogue, joined the New York Sons of Liberty, which favored the Patriot cause. After the British captured New York City in 1776, they arrested Salomon and other members of the Sons of Liberty.

Salomon was released when the British realized his fluency in German was such that they could use him as an interpreter with the many Hessians, German mercenaries serving the Crown in America. Salomon persuaded many of the Hessian soldiers to desert in exchange for free land that the American government was offering to any deserter. Salomon was arrested and, after an interval in a British prison, brought before a British court, where he was accused of giving financial help to the rebels, forwarding intelligence to the Patriot cause, and persuading the soldiers to desert. Salomon was sentenced to death but escaped the night before his execution[28].

Salomon made his way to Philadelphia. After recovering from illness contracted in prison, he wrote the Continental Congress asking for employment, stating, "Your memorialist was ... taken as a spy ... he has been of great service to the French and American prisoners and assisted them with money and helped them off to make their escape ... in these circumstances, he most humbly prayeth to grant him any employ ..." [29].

Turned down, Salomon quickly became a successful and wealthy broker. He then offered to put his fortune at the service of the Congress. Salomon wrote several times to Robert Morris, the treasurer of the Congress, but was ignored, probably due to Morris' prejudice against Jews. Morris even ignored a letter from George Washington suggesting he contact Salomon. Finally, Morris wrote to Salomon, who was at Yom Kippur services, saying, "The terrible emergency of the moment necessitates my turning to you at this hour. The office of finance has been unable to procure sufficient funds to cover the enclosed notes ... I must beg of you to act immediately with whatever resources you have to satisfy our distress" [30]. Salomon raised $20,000 from the congregation, money that was delivered to Morris that evening.

Salomon contributed vast sums that helped supply and pay the often ill-clothed, ill-fed, and ill-paid Continental Army. Salomon served as the official broker for the Office of Finance under Robert Morris, where Salomon arranged the sale of government bonds, handled bills of exchange, and obtained promissory notes to help pay for the war. Salomon handled all the funds for the support and maintenance of the French sea and land forces, investing all the money he made in commissions in the revolutionary cause.

Salomon also made personal loans to prominent American leaders, including Jefferson, Madison, and Monroe, but refused to take interest on the loans. Madison wrote to Edmund Randolph, "The kindness of our little friend [Salomon] in

Front Street, near the coffee house, is a fund that which will preserve me from extremities, but I never resort to it without great mortification as he obstinately refuses all recompense" [31]. Salomon also paid the salary of Baron von Steuben when the latter showed up at his door nearly destitute.

In 1781, the Americans had a chance to corner a British army at Yorktown in Virginia. With the troops balking at additional service due to not being paid for years, Washington asked for Salomon's help. Salomon donated the money to pay the troops and for their supplies, enabling the Americans to march to Yorktown and win the decisive battle for independence [32].

Salomon's contribution to the American cause was more than $650,000, an enormous fortune at the time. Largely impoverished at the time of independence, he tried to reestablish his business. However, he had contracted tuberculosis in the British prison and died from that in 1785. The Congress refused to give any money to his widow and three small children, who were rescued from poverty by the Jewish community in New York [33].

Robert Morris, the other financial leader for the Americans during the war, was also an immigrant. Morris, born in Britain in 1734, arrived in America in 1747. After his father's death a year later, Morris was apprenticed to the firm of Charles Willing, a leading merchant. After a seven-year apprenticeship, he became partners with Willing's son Thomas, dealing in shipping and marine insurance. Morris would be elected to the Continental Congress, where he chaired the Secret Committee on Commerce. Morris, along with Roger Sherman, was one of only two men to sign the Declaration of Independence (1776), the Articles of Confederation (1778), and the Constitution (1787) [34].

The Continental Congress had named several people as quartermaster generals in charge of getting supplies to the army. Yet the system of supply proved inadequate because many did not want to accept the amount Congress was offering, which was below market rates. Congress was further handicapped by unreliable financial support. Finally, in June 1781, Congress named Morris the Superintendent of Finance, giving an official role to what he had been doing. Morris was also given power to control supplies for the army. He ordered supplies collected at a great distance to be sold and the proceeds used to buy food and clothing as close as possible to the army. The supply to the army in the Yorktown campaign showed some improvement from prior campaigns[35]. Historian Thomas McCraw wrote of Morris, "His role in financing the war remained so vital that his power in the national government was second only to that of George Washington" [36].

Thaddeus Kosciuszko was born in Poland in 1746 to an impoverished noble family. After five years of school, he quit to help run his family's estate after the death of his father. He returned to school at age 19, entering the newly founded Royal Academy. After graduating near the top of his class, he joined the Polish military as a lieutenant in the artillery. In 1769, now a captain, he received one of four scholarships for further education in Paris.

In France and in travels to other European nations, Kosciuszko was exposed to the thinking of the Enlightenment, which argued that government should be for the benefit of all citizens. He wrote, "During the five years of my life spent in foreign countries, I ... endeavored to master those arts which pertain to a solid government, aiming at the happiness of all" [37].

In 1772, Russia, Austria, and Prussia forced Poland to surrender a third of its territory. Kosciuszko returned home to find that he was destitute, while the division left few options for employment in the military. He went back to France in 1775, where he learned of the start of the conflict between the thirteen colonies and the British government. Eager to weaken the British, the French government began aiding the Americans, surreptitiously sending money and volunteers.

Kosciuszko volunteered to aid the Americans. He arrived in August 1776 and presented himself to the Continental Congress, asking for a commission in the Continental Army. As one of a large number of foreigners who were applying, he was initially turned down.

The British capture of New York City meant that Philadelphia might be their next target. Kosciuszko secured a position with the Pennsylvania Council of Safety, where he proposed building fortifications on the Delaware River. George Washington had been disappointed with his military engineers, whose skills he felt were lacking. Retreating from New Jersey to Philadelphia, he was delighted to hear that there was a skilled engineer already working on fortifying the defenses of Philadelphia. Washington wrote John Hancock, President of the Congress, saying, "None of the French Gentlemen who I have seen with appointments seem to know anything of the Matter. There is one in Philadelphia who I am told is clever, but him I have never seen" [38]. Reluctant now to release Kosciuszko, the Congress employed him to build Fort Mercer on the New Jersey side of the Delaware River, which he connected to his earlier fort on the Pennsylvania side with a sharp-tipped row of fortifications that would rip out the bottom of any vessel attempting to pass.

The British decided to put off the attack on Philadelphia with the onset of the winter. Kosciuszko became friends with General Horatio Gates, who commanded Philadelphia's forces. When Gates was sent north to take over the forces opposing a British invasion into New York from Canada, Kosciuszko went with him in the spring of 1777.

The key American position was at Fort Ticonderoga, located near the junction of Lake Champlain and Lake George. Kosciuszko went there in May 1777, but the American commanders ignored his suggestion to fortify Sugar Loaf Hill, which overlooked the fort. On June 30, the British Army under General John Burgoyne arrived at the fort and proceeded to place artillery on the hill. Facing an untenable situation, the Americans evacuated the fort on July 5, leaving behind tons of supplies and ammunition.

Kosciuszko received orders to delay the British advance south. Commanding one thousand soldiers, Kosciuszko cut down trees and placed other obstacles to block the road. The British, who had previously advanced about eighteen miles a day, now barely covered a mile a day. The month-long delay allowed the Americans to rebuild their weakened forces.

Kosciuszko built up the American defense near Saratoga, New York. Fortifications were built stretching from the Hudson River to the nearby Bennis Heights. The British Army reached here but was unable to advance further. The Americans counterattacked and forced the surrender of Burgoyne's entire army.

Kosciuszko, in the spring of 1779, was assigned to fortify the heights overlooking the Hudson to prevent a British advance northward from New York City. Kosciuszko's fortifications at West Point won the commendation of General Washington. In the fall of 1779, Kosciuszko was appointed to command the Corps of Engineers of Washington's army. By July 1780, the defenses at West Point were complete. A contemporary noted, "[Kosciuszko] gave the fortifications [at West Point] such strength that they frightened the very enemy from all temptations of even trying to take the Highlands" [39].

Washington simply wrote about the accomplishment that "the American people are indebted (to Kosciuszko)" [40]. Kosciuszko was sent south that fall to join the Americans' southern army under General Nathanael Greene. His first task was to slow the British advance while he also built a fleet of flat-bottomed boats that allowed the Americans to escape across the Dan River.

After the British surrendered, Kosciuszko was promoted to brigadier general for "his long, faithful, and meritorious service" [41].

Friedrich Wilhelm von Steuben was born In Magdeburg in Germany in 1730. He entered military training at age 14, and at age 17, he found himself an officer in the Prussian army. Serving in battle under Frederick the Great, he would be twice wounded. By 1762, he had become a captain and aide-de-camp to the king. However, in 1763, he was suddenly dismissed from the Prussian army, which he later claimed was retaliation by a general with whom he had quarreled. He went to the court of the Prince of Hohenzollern-Hechingen, where he became Grand Marshall. In 1771, he was abruptly dismissed, with rumors claiming that he had had a series of homosexual liaisons[42].

Von Steuben traveled to Paris, where he met Benjamin Franklin. The initial meeting did not go well, but a subsequent meeting in 1777 led Franklin to feel that von Steuben's experience would be useful to the undisciplined Continental Army. Franklin sent von Steuben with an introduction to the Continental Congress as a former lieutenant general in the Prussian army. Von Steuben arrived in Portsmouth, New Hampshire, in November and, from there, traveled to Philadelphia. Von Steuben offered himself to Congress as a volunteer.

By the end of 1777, the British had captured Philadelphia. The Continental Army settled into winter quarters at Valley Forge, some twenty miles northwest of Philadelphia. There, they suffered from hunger, lack of warm clothing, and disease. It was feared that the army would disintegrate.

On February 5, 1778, von Steuben arrived. Rather than disparaging the army's desperate state, von Steuben found himself "admiring an army which held together under circumstances that no European army could have endured" [43]. Von Steuben started a regimen of training and morale-building while also dealing with basic sanitation. Von Steuben spoke no English, so he eventually issued instructions in French, which other officers translated into English. He created a manual of regulations for the army, which would be formally published in 1779 as the *Regulations for the Order and Disposition of the Troops of the United States*. It remained in use through the War of 1812.

Von Steuben recognized the difference between the Revolutionary army and the Europeans' armies, writing an old comrade, "In the first place, the genius of this nation is not in the least to be compared to that of the Prussians, Austrians, or French. You say to your soldier, 'Do this,' and he doeth it, but I am obliged to say, 'This is the reason you ought to do that,' and he does it" [44].

Within weeks, von Steuben had vastly improved the organization and training of the troops. He also kept track of weapons and supplies, appointing subordinate inspectors, with a resulting marked decrease in graft and war profiteering. The savings were such that von Steuben was appointed to the newly created post of Inspector General on May 5, 1778.

Thanks to their improved training, the Continental forces gained increased agility in maneuvers and the ability to better meet the British in open combat. Von Steuben was only disappointed by not being given a field command, although he had taken command and rallied fleeing troops in the Battle of Monmouth.

John Paul Jones is sometimes called "The Father of the American Navy." He was born the son of a gardener and with the name of John Paul, on July 6, 1747, in Scotland. In 1761, at age 13, he was apprenticed as a ship's boy in the merchant brig *Friendship*. After three years of trading, the ship was sold. Jones then served three years as second and then chief mate on a slave ship. He then obtained his discharge, saying that he would have no more of that "abominable trade" [45]. While sailing back to Scotland in 1768 as a passenger on the brig *John*, Jones took command upon the death of the master and mate from fever. When he reached home, the ship's owner named him, at age 21, master of the ship. He spent five years as master of first the *John* and then the *Betsy*. In 1773, on the island of Tobago, Jones got into a dispute with a mutinous seaman, whom he ran through with his sword. For reasons that remain unclear, Jones abandoned his ship and fled to America, changing his name to John Paul Jones to avoid extradition for murder. After two years in obscurity, he reached Philadelphia in the middle of 1775[46].

Jones was commissioned as a lieutenant in the fledging Continental Navy and, in December, appointed the second in command of a converted merchantman, the *Alfred*. In March, the *Alfred* was part of an American fleet that captured British artillery and supplies in the Bahamas. In May, Jones was given command of the sloop *Providence*. After some months of convoy duty, Jones took the *Providence* on an independent cruise, capturing seven British merchantmen in seven weeks. In October, he led another successful cruise, capturing several more British merchantmen. These included the British transport *Mellish* carrying 16,000 wool uniforms and 30,000 pairs of shoes that Jones declared was "the most valuable ship that hath been taken by the American arms" [47]. In July, Jones was given command of the newly built sloop *Ranger*, which finally sailed from New Hampshire on November 1, 1777, carrying to France the news of Burgoyne's surrender.

After a winter in France, Jones took the *Ranger* to bring the war home to Britain. After capturing several British merchantmen, Jones led 40 men from the ship to the British port of Whitehaven, where they spiked guns and burned ships. Historian Samuel Eliot Morrison wrote, "The damage done was inconsequential ... but the moral effect was stupendous. Nobody had done that sort of thing to an English seaport since 1667" [48]. Jones followed this by raiding St. Mary's Isle, hoping to abduct the Earl of Selkirk. Finding him absent, Jones allowed his crew to seize limited booty from his mansion. On the way back to France, the *Ranger* encountered the sloop HMS *Drake*. After a furious battle, *Drake* surrendered, and Jones returned with the captured ships to France in May 1778. Jones traded his prisoners for 228 American sailors imprisoned by the British.

With the *Ranger* having been sent home, Jones was without a command until February 1779, when he took command of the *Bonhomme Richard,* a converted merchantman of forty guns. After months of refitting, Jones sailed in command of the *Richard* and a squadron of smaller vessels. Yet, the other ships, largely under the control of French captains, often refused to obey orders. Such was the case when the squadron encountered two British warships escorting a large convoy. Jones, in the *Richard,* engaged *HMS Serapis,* a British frigate that outgunned the *Richard.* After repeated firing and maneuvers, the British captain called out, "Has your ship struck?" to which Jones reportedly replied, "I have not yet begun to fight" [49]. At last, the *Richard* grappled with her opponent. Of the three other ships in the squadron, one engaged the smaller British ship, one did nothing, and the last fired broadsides into the *Richard.* For two hours, the *Richard* and the *Serapis* fought, linked together. The *Richard* had few guns left and was starting to sink, but still she compelled the *Serapis* to surrender. The squadron then began sailing home, but the *Richard* had been damaged so much that she had to be abandoned to quickly sink thereafter. The casualties were severe on both sides: 150 killed or wounded out of a crew of 322 on the *Richard* and about 168 killed or wounded out of 325 on the *Serapis*[50].

The battle aroused a storm of indignation at their defeat in Britain and delight in France. Benjamin Franklin wrote Jones after receiving news of the battle, "For some days after the arrival of your express, scarce anything was talked of at Paris and Versailles, but your cool Conduct and persevering Bravery during the terrible Conflict" [51]. Yet infighting would prevent Jones from sailing again until September 1780, when he successfully sailed a ship full of supplies back to America. He would not get another ship to command before the war effectively ended with the British surrender at Yorktown.

Richard Montgomery was born in Ireland, the son of an Irish baronet. He served as a British army officer for 16 years, but the end of the wars with the French meant an end of rapid promotion. In 1772, he sold his captain's commission. He wrote a cousin, "I have cast my eyes on America, where my pride and poverty will be much more at their ease." [52].

Montgomery moved to America, bought a 70-acre farm north of Manhattan, and married the daughter of a prominent judge. When the Revolution broke out, Montgomery was appointed a brigadier general. He accepted command with reluctance, writing, "I have been dragged from obscurity much against my inclination and not without some struggle" [53].

When reports of British forces at St. Johns preparing to invade New York via Lake Champlain were received, Montgomery took command of 1,200 men to head them off. His superior, General Philip Schuyler, relinquished command in September due to illness. Montgomery began besieging the British in St. Johns. Montgomery turned back the British attempts to relieve the garrison. Finally, on November 3, the British surrendered. The Americans had captured three-quarters of the British regular troops in Canada, along with huge numbers of cannons and supplies. Montgomery wrote his wife, "If I live, you may depend on it that I will see you this winter" [54].

On November 18, Montgomery took Montreal. One fortress remained till Canada was won. Montgomery wrote his brother-in-law, "I need not tell you that till Quebec is taken, Canada is unconquered" [55]. Montgomery took three hundred of his ragged troops toward Quebec, where they joined up with 675 emaciated New Englanders whom Benedict Arnold had led through the Maine wilderness.

The Americans had few cannons, making a siege impracticable. Then, on December 6, smallpox broke out in the American ranks, reducing the number of fit troops to under eight hundred, less than half the size of the garrison. Nevertheless, Montgomery and Arnold decided to each lead a column of men to attack the lower town from different directions. On December 30, the Americans attacked in the midst of a snow-storm.

The result was disaster. Arnold was shot below the knee, leaving his troops leaderless. Montgomery, leading his troops, was killed. The American assault collapsed as some retreated while a vanguard was captured. Thus vanished the best chance that Canada would have joined the Thirteen Colonies in independence. Historian Rick Atkinson wrote, "Perhaps the best this dead, defeated general could hope for was martyrdom. In this, Montgomery succeeded spectacularly. Poems and songs were composed in his honor ... [and] streets, counties, and towns would be named for him" [56].

Paine had influence over more than the fight for independence. He was, in the words of historian James Mac Gregor Burns, "the political and intellectual luminary" among radicals in Philadelphia[57]. In 1776, the radicals had gained control of the Pennsylvania Constitutional Convention. The ensuing Pennsylvania Constitution went far beyond any other state in giving power to the common people. It abolished property ownership requirements for voting or for serving in government and created a single legislative body with annual elections that were open to the public and press. Burns wrote, "In one sweep, the colonial gentry had lost its political power" [58].

Following the end of the war in 1783, Paine went to England and then to France, where he defended the French Revolution in a series of pamphlets titled *The Rights of Man.* Within a decade, it sold over 1.5 million copies, more than any other book in the world, once again, except the Bible. His popularity in America was shaken both by his defense of the French Revolution and his arguments for deism in *The Age of Reason.* Paine also had attacked George Washington over what he felt was an insufficient effort to free him from prison. Paine returned to America in 1802 following ten months of imprisonment in France. He died forgotten in 1809 at his farm in

New Rochelle, New York. His reputation would be somewhat restored when Howard Fast published what became a bestselling work of historical fiction, *Citizen Tom Paine,* in 1943. With multiple editions and translations into at least twelve languages, a reviewer commented, "Mr. Fast's story of Tom Paine is a brilliant piece of fictional biography" [59].

Peter Francisco went back to school following the war. He became prosperous, married three times, and acquired a reputation for kindness and generosity. He died in 1831.

The Articles of Confederation provided for a financial superintendent. Morris was chosen for the post. Morris would be criticized for mixing his private business with that of the government. Yet he operated under the overwhelming obstacle that the national government was dependent on states for revenue but could not compel them to provide this. An attempt to allow Congress to control import duties was blocked by the veto of Rhode Island, for the Articles of Confederation allowed any state to block the actions of Congress.

Morris turned down George Washington's offer to be the first Treasury Secretary in 1789. Morris then made a series of disastrous investments in land that squandered his fortune. Facing debts of close to three million dollars by the late 1790s, he was arrested in 1798 for debt. He spent three and a half years in prison. Following his release, he lived in obscurity before dying in 1806[60].

Kosciuszko sailed back to Europe in 1784, after which he worked for the liberation of Poland. He died in Switzerland in 1817. On a trip to America in 1797, Kosciuszko became friends with Thomas Jefferson. In his will, Kosciuszko asked Jefferson to take the money from his estate to purchase freedom for slaves and for their education, "giving them Liberty in my name" [61].

Von Steuben was offered citizenship after the war and settled first in New Jersey and then in New York. He would suffer financial problems until he received an annual pension of

$2500 in 1790. He died at the age of 64 on November 28, 1794.

After the war, John Paul Jones spent three years in Paris trying to get paid the prize money from the ships he had captured. His hopes of promotion in the American Navy were blocked by factions hostile to him. In 1788, he became a Rear Admiral in the Russian Navy. He won a battle against the Turks but was dismissed in disgrace when he was accused of rape, a charge he denied. He returned to Paris in ill health. On June 1, 1792, President Washington appointed Jones to negotiate with the Dey of Algiers concerning American prisoners. By the time news of this reached Paris, John Paul Jones was dead. He died July 18, 1792, at the age of 45, of chronic kidney disease. In 1905, President Theodore Roosevelt sent a squadron of ships to bring his body back to America for burial. He would be buried at the Naval Academy.

Following the Revolution and signing of the Constitution, George Washington, elected the nation's first president, set the tone as to the nation's attitude towards immigrants, telling a group of Irish refugees that "the bosom of America is open to receive not only the Opulent and respectable Stranger, but the oppressed and persecuted of all Nations and Religions" [62]. Under his administration, Congress passed the first immigration law, the Naturalization Act of 1790, allowing any "free White person" to become a citizen after two years of residency.

---

1 Daniels, 66.

2 Daniels, 31.

3 Michael Barone. *Shaping Our Nation: How Surges of Migration Transformed America and its Politics*, Crown Forum, New York, 2013, 4-5.

4 Barone, 16.

5 Barone, 27.

6 Albert Marrin. *Thomas Paine: Crusader for Liberty*, Alfred A. Knopf, New York, 2014, 7.

7 Marrin, 20.

8 Thomas Paine. *The Collected Writings of Thomas Paine*, ed. Philip S. Foner, Citadel Press, New York, 1945, 610.

9 Marrin, 24.

10 Thomas Paine. "African Slavery in America," https://www.constitution.org/2-Authors/tp/afri.htm.

11 John Richard Alden. *The American* Revolution, Harper Touch Books, New York. 1954, 77.

12 Thomas Paine. *Common Sense*, Civic Classics, New York, 2012, 24.

13 Robert Middlekauff. *The Glorious Cause: The American Revolution 1763–1789*, Oxford University Press, New York, 2005, 324.

14 Middlekauff, 407.

15 Paine, *Common Sense, 56*.

16 Paine, *Common Sense, 85-86*.

17 Marrin, 47.

18 Kennedy, 9.

19 Rick Atkinson. *The British are Coming*, Henry Holt and Company, New York, 2019, 486.

20 Atkinson, 487.

21 Alden, 107.

22 Atkinson, 561.

23 Michael D. Hull. *Peter Francisco: American Revolutionary War Hero*, https://www.historynet.com/peter-franisco-america-revolutionary-war-hero.

24 Sara Novic. *America is Immigrants*, Random House, New York, 2019, 156.

25 Hull.

26 Hull.

27 Helen Miller Bailey. *Forty American* Biographies, California State Series, Sacramento, 1967, 35.

28 Bailey, 36.

29 Jacob Rader Marcus. *Early American Jewry: The Jews of Pennsylvania and the South 1655-1790, Jewish* Publication Society, Philadelphia, 1953, 139.

30 David Allen Lewis. *Forgotten Patriot: The Story of Haym Salomon*, Bridges for Peace, Jerusalem, 2007, 26.

31 Lewis, 15.

32 Bailey, 39.

33 Middlekauff, 524.

34 Bailey, 39.

35 Thomas K. McCraw. *The Founders and Finance: How Hamilton, Gallatin, and Other Immigrants Forged a New Economy.* Belknap Press, 2013, 61.

36 McCraw, 61.

37 Meg Greene. *Thaddeus Kosciuszko: Polish General and Patriot,* Chelsea House Publishers, Philadelphia, 2002, 18-19.

38 Greene, 33-34.

39 Greene, 62.

40 Greene, 63.

41 Middlekauff, 425.

42 Greene, 70-71.

43 Charles River Editors. *Baron Von Steuben,* Charles River Editors.

44 Allen French. Review of John McAuley Palmer's *General von Steuben, The American Historical Review,* July 1938, 43(4): 894-5.

45 Samuel Elliot Morrison. *John Paul Jones,* Time Incorporated, New York, 1959, 13.

46 Middlekauff, 543.

47 Morrison, 26.

48 Atkinson, 468.

49 Morrison, 141.

50 Morrison, 231.

51 Morrison, 250.

52 Atkinson, 150.

53 Atkinson, 150.

54 Atkinson, 149.

55 Atkinson, 152.

56 Atkinson, 213-214.

57 James MacGregor Burns. *The Vineyard of Liberty,* Random House, New York, 1982, 117.

58 Burns, 118.

59 Howard Fast. *Citizen Tom Paine*, Grove Press, New York, 1943, back cover.

60 McCraw, 86.

61 Greene, 72.

62 Kane, 76.

31

Alexander Hamilton

Albert Gallatin

CHAPTER 2

Creating a New Financial System

Alexander Hamilton, an immigrant from the Caribbean island of Nevis, is famous for his role in creating a new financial system for the new United States after the adoption of the Constitution. Another immigrant, Albert Gallatin from Switzerland, played almost as important role in assuring American prosperity. Without the efforts of these two immigrants, the new nation may have foundered. In fact, four of the first six Secretaries of the Treasury were born overseas, serving for a total of 21 of the first 27 years under the Constitution[1].

Hamilton was born on the island of Nevis sometime in 1755–7. He was the illegitimate child of Rachel Lavien, who had left her husband and moved to St. Croix, where she began living with James Hamilton, the ne'er-do-well child of an aristocratic family. Rachel bore James Hamilton two sons before he deserted her. Rachel was imprisoned for two months for adultery. Shortly afterward, Rachel and Alexander fell ill, possibly of yellow fever. Rachel died, leaving Alexander, age nine, and his brother, James Jr., alone. The boys were split up. Due to his parents' status, Hamilton was denied an education in the local church school as well as in the Church of England. Hamilton would become self-taught and a voracious reader. John Adams reportedly described him as "the bastard brat of a Scottish peddler"[2].

Slavery was the all-important feature of St. Croix, with Blacks far outnumbering Whites. Biographer Ron Chernow would note, "Hamilton ... would be conspicuous among the founding fathers for his fierce abolitionism"[3].

At age 14, Hamilton began working for a local merchant specializing in the import-export trade, impressing the locals with his intelligence and writing skills. At age 15 and a half, locals helped him go to the Thirteen Colonies for further education. After a year in a private school, he entered King's College (now Columbia University) in New York City in the fall of 1773.

The growing unrest between Britain and the colonies soon became the great issue of the day. At a 1774 mass meeting organized by the anti-British Sons of Liberty, the 19-year-old Hamilton transfixed the crowd with his rhetoric against the British. Hamilton began writing pamphlets. Chernow observed that his "slashing style of attack would make Hamilton the most feared polemicist in America, but it won enemies as well as admirers"[4].

In January 1776, half a year into the Revolutionary War, Hamilton joined an artillery company in New York, being promoted to captain in March while still a teenager.

After impressive performances in the Battles of Trenton and Princeton, George Washington requested Hamilton join his staff in January 1777, promoting him to lieutenant colonel. Hamilton remained by his side for the next four years, often writing Washington's messages and carrying out the hardest assignments[5]. He gained a long-desired field command at the Battle of Yorktown, leading the American assault that captured the key British redoubt.

Leaving the Army, Hamilton married the daughter of the influential General Philip Schuyler and then gained a law degree after a few months' study. He was elected to the New York legislature while many believed him the best trial lawyer of his generation. As a new immigrant, Hamilton lacked strong allegiance to a single state, instead thinking of the colonies as a whole, as when he wrote in 1782, "There is something noble and magnificent in the perspective of a great Federal republic ... but there is something proportionally diminutive and contemptible in the prospect of a number of petty states" [6].

The financial instability following the war demonstrated to Hamilton and others the weakness of the Articles of Confederation, for each state had a veto over national actions. Hamilton, along with James Madison, helped orchestrate the Annapolis Convention of 1786. Attended by only nine states, the Convention's main accomplishment was to call for a meeting of all the states. Writing the address of the Convention, Hamilton wrote that the national circumstances "render the Situation of the United States delicate and critical" [7].

Hamilton was chosen as one of New York's delegates to the Constitutional Convention, which opened on May 14, 1787. Every state except Rhode Island sent delegates. The fifty-five delegates deliberated in secret for four months. Eight of the delegates were immigrants, all but one of whom signed their support of the proposed Constitution[8]. When Franklin proposed that the Convention start each session with a prayer, Hamilton reportedly said that they did not need "foreign aid" [9].

Following the writing of the Constitution, Hamilton, along with James Madison and John Jay, wrote *The Federalist Papers*, a series of articles to be published in newspapers, explaining and defending the proposed Constitution. Chernow commented, "Hamilton supervised the entire *Federalist* project. He dreamed up the idea, enlisted the participants, wrote the overwhelming bulk of the essays, and oversaw the publication" [10]. Thanks to this and the effort of those supporting the Constitution in every state, the required nine states ratified the document, which took effect in 1789.

George Washington was elected the first President, and Hamilton was named Secretary of the Treasury. Hamilton was nominated and confirmed on the same day, September 11, 1789. Chernow wrote of Washington and Hamilton, "The two men had complementary talents, values and opinions that survived many strains ... Washington possessed the outstanding judgement, sterling character and clear sense of purpose needed to guide his sometimes wayward protégé; he saw that the volatile Hamilton needed a steadying hand. Hamilton contributed philosophical depth, administrative expertise, and comprehensive policy knowledge that nobody in Washington's orbit ever matched" [11].

One of the first actions of the new government was the passage of the Tariff Act, which gave the national government a source of funding and, in fact, was the principal source of funding until the Sixteenth Amendment legalized the income tax in 1913. Congress set the tariff on imports at 5–10% of the value of the goods with additional duties on goods carried by foreign ships, thus also promoting the American merchant marine[12].

At this point, there were at least 50 forms of coinage and currencies in circulation from different countries and states. Another problem was the vast debts, about $74 million, owed both by states and the national government to foreigners and Americans alike. Hamilton proposed a series of measures to pay off the debt and to establish the United States as creditworthy. He persuaded Congress to borrow money from abroad to refinance and immediately pay off the $12 million dollars owed to foreign creditors. Hamilton also proposed creating new federal bonds that would allow payment of all of the national and state debts. The money to pay off the interest would come from the import duties, while the total amount of the new bonds exceeded the debts, creating a source of liquidity.

Hamilton had noted how Great Britain used its public debt to build up the Royal Navy and stimulate industry. Rather than make America a pawn of Britain, as his opponents claimed, Hamilton wanted to use British methods to build up the United States to make it less dependent on Britain. Hamilton argued, "States, like individuals, who observe their engagements are respected and trusted" [13].

Madison and others opposed paying off the debts at face value because much of the debt had been bought by speculators. Hamilton noted that figuring out the ownership of the debt would be an administrative nightmare, while failing to pay at face value would be "a breach of contract" [14]. Finally, Hamilton gained Madison's support for his proposal in exchange for a promise that the capital would be moved southward to what later became Washington, DC.

The passage of the measure ensured the creditworthiness of the United States, while the resulting economic growth led to a faster reduction in debt payments than expected. Contrary to those who thought Hamilton wanted the nation to always be in debt, Hamilton had instead written that it should be incorporated "as a fundamental maxim in the system of public credit of the United States that the creation of debt should always be accompanied with the means of extinguishment" [15].

Hamilton now proposed creating a national bank that could increase the amount of money in circulation and replace the various currencies with dollars issued by the Bank of the United States. Hamilton proposed that the government would deposit not only gold and silver but also other bonds in the Bank, thus expanding the amount of money it could lend. Hamilton persuaded Washington to sign the bill over the objections of Jefferson and Madison, arguing that the Constitution established "implied powers" of the federal government as necessary to achieve the goals of the government[16].

Hamilton now turned his attention to diversifying the American economy. In his "Report on the Subject of Manufactures," Hamilton argued that America would benefit from strong manufacturing and financial, as well as agricultural, sectors.

Hamilton wrote that every nation needed "the means of subsistence, habitation, clothing and defence" [17]. Hamilton persuaded Congress to raise certain tariffs to allow for the establishment of domestic manufacturers of these goods.

By the time Hamilton left office in 1795, the United States had a stable currency, a central bank, and among the best credit in the world. McCraw concluded, "The American financial system was now on its way to becoming the best in the world" [18]. Theodore Roosevelt concluded that Hamilton was "the most brilliant American statesman who ever lived, possessing the loftiest and keenest intellect of his time" [19]. Chernow wrote, "Hamilton was that rare revolutionary: a master administrator and as competent a public servant as American politics ever produced" [20].

Yet the lofty rhetoric of Constitutional issues was marred in these early years by vicious personal attacks and jockeying for power. Exhausted by the attacks, particularly from adherents of Jefferson and Madison, Hamilton resigned his post in 1795.

Hamilton's future following his resignation was one of increasing problems. He severely suffered from the loss of Washington's restraining influence. In 1797, his political opponents published details of his adulterous affair with Maria Reynolds. Hamilton had paid blackmail to Reynolds and her husband to prevent disclosure of the affair. Against the advice of allies, Hamilton published a long reply to the attack, admitting the affair but denying corruption in office. Hamilton's reputation never recovered from the scandal, although he remained a leader in the Federalist Party. Chernow wrote, "Without Washington's guidance of public responsibility, he had again revealed a blazing, ungovernable temper that was unworthy of him and rendered him less effective" [21].

Hamilton further wounded his reputation with a searing attack on the Federalist President John Adams, with whom Hamilton had fallen out after Hamilton was found to be behind an effort to replace Adams with Charles Pinckney as the Federalist candidate. Then in 1804, Hamilton was challenged to a duel by Aaron Burr, the then Vice President of the United States, who Hamilton had disparaged as corrupt. Burr blamed Hamilton for preventing him from gaining the Presidency and then the Governorship of New York. Three years earlier, Hamilton's oldest son, Philip, had been killed in a duel trying to protect his father's honor. Burr now challenged Hamilton to a duel. On July 11, 1804, Burr killed Hamilton in the duel. Thomas Jefferson, long Hamilton's greatest political opponent, would later write, "Hamilton was indeed a singular character of acute understanding, disinterested, honest, and honorable in all private transactions, amiable in society and duly valuing virtue in private life—yet so bewitched and perverted by the British example to be under the thorough conviction that corruption was essential to the government of a nation" [22].

Another immigrant, Albert Gallatin, would dominate financial affairs through the presidencies of Jefferson and Madison, from 1801–1813. Congressman Josiah Quincy would comment in 1813 that the country had been governed in the previous twelve years by "two Virginians and a foreigner" [23].

Albert Gallatin was born in Geneva, Switzerland in 1761. Gallatin was educated at the elite Academy of Geneva. After graduation, he decided, along with two classmates, to move to America, then still in the throes of the battle for independence against Britain. Gallatin arrived in 1780. After his initial misadventures, he spent two years tutoring students at Harvard in French and improving his English.

Gallatin became an American citizen in 1785. Upon receiving his inheritance in 1786, he bought a four-hundred-acre plot of land in western Pennsylvania. In 1788, he was elected a delegate to a Pennsylvania Convention to discuss revisions of the not yet ratified Constitution. He was married in May 1789, but his wife suddenly died a bare five months later. Following her death, Gallatin devoted most of the rest of his life to public service.

Gallatin was elected to the Pennsylvania House of Representatives in 1790. He found that he excelled in the understanding of finance and became very influential. He later recalled, "In the session of 1791–92, I was put on 35 Committees, prepared all the reports and drew all their bills" [24]. His plan to refinance the state debt succeeded brilliantly. He also supported chartering the Bank of Pennsylvania. Gallatin's measures also included a measure that limited land claims to four hundred acres and required buyers to actually settle the land. To the protests of land speculators, Gallatin replied, "The happiness of a country [depended] on the poorer class of people having it in their power to become freeholders" [25].

In 1793, Gallatin was elected by the legislature to the United States Senate, where he attacked Hamilton's financial management. The majority Federalists challenged his eligibility, claiming he had not been a citizen for the required nine years before his election, and expelled him on a party-line vote. However, the next year, having been a citizen for nine years, he was elected to the US House of Representatives, where he took his seat at the start of 1795. Gallatin was the leading financial expert among the Democratic-Republicans who had won a majority in 1794. Madison wrote Jefferson, "Gallatin is a real Treasure ... He is sound in his principles, accurate in his calculations and indefatigable in his researches" [26].

In 1796, Gallatin published "A Sketch of the Finances of the United States," in which he attacked most of Hamilton's program. He argued that the United States should work to abolish its debt by practicing extreme frugality while raising money from the tariffs and sales of Western lands. McCraw wrote, "Gallatin's Sketch was an attack by one immigrant financial expert on the program of another. Each had proven himself the preeminent economic expert within one of the two emerging political parties: Hamilton for the Federalists,

Gallatin for the Republicans" [27]. Biographer Gregory May wrote, "Gallatin demystified Treasury operations, showed how the Washington administration had increased the public debt, and exposed the administration's financial proposals to more open debate" [28].

By 1796, Gallatin assumed much of the leadership of the Republicans in the House. Gallatin persuaded the House to establish a standing Ways and Means Committee to monitor federal spending. Federalist Harrison Grey Otis, who had studied French from Gallatin at Harvard, spoke for many of his party when he attacked Gallatin at a public meeting, saying, "Shall we join a vagrant foreigner in opposition to Washington, a foreigner who to [my] knowledge ten years ago came to this country without a second shirt to his back?" [29].

John Adams had been elected president in 1796 and quarreled with both the Republicans and Hamilton. Adams remarked that Hamilton "was a bastard and as much a foreigner as Gallatin" [30]. Federalists, besides attacking Gallatin as a foreigner, also attacked him for his links to the protests against the whiskey excise tax that had led to the Whiskey Rebellion, an armed protest quelled by federal forces in 1794. Gallatin was unsuccessful in preventing the Federalist majority in Congress from passing the Alien and Sedition Acts, which allowed the president to deport immigrants whom the president viewed as dangerous and criminalized opposition to government measures. Abigail Adams wrote that the "Jesuit Gallatin is as subtle and artful and designing as ever but meets with more decided opposition" [31]. The Federalists, reflecting their suspicion of new immigrants, also passed an act lengthening the period of residence required for citizenship from 5 to 14 years.

When Thomas Jefferson defeated Adams in the presidential election of 1800, he named Gallatin Secretary of the Treasury, writing that Gallatin was "the only man in the United States who understands, through all the laberinths that Hamilton involved it, the precise state of the Treasury and the resources of the Country"[32]. Jefferson, Secretary of State James Madison, and Gallatin would work closely together to accomplish the administration's goals. Much of the actual work of administration was left to Gallatin, who was the only one of the three to spend the hot summers in Washington, DC. The Treasury was the largest of the Federal departments, responsible not only for revenues and spending but also for the Mint, the Post Office, and the management of public lands, harbors, lighthouses, and hospitals for seamen.

Jefferson did not always accept Gallatin's recommendations, rejecting his suggestion that federal employees be chosen on merit rather than politics and that a woman might be appointed to a position. Jefferson wrote, "The appointment of a woman to office is an innovation for which the public is not prepared, nor am I"[33].

Gallatin persuaded Jefferson of the need for a national bank and at least temporary internal taxes. Jefferson replied, "It mortifies me to be strengthening principles which I deem radically vicious," yet agreed to continue these measures at Gallatin's behest[34].

Jefferson and Gallatin emphasized paying off the national debt, which they proposed to do by reducing taxes and spending, including eliminating a standing army and navy. Jefferson had exhorted Gallatin to expose "the blunders and frauds of Hamilton," but after research, Gallatin would conclude, "Hamilton made no blunders, committed no frauds; he did nothing wrong"[35].

Gallatin secured the elimination of internal taxes by Congress, most notably the unpopular tax on whiskey. He also made substantial progress in paying down the national debt, which decreased from $83 million in 1801 to $45 million in 1812. Gallatin's reduction in military spending was predicated on the nation remaining uninvolved in the war between Britain and France.

One of Gallatin's most significant contributions was persuading Jefferson of the constitutionality of the Louisiana

Purchase and creatively producing the funding to complete the purchase, which almost doubled the territory of the United States. Gallatin also played a major role in championing the Lewis and Clark expedition.

Gallatin broke from Republican orthodoxy in championing the development of infrastructure. In 1808, he presented his "Report on Roads and Canals," in which he proposed spending $2 million a year for the next decade to develop new and better roads and canals to improve transportation and communications between the different parts of the nation. The plan would be rejected by those opposed to spending federal money on internal improvements, but it was also thwarted by the outbreak of the War of 1812, which swallowed up the available money.

In 1810, Gallatin emulated Hamilton's "Report on the Subject of Manufactures" with his own "Report on Manufactures." Gallatin proposed a $20 million federal program to make loans to manufacturers to help spur the development of manufacturing in the nation. Unfortunately, the plan did not come to fruition as the War of 1812 consumed the surplus in federal revenues that Gallatin had envisioned using for the program.

Jefferson's first term was marked by a flourishing economy and the Louisiana Purchase. His second term would be less successful. Great Britain, desperate for sailors for its large navy, had increasingly seized British immigrants and deserters off American ships. In 1807, the HMS *Leopard* fired at the USS *Chesapeake* when denied permission to search the ship, killing three Americans and wounding 18. Rather than declaring war, Jefferson proposed an Embargo Act that would remove American ships from the seas. Gallatin strongly opposed the plan, commenting, "Governmental prohibitions do always more mischief than had been calculated ... as to the hope that it may ... induce England to treat us better, I think it entirely groundless" [36].

Congress passed the Embargo Act on December 22, 1807,

banning all American merchant ships from traveling to a foreign destination. British ships could continue to enter and leave American ports, ensuring that the biggest loser would be American shippers and exporters. The embargo would last for 15 months despite Gallatin urging the President to reconsider. Maritime smuggling skyrocketed. American exports declined 80% in a year while federal revenues plummeted. Jefferson left office with his popularity dashed.

He was succeeded by James Madison, who wanted to make Gallatin Secretary of State, but members of Congress objected to making a "foreigner" the nation's top diplomat. Madison instead named Robert Smith, who proved to be a disastrous choice. John Quincy Adams later wrote that if Gallatin had been appointed instead, "it is highly probable that the war [of 1812] with Great Britain would not have taken place" [37].

Madison, a brilliant political thinker, proved an ineffective executive. The embargo was tweaked but not repealed. Meanwhile, the charter of the Bank of the United States came up for renewal in 1811. Gallatin had strongly endorsed its continued operation, but Madison remained on the fence in the face of strong opposition from those who felt that their local banks would prosper if the operation of the Bank ceased and they could scoop up its profitable business. On January 24, 1811, the motion for the recharter was put off indefinitely in the House by a vote of 65 to 64. In the Senate, a 15–15 tie was broken by the negative vote of the vice president. Gallatin resigned in protest but was persuaded to withdraw his resignation.

In 1812, after years of frustrations, the United States declared war on Great Britain by a close Congressional margin. Gallatin had been preparing to raise additional financing in case of war, but the end of the Bank of the United States the prior year made this exceedingly difficult, for state banks were reluctant to help. Congress at last accepted Gallatin's proposals for new taxes, but the war had seen the revenue from import duties collapse due to a British blockade.

The six men most responsible for securing the financing for the United States for the War of 1812 were all immigrants, including three Secretaries of the Treasury and three financiers. Gallatin served as Treasury Secretary until May 1813, when Madison sent him to Europe as a peace negotiator. He was succeeded as Secretary of the Treasury by George Campbell, originally from Scotland, and then Alexander Dallas, who hailed from Jamaica. The three largest investors in wartime securities were also immigrants. Stephen Girard arrived from France in 1774, while John Jacob Astor and David Parish immigrated to the United States from Germany in 1784 and 1805, respectively. The three investors supplied the majority of the money to purchase war bonds in April 1813, a month after Gallatin had informed Madison that "we have hardly enough money to last till the end of the month" [38].

The war itself showed a series of American military disasters interrupted by rare victories. Peace negotiations began in March 1813. Gallatin helped hold the quarreling American negotiators together in the face of British intransigence and delay. Finally, after 21 months of negotiations, a peace treaty was signed on December 24, 1814, ending the war. For the Americans, avoiding defeat felt like a victory, while the end of the war allowed the resumption of trade between Britain and America. John Quincy Adams' grandson Henry Adams called the treaty "the special work and the peculiar triumph of Mr. Gallatin" [39]. Gallatin wrote about the peace treaty, "Whatever objections may be made to it, and objections there will be, it is as good as could be obtained" and as good as "we had ... a right to expect" [40].

Gallatin refused to return to his position at the Treasury but reluctantly agreed to serve as the American Ambassador to France. He stayed in this post from 1816–23. During this time, he helped negotiate a new commercial treaty with Britain that also settled the boundary between Canada and the

United States and resolved several other outstanding issues. After two years of retirement, he became the Ambassador to Great Britain in 1826. Finally, he left public service in 1828 at age 67. He moved to New York City to become the president of the new National Bank of New York, funded by Astor. Gallatin helped found in 1831 what became New York University. Gallatin also wrote a series of works on Native American ethnology, co-founding the American Ethnological Society and then serving as the president of the New York Historical Society. He died in 1848 at the age of 88. He was buried in Trinity Cemetery in New York, close to the grave of Alexander Hamilton. Gallatin biographer Henry Adams wrote that Gallatin "was the most fully and perfectly equipped statesman we can show ... I cannot say as much for his friends Jefferson, Madison and Monroe" [41].

Despite serious ideological differences, both Hamilton and Gallatin agreed on a variety of issues that would be key to the growth of the American economy. These included the importance of credit, having money available to support new enterprises, a national bank to supply and regulate this credit, the importance of manufacturing as well as agriculture to the United States, and the need for internal improvements. Without the successful deliverance of much of this in the nation's first quarter century, the United States may well not have survived.

It is worth noting that the Constitution allowed immigrants to serve in any position except President. The Constitution set limits on how long a person had to be a citizen before serving in Congress (seven years for the House, nine years for the Senate). It mandated that the federal government create rules for how people needed to be residents before they could become citizens. After a period, when this time was changed from two years to five to 14, the Naturalization Act of 1801 set this period at five years, which has subsequently stayed the law[42].

1 Thomas K. McCraw. *The Founders and Finance: How Hamilton, Gallatin and Other Immigrants Forged a New Economy*, Belknap Press, 2012, 3.

2 Novic, 38.

3 Ron Chernow. *Alexander Hamilton*, Penguin Books, New York, 2004, 23.

4 Chernow, 60.

5 McCraw, 28.

6 McCraw, 43.

7 Chernow, 88.

8 McCraw, 77.

9 Chernow, 235.

10 Chernow, 247.

11 McCraw, 83.

12 McCraw, 89.

13 Chernow, 297.

14 McCraw, 101.

15 Chernow, 300.

16 McCraw, 118.

17 McCraw, 124.

18 McCraw, 121.

19 Chernow, 492.

20 Chernow, 319.

21 McCraw, 133.

22 Chernow, 288.

23 McCraw, 181.

24 McCraw, 196.

25 May. *Jefferson's Treasure*, Regnery History, Washington, DC, 2018, 35.

26 McCraw, 205.

27 McCraw, 214.

28 May, xxiv.

29 May, 72.

30 McCraw, 217.

31 Chernow, 646.

32 May, 79.

33 McCraw, 227.

34 McCraw, 230.

35 McCraw, 232.

36 McCraw, 275.

37 McCraw, 287.

38 McCraw. 302.

39 McCraw, 314.

40 May, 242.

41 May, xxviii.

42 Daniels, 113-115.

John Ericsson

Elijah McCoy

CHAPTER 3

Immigrants: Rich, Poor, and Inventive

The years from the American Revolution to the Civil War were marked by a rapid growth of the population, in large part due to immigrants. Immigrants also helped bring technological advances and new businesses that led to rapid economic growth.

At the start of this period, Britain, the leader of the Industrial Revolution, had laws prohibiting the emigration of skilled artisans or the export of machinery. Nevertheless, many of these men began to leave Britain to immigrate to the new nation. One of the most important was Samuel Slater. Slater had been an apprentice at a water-powered cotton mill in Britain that had been designed by Richard Arkwright, the inventor of the British textile industry. Slater memorized details of the mill and machinery. Disguised as a farm laborer, he took a ship to America in 1789. After immigrating, Slater moved to Providence, Rhode Island. Nearby, he erected the first cotton mill in the United States at Pawtucket Falls. Other mills soon followed. The machine produced cotton thread, helping make cotton the dominant material in clothing in the United States within two decades. Slater's mills also marked the beginning of the Industrial Revolution in America[1].

Slater pioneered the factory system in America. He copied

an English concept in dividing the work into a variety of simple tasks rather than requiring skilled artisans who could do everything. He also opened the first American mill powered by steam. President Andrew Jackson, when visiting the mill, asked Slater if it was true that "you taught us how to spin so as to rival Great Britain in her manufactures." Slater reportedly replied, "Yes sir, I suppose that I gave out the psalm, and they have been singing the tune ever since" [2].

Douglas McKay was born in Canada, the oldest of ten children of a Scottish farmer. In 1827, he moved to New York, determined to learn the shipbuilding trade. His family all joined together to pay for his passage from Nova Scotia. At age 17, McKay found a job as a laborer in a shipyard. By the time he was twenty-one, he was a skilled shipwright. McKay started working on ship design with a friend, John Griffiths. Before long, McKay was building his own ships. His first ship, the *Courier*, outdistanced the other ships on the Liverpool–New York run. Impressed, a Boston shipowner, Enoch Train, formed a partnership with McKay. From 1844–48, McKay built five ships for Train. Then gold was discovered in California. This put a premium on ships that could travel quickly to California.

In 1848, McKay built the *Stag Hound, the* first of a new class of ships that would be called the Yankee Clippers. The largest merchant ship ever built, the *Stag Hound* traveled back and forth from San Francisco in 118 days, setting a record and paying for itself in a single voyage. McKay's next ship, the *Flying Cloud*, broke that record. *The Flying Cloud,* unusual in that the ship's navigator was Ellen Creasy, the wife of her captain, Josiah Creesy, did the journey in 89 days[3].

McKay's next ship, the *Sovereign of the Seas,* completed the journey in 103 days despite losing two masts in a storm. By 1853, alternative modes of transportation decreased the market for the great clipper ships. McKay built several more clipper ships before their day ended when they could not compete with the new steamships. With the onset of the Civil

War, McKay reorganized his shipyard to build iron-hulled steamships. McKay would later say, "I never yet built a vessel that came up to my own ideal. I saw something in each ship which I desired to improve"[4].

Eleuthere DuPont de Nemours was the son of Pierre DuPont de Nemours, a French intellectual who served as president of the Constituent Assembly during the French Revolution. When the revolution turned more radical, the DuPonts were condemned to death. Reprieved by the death of Robespierre, they fled to America. Eleuthere was born in Paris in 1771, where he studied the production of gunpowder. He came to the United States in 1800 and, by 1802, had established his business, the Eleutherin Mills, along the Brandywine River in Delaware. DuPont found the American production of gunpowder to be inefficient and of poor quality. Going into the production of gunpowder, DuPont became wildly successful. The firm owned the houses of its employees and managed their lives. DuPont became the major source of gunpowder for the Union in the Civil War[5].

The new inventors were joined by other immigrants, a few of whom went from rags to riches. John Jacob Astor, the son of a German butcher, arrived in New York in 1784. He became a merchant specializing in furs. Initially, Astor himself would travel into the interior to buy furs. He would travel to the western shore of Lake Superior in the 1790s to see Grand Portage, the Canadian Northwest Company's trading post for western furs. Within two decades, Astor had become the dominant fur trader in America, combining this business with owning ships trading for tea in China. His American Fur Company sought out furs throughout the nation, mostly in the West, and in Canada.

In 1808, Astor wrote to President Jefferson asking for a meeting. Astor wrote, "It is my intention to have presented myself before you my wish of engaging in an extensive trade with the Indians ... [that] may in time embrace the greater part of the fur trade on this continent, the most of which passes now through Canada"[6]. The result of their meeting was a plan by Astor, with Jefferson's rhetorical support, to establish an American colony and trading post on the Pacific Ocean at the mouth of the Columbia River in what is now Oregon. In 1810, Astor dispatched two parties of men, one overland and one by sea around Cape Horn at the bottom of South America, to establish this outpost, which would be named Astoria. From there, furs would be gathered and transported to China to be sold for Chinese goods to be, in turn, brought back to New York. Jefferson wrote Astor, "I view [your undertaking] as the germ of a great, free and independent empire on that side of our continent"[7].

Both parties would suffer multiple hardships and casualties before finally reaching and establishing the outpost, which they named Astoria. Despite the hardships, Astoria initially flourished with parties sent in all directions to trade for furs with the Indians.

The War of 1812 would dash Astor's dreams. Astor opposed the war, knowing that the British Navy could prevent American trade from reaching the post, but to no avail. Astor spoke to Secretary of the Treasury Gallatin. Gallatin proposed to President Madison that an American frigate be sent to the Pacific, dropping off Marines to protect Astoria "so as to embrace this opportunity of taking possession"[8]. However, no action was taken. Under British threats, those in charge at Astoria, many of them Scots and former employees of the British Northwest Company, agreed to abandon the post.

Hearing of the debacle, Astor reportedly concluded, "My plan was right, but my men were weak. Time will vindicate my reasoning"[9]. Astor spent the next two decades building up a fur trading empire east of the Rockies. Much of his profits were sunk into the purchase of land. The amount of property was such that his heir, William B. Astor, became known as "the landlord of New York"[10].

With the end of the war, Britain and the United States agreed to a joint occupation of the disputed "Oregon" territory along the Northern Pacific coast, which stretched from Spanish-owned California to Russian Alaska. While the British dominated the fur trade in the area, a growing number of American settlers took residence. Finally, in 1846, Britain and the United States settled on the current American-Canadian border.

When Astor died in 1848 at age 84, he was the richest man in the nation. His fortune of $20 million dollars would be worth $110 billion in today's dollars[11]. His contribution would form the foundation for the New York Public Library.

Another successful immigrant was Alexander Stewart, who arrived from Ireland in 1823. Stewart started as a seller of linens. Within a few years, he was successful enough to build a huge dry goods store In New York. At his peak, Stewart employed two thousand persons, earning a fantastic income, for the day, of over $1 million dollars a year[12].

Of course, there were a multitude of immigrants who arrived in America but did not become millionaires.

The first years of the new nation saw a variety of immigrants arrive. The large number of immigrants landing there had, by 1790, allowed New York to overtake Philadelphia as the most populous city. Historian James MacGregor Burns wrote, "The city was already turning into the human salmagundi of the new nation ... so many exiles from France had settled in Manhattan that newspapers printed some advertisements in their language. Germans and British—especially Irish—were landing by the boatload ... New York did not yet contain a ghetto for Blacks, Jews, Irish or any other race or nationality"[13].

Nevertheless, immigration was relatively slow in the years between Yorktown and the end of the War of 1812, averaging about ten thousand a year. The increase in the American population from 3.9 to 9.6 million from 1790–1820 was almost entirely due to births exceeding deaths among the existing population[14].

Before the Revolution and in the early years of the Republic, the majority were of British stock. From 1815–30, some 220,000 immigrants arrived, three-fourths from the British Isles. This began to change as the nineteenth century progressed. Immigration increased almost tenfold as the years 1830–1850 saw the arrival of 2.5 million people[15].

One of the biggest factors in European immigration was the rapid growth of the population in Europe. From 140 million in 1750, the European population reached 260 million by 1850 and 400 million by WWI[16]. The limited amount of land available for the growing population in Europe helped, for many, drive the decision to move.

A huge wave of immigrants, driven by disease, famine, and poverty, fled Ireland for America. By 1850, they outnumbered the British as the major source of new settlers. Hunger, which reached its height in the Great Famine of the mid-1840s when the potato crop failed, would be a principal driver of Irish emigration. A half million Irish would immigrate to the United States prior to the famine, while another 1.5 million would arrive in the famine decade from 1845–55[17]. This does not include an estimated 9% of those fleeing Ireland who, weakened by hunger and disease, died on the voyage to America[18]. In the worst year, 1847, the death toll was 20% of Irish emigrants, compared to the average death toll of 9% on slave ships[19]. A higher proportion of the population would emigrate from Ireland than any other nation[20].

From 1820 to 1920, some 4.5 million Irish would immigrate to America[21]. The Irish tended to congregate along the Eastern seaboard in the coastal cities. Irish American author Frank McCourt wrote, "Our forebears, landing on the eastern seaboard of the United States, hesitated to move inland, where they could have farmed to their hearts' content. Oh no, they weren't going to be caught again. Look at what the land had done to them in Ireland. They'd stay in the big cities, never again to become victims of the treacherous spud" [22].

It was not the poorest proportion of the Irish population that emigrated, for they could not afford the cost of passage, but the strata just above, many aided by money sent by relatives already in the United States. Over half of the Irish would settle in just four states: Massachusetts, New York, Pennsylvania, and Illinois, with four-fifths living in cities [23].

The Irish would suffer the prejudice that would later befall other immigrants. The native American population was suspicious of their numbers, their Catholicism, and their Gaelic language. The Know Nothing Party was a political movement formed largely in opposition to the Irish immigrants. When looking for work, many of the Irish would encounter signs saying, "No Irish Need Apply" [24]. A help-wanted ad in the *New York Herald* read, "A cook, washer, and ironer, who perfectly understands her business; any color or country except Irish" [25].

The Know Nothings reached their peak in 1855 when they became the second-largest political party in the nation. The prior year saw them capture six governorships and win near-majorities in the Massachusetts and New York legislatures. Members promised to support only American-born Protestants and pushed Congressional legislation that would require immigrants to live for 25 years in the United States before they could become citizens. Abraham Lincoln wrote a friend, "As a nation, we began by declaring that 'all men are created equal.' We now practically read it 'all men are created equal except Negroes.' When the Know-Nothings get control, it will read that 'all men are created equal except Negroes, and foreigners and Catholics'" [26].

Prejudice against the Irish was not limited to the less educated. The prominent cleric Reverend Lyman Beecher, father of Harriet Beecher Stowe, author of *Uncle Tom's Cabin*, frequently preached violently anti-Catholic sermons. After three such sermons one day in Boston, a mob burned down the

Ursuline convent and school, setting off a wave of burnings of Catholic churches[27]. Ralph Waldo Emerson, the nation's leading intellectual before the Civil War, put the Irish among the lower races, writing in 1829, "I think it cannot be maintained by any candid person that the African race have ever occupied or do promise ever to occupy any very high place in the human family. Their present condition is the strongest proof that they cannot. The Irish cannot, the American Indian cannot, the Chinese cannot ..." [28].

Rhetoric against the Irish sometimes turned to violence. A mob in Ellsworth, Maine, in 1854, tarred and feathered and nearly burned to death a priest. After the election riots of 1855 in Louisville, a priest reported, "a reign of terror ... nearly one hundred poor Irish have been butchered or burned, and some twenty houses have been consumed in the flames" [29].

The Irish found employment, particularly in manual labor. The majority of those who built the Erie Canal in 1825 and other canals were Irish[30]. Historian James MacGregor Burns wrote, "Canal builders lacked excavating machines, so the canals were built by crowds of men with shovels and crude derricks. Hundreds of 'Irish bogtrotters' were kept at work for long hours amid the muck" [31]. Historian Kevin Baker described the Irish role, writing, "At eighty cents a day, Irish immigrants made five times the wages they could get at home, but contractors fed them swill, housed them in shanties and dosed them with twelve to twenty ounces of whiskey a day ... They died in droves from dysentery, yellow fever, typhus, pneumonia, dehydration and falling trees and faulty equipment and were despised by people in the towns they were about to enrich" [32].

Irish labor also played a major role in the building of the railroads, with so many deaths among them that it was said that there was "an Irishman buried under every [railroad] tie" [33]. Others found employment in Pennsylvania mines and other construction projects. Economist Thomas Sowell wrote,

"The hardships of their lives may be summed up in a nineteenth-century observation, 'You seldom see a gray-haired Irishman.'" [34].

Women increased as a percentage of Irish immigrants over time. Many found work as domestic servants. Historian Roger Daniels commented, "The great reluctance of native-born Americans to work as servants created an endemic servant problem in the United States from the era of Andrew Jackson to the Great Depression. It was a problem whose solution was almost always immigrant 'help,' who—when not Irish—were usually German or Swedish immigrant women" [35].

Most Irish arrived in New York, where the population density of the seven lower wards of Manhattan almost doubled from 1820 to 1850. Historian Burns wrote, "New Jersey contractors recruited construction gangs among the Irish of New York City, and for sixty cents a day, tens of thousands labored from sunrise to sunset in the swampy, disease-ridden lowlands" [36].

Some of the Irish turned to politics. Mike Walsh was born in Ireland in 1815. In 1841, he challenged the Democratic Party in New York City, which was dominated at the time by old-line Protestant leaders. Their nominating committee refused to choose Walsh for a seat in the state legislature and refused to let him speak. Walsh worked to organize the Irish workers, founding his own newspaper, the *Subterranean*, to aid the campaign. Before the decade was over, he won a seat in the state legislature and then a seat in Congress. Walsh remained an advocate for the poor, telling Congress, "The only difference between the Negro slave of the South and the White wage slave of the North is that one has a master without asking for him and the other has to beg for the privilege of becoming a slave" [37].

The success of the Irish in urban politics meant that they assumed control of municipal political machines well into the twentieth century. Sowell noted, "The Irish political machines were accessible to people still in the working class and the slums ... the bewildering bureaucracies, regulations and red tape confronting the poor and uneducated could be made responsive or could be circumvented through the episodic interventions of political bosses" [38].

The Irish immigration expanded the proportion of the American population that was Catholic from 5% in 1840 to 12% in 1860[39].

Daniels noted how the Irish immigrants, along with German Catholic immigrants, transformed the Catholic Church in America, commenting that these immigrants and their children "made up the vast majority of church membership and the Roman Catholic church [became] ... an immigrant church" [40].

The most consequential leader of the Catholic Church of the day was John Hughes, born in Ireland in 1797, the son of a tenant farmer. Hughes immigrated to the United States in 1817. Initially turned down in his application to study at Mount St. Mary's Seminary, he secured work there as a gardener and persuaded them to allow him entry in 1820. At age 26, he was ordained as a priest. In 1837, he was called on to be a bishop in New York. Hughes conducted an unsuccessful battle to secure funding for Catholic schools but was nonetheless successful in setting up an extensive system of Catholic schools in the city.

When anti-Catholic agitators burned churches elsewhere, Hughes put armed guards on the churches and announced that "if a single Catholic church was burned in New York, the city would become a second Moscow," which had burned down thirty years earlier[41]. There were no attacks on churches in New York City.

Hughes tripled the number of churches in the city, encouraged Catholic charitable organizations to serve the poor, and laid the cornerstone for St. Patrick's Cathedral.

The dominance of the Catholic Church was not without critics. As a critic of Irish descent, a sociologist, and later a United States senator, Daniel Patrick Moynihan pointed out the negative aspects in the 1960s, writing, "In secular terms, it has cost [the Irish] dearly in men and money. A good part of the surplus that might have gone into family property has gone into the building of the Church. This has almost certainly inhibited the development of the solid middle-class dynamics that produce so many of the important people in America" [42].

The 1850s saw another 2.75 million immigrants arrive, a slight majority being from Ireland, with the next most common group being Germans. Irish immigration continued in large numbers through the nineteenth century. Of the roughly 4.5 million Irish who came to the United States between 1820 and 1930, half were women[43]. Contrary to popular belief, the majority of Irish arrived after 1860, although they made up a smaller percentage of the arriving immigrants as the century progressed[44].

Early German immigration was disproportionately from various pacifist sects that then settled across the nation. German immigration rose in the 1850s. 1848 had seen the suppression of liberal movements throughout Europe. Many of the liberal Germans found their way to the United States. Others came to escape the hunger, population growth, and oppression that was widespread across Germany. While one in four Germans became farmers, others settled in the cities, particularly in the Midwest. Germans were more often (when compared to the Irish) skilled artisans, and they dominated the beer industry. Close to six million Germans would immigrate from 1820–1924[45].

Prejudice against the Germans was less as the majority were Protestants and their settlements were more diffused across the nation, with only a minority settling in large cities. Despite the increased diffusion, the so-called German triangle made up of the midwestern cities of Cincinnati, St. Louis, and Milwaukee would include the majority of Germans in the United States[46]. In 1860, 15% of New York City residents were

German immigrants, while they made up 20% of Chicago and 35% of the population of Milwaukee[47].

Germans brought many of their customs into America, where these traditions would be adopted by the new nation. German immigrants started the first orchestras and kindergartens. The first singing group, or glee club, was founded by German immigrants in Philadelphia in 1835. American universities had mainly been places for upper-class men to get a "liberal" education. Reflecting German universities, Germans married this concept to vocational training in new universities, starting with the University of Michigan in 1837[48]. Daniels concluded, "The major cultural enterprises of German America between 1850 and the outbreak of World War I ... was and remains unrivaled by any other American ethnic group" [49].

German language instruction in schools with large numbers of German immigrants would continue, in many cases, up to WWI. Among other things, German immigrants introduced the Christmas tree to America.

The Germans also changed the attitude that had come down from the Puritans that organized recreation was sinful and even more sinful if done on Sunday. German beer gardens catered to families, offering music, plays, and sports. In 1883, an observer noted, "The German notion that it is a good thing to have a good time has found a lodgment in the American mind ... There is no longer any such feeling about dancing, social games and dramatic performances as was almost universal among respectable people thirty years ago[50].

Some 250,00 of the German immigrants were Jews, numbers which far exceeded the preexisting Jewish community in America. The Jewish population of New York went from around five hundred in 1825 to an estimated 40,000 in 1860. The German Jews were unlikely to become farmers, becoming instead merchants and artisans, particularly tailors[51].

A number of nineteenth-century German immigrants achieved fame and success. Two German immigrants, John

Jacob Bausch and Henry Lomb, established an optical firm in 1849 that became the world's largest producer of lenses for products ranging from glasses to microscopes. Another German immigrant, John Augustus Roebling, built the world's first suspension bridges, including starting the work on the Brooklyn Bridge. Frederick Weyerhaeuser and Henry J. Heinz built giant companies in wood and food products, respectively[52].

Maximilian Berlitz was a German professor who immigrated to the United States in 1869. In less than a decade, he opened the first of what would be hundreds of schools teaching foreign languages[53].

A third major source of new immigrants were Scandinavians, drawn to the opportunities for free land for farms. Crop failures and declines in the fishing and timber industries helped motivate many[54]. The biggest driver, however, was the increasing population, which left much of the farm population landless.

The first large group to arrive were Swedes, who settled in Wisconsin in 1841. They would be joined by Norwegians, Danes, and Finns, who then dominated the lumber industry of the Northern frontier. Most were drawn by better economic opportunities than were found at home.

Estimates are that, of the Scandinavian immigrants before the Civil War, one-third were skilled artisans, one-third were unskilled workers, and the other third were farmers attracted by the prospect of land[55]. While only about 125,000 Scandinavians came before the Civil War, they would be joined by another two million before WWI, with the peak decade in the 1880s[56].

Of these immigrants, about half were Swedish, a third Norwegian, and the remainder Danish. They settled mostly in rural areas of the upper Midwest, although the 150,000 Swedes made up 9% of Chicago's population in 1900[57].

Sweden, in the nineteenth century, conducted intelligence

tests of its population. A scholar commented, "A comparison of those Swedes, rural as well as urban people, who emigrated later on, with those who remained in Sweden, reveals that ... emigrants generally made higher marks than the rest of the population. They were brighter in school, had a wider picture of the world, and were the kind of persons to whom it would occur to leave their habitual surroundings" [58].

One of the most influential Scandinavian immigrants was another inventor, John Ericsson. Ericsson was born on July 31, 1803, in Sweden. His father, an inspector of mines, helped teach John and his brother Nils the principles of mechanics, engaging other professional men to further their education. He also arranged for the boys to be appointed as cadets in the Mechanical Corps of the Swedish Navy in 1815. John Ericsson was assigned to work on the Gota Canal project. By age 14, he was the supervisor of some six hundred men. At 17, he transferred to a rifle regiment in the far north, where he surveyed the Jämtland region and, in his spare time, authored a book on the engineering of the Gota Canal. At age 22, he invented an engine that used heated air rather than steam to move a piston. Finding opportunities too limited in Sweden, he left for England in May 1826, never to return home[59].

Ericsson's demonstration of his flame engine failed. Still, John Braithwaite, owner of an engineering firm, offered Ericsson a job. Before long, the company was renamed Braithwaite and Ericsson. In the next decade, Ericsson patented thirty inventions, including a new pumping system for mines, new boilers, a steam fire engine, and a surface condenser for the maritime steam engine[60].

His greatest invention was the development of a screw propeller that replaced the paddle wheels of earlier steamships. Ericsson wrote to a friend, "1835. Designed a rotary propeller to be actuated by steam power" [61].

To demonstrate the invention, Ericsson built the *Frances B. Ogden*, a screw-propelled steamer named after the American consul in Liverpool who helped finance the venture. Despite the ship steaming faster than a comparable paddle-wheeled ship, the British Admiralty was indifferent.

Ericsson's inventions did not make much money. The construction of the *Ogden* pushed the company to the brink of bankruptcy. Ericsson was tossed into debtors' prison but was freed when Parliament fortunately passed an act "for the relief of insolvent debtors" [62].

Soon after his release from prison, Ericsson met Lieutenant Robert Stockton, a visiting American naval officer. Stockton realized the importance of the screw propeller, telling Ericsson, "I do not want the opinions of your scientific men; what I have seen this day satisfies me" [63]. Stockton commissioned Ericsson to build two screw-propelled ships.

In March 1839, Congress passed authorization to build three new men-of-war. Stockton was assured that one of the ships would be built on Ericsson's design. At the end of 1839, Ericsson moved to the United States. It would not be until 1841 that construction began on the large frigate. Ericsson designed not only the engine and propeller but also the guns and gun mounts.

Ericsson was not a very shrewd businessman, telling Stockton, "I shall be satisfied with whatever sum you may plan to recommend, or the Government sees fit to pay for the patent rights" [64]. The USS *Princeton*, as the ship was named, was the first iron propeller-driven man of war, the first to have its machinery below the water line, safe from enemy shot, the first to burn smokeless anthracite coal, the first with a collapsible smokestack, and several other innovations. Yet Ericsson remained unpaid for his work.

Ericsson had designed guns for the ship. Stockton had his own gun built, one that neglected some of Ericsson's design. On February 28, 1844, Stockton hosted President Tyler and much of the Cabinet on the *Princeton*. Stockton was persuaded to demonstrate his gun, which proceeded to explode, killing the Secretaries of State and the Navy and four others. Stockton blamed Ericsson and refused to pay him for his services. An 1855 court found in Ericsson's favor, but he remained unpaid for the work.

Nevertheless, Ericsson was able to get his "caloric" heated air engine to work, resulting in the production and sale of thousands of these engines. Ericsson also developed plans for a shot-proof, turreted main battery of guns. At the start of 1861, a friend of a friend, Cornelius Bushnell, asked to be able to present the idea to the Navy. Although Ericsson had known Bushnell for less than a day, he allowed Bushnell to make the presentation, again saying he would accept whatever compensation Bushnell thought was fair.

Bushnell showed the model to the new Secretary of the Navy, Gideon Welles, saying that "he had found a battery which would make us masters of the situation, as far as the ocean was concerned" [65].

Although the onset of the Civil War was imminent, both Welles and Bushnell knew that selling the idea to the conservative Navy board would be difficult. Bushnell arranged for Ericsson and himself to enter into partnership with two New York ironmakers who were friends of Secretary of State Seward. Bushnell and the two partners met first with Seward and Lincoln. Lincoln accompanied them to the Navy board meeting. Asked his opinion, Lincoln said, "All I have to say is what the girl said when she stuck her foot in the stocking. It strikes me there's something in it" [66]. Nevertheless, the board turned down the idea, with one member telling Bushnell, "Take the little thing home and worship it, as it would not be idolatry because it was made in the image of nothing in the heaven above or in the earth below or in the waters under the earth" [67]. Bushnell persuaded Ericsson to go to Washington, where he finally won the board's support for his *Monitor* plan, promising it could be built in a hundred days.

The Confederate Navy was building their own ironclad ship, the CSS *Virginia*, constructed on the top of the half-burned frigate *Merrimack*. On March 8, 1862, *Virginia* sortied out to attack the wooden ships of the Union Navy blockading Hampton Roads off northern Virginia. The *Virginia* destroyed two Union frigates while a third, the USS *Minnesota*, ran aground. It seemed like the Union blockade would soon be broken.

Yet the USS *Monitor*, the ironclad built by John Ericsson, was already en route. It arrived at the Union base at Fortress Monroe at 9 p.m. on the eighth. On March 9, the *Virginia* steamed out to finish destroying the Union fleet. Standing between it and its goal was the *Monitor*. Thus began the world's first battle between ironclad ships. William Keeler, an officer on the *Monitor*, wrote, "The sounds of the conflict at this time were terrible. The rapid firing of own guns amid the clouds of smoke ... mingled with the crash of solid shot against our sides and the bursting of shells all around us" [68]. Neither ship could destroy the other. At last, the *Virginia* retreated back to its base. John Ericsson's creation had saved the rest of the Union fleet and kept the blockade intact. The New York legislature and the US Congress both passed resolutions of thanks to Ericsson.

Ericsson would go on to build more ironclads for the Union. In the 1870s, he designed the USS *Destroyer*, the first ship to fire underwater torpedoes. John Ericsson died on March 8, 1889, at the age of eighty-six.

Another immigrant inventor faced an even harder path than Ericsson. Elijah McCoy was born in Canada in 1844, the son of two escaped slaves. At age 16, his parents sent him to Scotland to study mechanical engineering. Shortly thereafter, his parents moved back to the United States, settling in Michigan. When Elijah McCoy returned home, he could only get work as a fireman and oiler on the railroad. In his spare time, he worked in a home machine shop that he had set up.

In 1872, McCoy invented an automatic lubricator that oiled the engine even when it was moving[69]. Within a few years, his invention was being used on almost all American railroads.

McCoy continued perfecting the lubricators. When buyers were offered copies made by others, they might ask, "Is this the real McCoy?" reportedly introducing the phrase into the language[70]. In 1916, McCoy invented the graphite lubricator. McCoy also invented the folding ironing board, the first lawn sprinkler, and treads for tires to improve traction[71]. He would patent fifty-seven inventions and win election to the National Inventors Hall of Fame. McCoy died at age 85 in 1929.

---

1 McCraw, 126-7.

2 Harold Evans. *They Made America*, Little, Brown and Company, New York, 2004, 56

3 Kevin Baker. *America the Ingenious: How a Nation of Dreamers, Immigrants, and Tinkerers Changed the World*, Workman Publishing, New York, 2016, 15.

4 Bailey, 89.

5 Burns, 430.

6 Peter Stark. *Astoria*, HarperCollins, New York, 2015, 17.

7 Stark, 26.

8 Stark, 165.

9 Stark, 288.

10 Matthew Josephson. *The Robber Barons*, Harcourt, Brace and Jovanovich, Orland, 1914, 12.

11 Stark, 301.

12 Josephson, 12.

13 Burns, 80-81.

14 Daniels, 117.

15 Burns, 405.

16 Oscar Handlin. *The Uprooted.* Little, Brown and Company, Boston, second edition, 1979, 23.

17 Daniels, 135.

18 Barone, 110.

19 Sowell, 22.

20 Sowell, 21.

21 Kennedy, 18.

22 Frank McCourt. "Scraps and Leftovers: A Meditation." In Michael Coffey and Terry Golway, eds. *The Irish in America*, Hyperion, New York, 1997, 41.

23 Sowell, 25.

24 Burns, 406.

25 Tim Egan. *The Immortal Irishman: The Irish Revolutionary Who Became an American Hero*, Houghton Mifflin Harcourt, New York, 2016, 151.

26 Kennedy, 19.

27 Nell Irwin Painter. *A History of White People*, W.W. Norton and Company, New York, 2010, 136.

28 Painter, 139.

29 Painter, 148.

30 Burns, 303.

31 Burns, 405.

32 Baker, 10.

33 Sowell, 27.

34 Sowell, 1.

35 Daniels, 131.

36 Burns, 408.

37 Burns, 405.

38 Sowell, 31.

39 Barone, 107.

40 Meltzer, *Bound for America*, 33.

41 Barone, 120.

42 Barone, 121.

43 Meltzer, *Bound for America*, 57.

44 Daniels, 139.

45 Meltzer, *Bound for America*, 36, 38.

46 Daniels, 150.

47 Barone, 127.

48 Handlin, 32.

49 Daniels, 161.

50 Sowell, 60.

51 Daniels, 155.

52 Sowell, 59.

53 Sowell, 61.

54 Kennedy, 21.

55 Meltzer, *Bound for America*, 29.

56 Daniels, 165.

57 Daniels, 168-9.

58 Daniels, 166.

59 James L. Nelson. *Reign of Iron*, HarperCollins, New York, 2004, 116.

60 Nelson, 117.

61 Nelson, 118.

62 Nelson, 119.

63 Nelson, 120.

64 Nelson, 123.

65 Nelson, 130.

66 Nelson, 132.

67 Nelson, 133.

68 Milton Meltzer. *Voices from the Civil War*, HarperCollins, New York, 1989.

69 Debra J. Housel. *Famous Immigrants*. Teacher Created Materials, Huntington Beach, CA, 2008, 8.

70 Housel, 8.

71 Housel, 9.

Thomas Francis Meagher

Carl Schurz

CHAPTER 4

Preserving the Union

Immigrants are not a big part of the books on the Civil War. Yet their role in preserving the Union was pivotal.

The large-scale immigration to the United States in the years before the war was not spread evenly. In 1860, the United States had some four million foreign-born inhabitants, comprising 13% of the population. The immigrants lived overwhelmingly in the free states of the North. Less than 6% of the immigrants lived in the states that became the Confederacy[1].

Some immigrants were opposed to slavery, while others did not want to compete with slave labor. Most of the larger cities and most of the industry were in the north. These offered jobs and a chance to be near others who had immigrated from their homeland. Irish immigrants tended to congregate in the cities of the East Coast, while many of the German immigrants opposed slavery.

This disparity would make itself felt when the Civil War broke out. Immigrants and sons of immigrants made up over 40% of the Union's armed forces. Nearly two-thirds were Germans and Irish, but others came from all over the world. Among the Union dead at Gettysburg was John Tommy, a Chinese immigrant[2].

Despite their numbers, the role of immigrants has been minimized. The Confederacy tried to emphasize their role, claiming that the Union armies were filled with foreign mercenaries, the "dregs" of Europe. John Slidell, the Confederate envoy to France, told Emperor Napoleon III that "probably one-half of the [Union] privates were foreigners, principally German and Irish," while the Confederate troops "were almost exclusively born on our soil"[3].

Embarrassed by these claims, Union representatives tended to downplay the role of immigrants, while prejudice against immigrants also led to a minimization of their contributions. The most detailed record came from Benjamin Gould, who compiled *Investigations in the Military and Anthropological Statistics of American Soldiers*. Gould estimated that 495,000 of the 2.2 million men in the Union Army were born outside of the United States, while other estimates raise this to over 543,000. Immigrants played an even bigger role in the Union Navy, making up 43% of its 84,000 sailors. Another 18% of the Union soldiers and sailors, in Gould's calculations, were born in the United States but had at least one foreign-born parent[4]. Gould credited the immigrant enlistees with a "spirit of sympathy with a republic struggling for the maintenance of free institutions"[5].

Recruitment of immigrants was often made in their own languages. New York's 39th regiment, the Garibaldi Guard, appealed to "Italian Patriots! Hungarians! Friends of liberty! German freedom fighters! Arouse, arouse, arouse," in their own tongues[6]. To those who criticized the recruitment of those with limited English, Secretary of State William Seward replied, "The contest for the Union is regarded, as it ought to be, a battle of the freemen of the world for the institutions of self-government"[7].

The New York 39th Regiment would be comprised of four companies of Germans, two of Hungarians, one of Spanish, one of Italians, and one of Swiss and other volunteers from around the world. The regiment pledged allegiance in fourteen different languages. Their marching song proclaimed, "Ye come from many a far-off clime / And speak in many a tongue / But Freedom's song will reach the heart / In whatever language sung"[8].

The areas settled by German immigrants were among the most opposed to slavery. Historian Michael Barone commented, "The German presence on the major river cities on the border between slave and free states—Cincinnati, Louisville, St. Louis—had significant political repercussions. The cities were almost German islands in a Southern-settled sea, profoundly out of sympathy with the mores and opinions of their near neighbors" [9].

While the Germans supported the Republicans' anti-slavery positions, they were repelled by the temperance movement, which had many supporters among the Republicans. Barone argued that one of the reasons for Lincoln's nomination in 1860 was his opposition to the anti-immigrant Know Nothings and his skepticism about temperance laws. These stands helped him win German support and contributed to his victories in Pennsylvania, Indiana, and Illinois[10].

Those few areas in the South with large numbers of German immigrants tended to be less hostile to Blacks, both before and after the war. The large number of German immigrants in Missouri played a major role in preventing that slave state from joining the Confederacy[11].

No immigrants contributed more men to the Union than the Germans. Some 200,000 Germans fought in the Union army. Many had undergone compulsory military training in their homeland, while others brought experience from the unsuccessful revolutions of 1848 in Europe. Confederate envoy Dudley Mann wrote from Belgium, "The Germans, trained to war by the military system of their own little kingdoms and duchies, seem to sniff the carnage from afar. They come over … ready material for the rough work of war" [12].

Letters from German veterans explained their reasons for fighting. August Horstmann wrote his parents in Germany, "The freedom of the oppressed and the equality of human rights must first be fought for here. To us, the war is a war of sacred principles, a war that should deal the fatal blow to slavery and bow down the necks of the southern aristocracy" [13].

Manus Brucker had immigrated from Baden after the Revolution of 1848. He wrote to his wife that he did not care if neighbors called him "a Black Republicaner Abolitionist, Lincolnite or Yankee Vandal. I am satisfied with myself and am doing my duty as a citizen of this republic" [14].

Friedrich Martens wrote his family in Germany, "I don't have the space or the time to explain all about the cause, only that the states that are rebelling are slave states and they want to slavery to be expanded but the Northern states are against this" [15].

German immigrants supplied several generals for the Union army, most notably Franz Sigel and Carl Schurz, while many German immigrants won the Congressional Medal of Honor. Nevertheless, although they fought valiantly in many battles, Germans would be seen by some as not fighting well, most notably at Chancellorsville, where the Confederate assault struck the largely German XI (Eleventh) Corps. Sigel would play a role in the Union victory at Pea Ridge in 1861 but would be less successful in command of a corps at the Second Battle of Bull Run and when given an independent command in the Shenandoah Valley [16]. There would be over five hundred German-born officers in the Union army, including nine major generals [17].

Schurz would be one of the most prominent German immigrants. He had been a 19-year-old student when the 1848 revolution broke out in Germany and other nations. He founded a newspaper calling for democratic reforms and then joined a rebel army. He led an artillery company in 1849. When the last rebel forces surrendered in 1850, Schurz fled to Switzerland. From there, he made his way to Philadelphia in 1852. In 1855, Schurz moved to Wisconsin. He joined the new Republican party while his wife promoted kindergarten to be part of American education. At age 28, he was nominated as the Republican party's candidate for lieutenant governor, losing by 454 votes. He served as a spokesman for the Wisconsin delegation at the 1860 Republican Convention.

Schurz was appointed Ambassador to Spain in 1861 but returned, at his request, to join the Union army as a brigadier general in 1862. He would serve in multiple campaigns. Following the war, President Andrew Johnson, who succeeded Lincoln, asked Schurz to survey conditions in the South during Reconstruction. Johnson, feeling the report by Schurz was too favorable to Blacks, attempted to suppress it.

Schurz would be elected to the United States Senate in 1869. He soon turned to oppose the corruption in the Grant administration as well as its Reconstruction policy. He would preside over the "Liberal Republican" Convention in 1872, which nominated Horace Greeley. After supporting Rutherford B. Hayes in 1876, he was appointed Secretary of the Interior, where he tried to promote nonpartisan civil service and provide a more humane treatment of the Indians. Afterward, he would have a wide-ranging career, editing the *New York Post* and *Harpers Weekley*, serving as president of the National Civil Service Reform League, and opposing American annexation of the Philippines. He died in 1906[18].

Irish immigrants also joined the Union army in large numbers. This was despite the Irish being largely loyal to the Democratic Party and a target of widespread anti-Catholic prejudice. It did not help that Pope Pius IX and much of the Church leadership were stridently anti-Republican. The Irish were disparaged as ignorant "with a proclivity toward alcohol and violence and their slavish obedience to the Church and the Democratic Party" [19].

Yet many of the Irish would support the Union and fight for its cause. The Fenian Brotherhood, a group formed among Irish soldiers, saw the fight as a prelude toward battling for Irish independence. The flag of the Union's Irish Brigade carried the words, "Remember Ireland and Fontenay," the latter being a battle in which Irish volunteers had fought against the English in 1745[20].

Peter Welch wrote to his family in Ireland, saying it "should seem very strange that I should voluntarily joine in the bloody strife of the battlefield ... Here thousands of the sons and daughters of Ireland have come to seek a refuge from tyranny and persecution at home ... America is Irland's refuge, Irland's last hope ... When we are fighting for America we are fighting in the interest of Ireland" [21].

Thomas Francis Meagher was born to a wealthy family in Waterford, Ireland, in 1823. He was sent to be educated in England, returning home in August 1843. He rejected recent Catholic emancipation as insufficient, stating, "It has brought a handful of slaves from field and gives them appointments in the master's house" [22].

Meagher joined the nationalist Young Ireland movement. The outbreak of the potato blight in 1845 soon led to large-scale starvation. Meagher became increasingly prominent as a critic of British rule, noting that amidst the widespread starvation, British absentee landlords continued to export food from Ireland. At a Dublin forum, Meagher declared, "The people will not consent to live another year in a graveyard" [23].

The British government moved in 1848 to arrest all the leaders of Young Ireland on grounds of treason. Having been convicted, before sentencing, Meagher told the court, "I am here to regret nothing I have ever done, to retract nothing I have already said. I am here to crave with no lying lip the life I consecrate to the liberty of my country" [24].

Initially sentenced to death, the British government instead exiled Meagher to a penal colony in Van Diemen's Land, which later became the current Australian state of Tasmania. After several years in exile, he escaped, reaching New York on May 27, 1852. At the time, New York City held some 160,000 Irish, a quarter of its population.

Meagher was given a hero's welcome. A supporter, Michael Cavanagh, wrote, "Frank and free, he was Tom Meagher—the best beloved of his race and generation ...On him centered the hopes of his exiled countrymen" [25]. *The New York Times* noted,

"His arrival has created universal satisfaction here" [26].

Yet it was not to universal satisfaction. The Know Nothings, derived from the American Nativist Party, were violently anti-Irish. In 1844, they had rioted in Philadelphia against the Irish immigrants, causing injuries and burning churches. In the 1850s, they joined the temperance movement to campaign against alcohol and immigration. They numbered over a million members. They now attacked Meagher as "this reptile snake ... this wordy warrior knave" [27].

Meagher became a prominent speaker. In 1854, he was traveling when his train crashed, killing forty-eight people and injuring scores of others. Meagher was hailed for his heroism by witnesses and the press. He passed the bar, became a citizen, and married. He opened a newspaper in 1856, the *Irish News*. Yet Meagher was conflicted on the great issue of the day: slavery.

The secession of the South did not initially impel him to take a position. Then, on April 12, 1861, the South attacked the Union garrison at Fort Sumter in Charleston Harbor. The attack convinced many in the North, including Thomas Meagher, to join the Union cause.

Following the attack on Fort Sumter, he threw his support behind the Union, telling his fellow Irish, "The Republic that gave us an asylum and ... is the mainstay of human freedom the world over, is threatened with disruption ... [Defending it] is not only our duty to America but also to Ireland" [28].

Meagher then decided to form his own unit, taking out an ad: "Young Irishmen to Arms ... one hundred young Irishmen—healthy, intelligent and active—Wanted at once to form a Company under command of Thomas Francis Meagher" [29].

Part of the 69th New York regiment, the unit and the rest of the regiment fought well in the Battle of Bull Run, which ended in a Union rout. When the commander of the Irish was captured in the battle, Meagher took over, proposing to form a four-regiment Irish brigade made up completely of immigrants. Speaking to a meeting of some 60,000 in New

York, Meagher said, "My heart, my arm, my life is pledged to the national cause ... Every blow that clears the way for the stars and stripes deals to this English aristocracy [which was sympathetic to the South] a deadly mortification and discouragement" [30]. In Boston, Meagher proclaimed, "This is the only nation where the Irish can reconstruct themselves and become a power." [31].

Soon, the Irish Brigade numbered three thousand men. Meagher was promoted to Brigadier General in February 1862. The Irish Brigade had their baptism of fire at the Battle of Fair Oaks, winning commendation from the commander, General McClellan. During the Seven Days Battles that followed, the Irish Brigade performed valiantly time after time but lost nearly a third of their men. The *New York Herald* reported, "When anything absurd, forlorn or desperate was to be attempted, the Irish Brigade was called upon" [32].

At Antietam, the Irish Brigade once more was in the thick of the fighting, suffering horrendous casualties. Meagher suffered a concussion. At Fredericksburg, the Brigade lost half its men in hopeless charges. Refused a chance to rest and recruit more men, the Brigade took part in the Union defeat at Chancellorsville. Meagher had had enough, writing, "the ungenerous and inconsiderate treatment of a gallant remnant of a brigade that had never once failed to do his duty" left him demoralized[33]. He resigned command on May 14, 1863.

The announcement of a draft led to a bloody riot in New York City, with a large number of Irish among the rioters. The earlier Emancipation Proclamation had led many who were hostile to Blacks to abandon their support of the Union. Meagher urged the Irish to stand by the Union, attacking those who had participated in the riots, saying, "To their own discredit and degradation, they have suffered themselves to be bamboozled into being obstinate herds" [34]. The Irish press now reviled Meagher, calling him a fool and a Lincoln lover. Meagher returned to Army service. He earned further criticism when he spoke up for the Black soldiers now serving the Union, saying, "The Black heroes of the Union Army have not only entitled themselves to liberty, but to citizenship" [35].

By the end of the conflict, more than 144,000 Irish-born soldiers would be counted in the Union ranks, while another 90,000 had at least one parent born in Ireland[36].

Soldiers from other nations also played a large role on the Union side. Colonel Joseph Smolinski was the son of a Polish war hero. He evoked his father's memory to recruit for the First United States Lancers. Many Hungarian refugees had settled in the United States following the failed revolution of 1848. Some eight hundred Hungarians, many of them military veterans of the 1848 conflict, would serve in the Union Army[37].

The generals on both sides were well aware of the immigrants' role. General Robert E. Lee reportedly grumbled that he could have beaten the Yankees were it not for the "dammed Dutch" (a common term for Germans)[38]. Union General George McClellan told of returning to camp but being unable to make himself understood by the sentries, saying, "I tried English, French, Spanish, Italian, German, Indian, a little Russian and Turkish" without success[39].

The start of the Civil War initially resulted in a large drop in immigration. While there were about 500,000 immigrants yearly during the 1850s, this dropped to 92,000 a year during 1861 and 1862. It is notable that a high percentage of immigrants in the 1850s, perhaps one-third, were men of military age (age 18–44)[40].

While the drop in immigration may have reflected an unwillingness to be dragged into the war or concerns about wartime economic conditions in the United States, there were many new immigrants who came specifically to aid the Union. An American diplomat in Berlin wrote the State Department, "I am in receipt of hundreds of letters and personal calls seeking positions in the American army and asking for a means of conveyance to our shores," before hanging up a sign that read,

"This is the legation of the United States and not a recruiting office" [41]. American diplomatic outposts in Paris, London, and Hamburg also were besieged by men wanting to go to America to fight for the Union.

Orlando E. Caruana was born in Malta in 1844. In 1861, he joined the Union army in New York City, claiming to be twenty years old. In 1862, he won the nation's highest honor, the Congressional Medal of Honor, for his actions in two battles. Caruana was discharged from his regiment as a sergeant in September 1864.

Liberals and radicals had seen the revolutions of 1848 crushed and conservative autocracy ascendant throughout Europe. Many saw America as the counter-example, a democratic republic almost unique in the world at the time. Once the Union made it more explicit that the fight was against slavery, European support soared.

In 1862, Congress passed the Homestead Act, offering 160 acres of free land to any settler. On August 8, 1862, Secretary of State Seward sent Circular 19 to all diplomatic posts, urging them to publicize the opportunity for free land as well as the fact that the war had expanded the demand for labor. Seward wrote, "Nowhere else can the industrious laboring man and artisan expect so liberal a recompense for his services" [42].

In Paris, American counsel John Bigelow had the announcement printed in all the leading journals in Europe. Almost immediately, the number of those wishing to immigrate to America soared. Immigration in 1863 almost doubled to 176,000 and continued to rise to 248,000 in 1865, the last year of the war. Bigelow later wrote, "This circular deserves a place in the record if for no other reason than the light it throws upon the mysterious repletion of our army during the four years of war" [43].

Immigrants also served the Union cause outside of its Army. As ambassador to Spain, Carl Schurz was among the first to argue that making the Union cause one against slavery would rally support among the ordinary European people and make it impossible for aristocratic governments who were more sympathetic to the Confederacy to dare intervene. Returning to the United States in the winter of 1862, Schurz met with Abraham Lincoln. Lincoln, after listening to Schurz's arguments, answered, "You may be right ... I cannot imagine that any European power would dare to recognize and aid the Southern Confederacy if it became clear that the Confederacy stands for slavery and the Union for freedom" [44]. The Emancipation Proclamation would follow later that year.

Abraham Lincoln advocated for increased immigration, arguing, "There is still a great deficiency of laborers in every field of industry" [45]. On July 4, 1864, Congress passed the Act to Encourage Immigration, allowing immigrants to pay for their travel to America out of future earnings.

The Republican party stressed their support for immigration in their 1864 platform, which stated, "Foreign immigration which in the past has added so much to the wealth, resources and increase of power to this nation—the asylum of the oppressed of all nations—should be fostered and encouraged by a liberal and just policy" [46].

After the war, Meagher and his wife left New York to travel to Montana Territory. There, Meagher was named the second-ranking official. When he arrived, the governor resigned, making Meagher the acting governor of an area twice the size of England. Yet the real power in the territory belonged to others. Vigilantes had murdered thirty-seven citizens by the end of 1865. Meagher soon found himself an enemy of the vigilantes when he pardoned a man they had seized. Soon after his release, the man was brutally murdered and found with a note pinned to his chest saying that Meagher would be next. On July 1, 1867, Meagher was aboard a ship on the Missouri River when he mysteriously vanished overboard.

A Hungarian Jewish immigrant who fought for the Union

would gain his fame after the war. Joseph Pulitzer was born in Hungary in 1847. When his father died, the family fell on hard times. In 1864, recruiters from the Union Army recruited Pulitzer to come to the United States to join the army. The seventeen-year-old Pulitzer joined the 1st New York Cavalry, a regiment made up largely of German immigrants. He fought under General Phillip Sheridan for the last eight months of the war[47].

Following the war, Pulitzer, who spoke little English at this point, moved to St. Louis. He worked a variety of jobs before becoming a lawyer in 1868. He had become a US citizen the year before. Struggling to manage a law practice with his limited English, he took a job as a reporter for a German-language newspaper. An admirer of Carl Schurz, Pulitzer joined the Republican Party and served a term in the state legislature. Meanwhile, he moved up in the newspaper and became managing editor.

In 1878, Pulitzer purchased and merged two struggling newspapers to form the *St. Louis Post-Dispatch*. Pulitzer featured advocacy for the common people along with exposés and sensational stories, which led to the papers being highly successful. The difficulties of politics in St. Louis led Pulitzer to move to New York in 1883 and purchase the *New York World*. Pulitzer featured stories of disasters and crime along with exposés of scandals. The paper's subscriptions grew from 15,000 to 600,00. In 1884, Pulitzer, who had become a Democrat, served one term in Congress. Declining health forced Pulitzer to give up day-to-day management of the paper. Joseph Pulitzer died in 1911, but he left $2 million dollars to found schools of journalism at the University of Missouri and Columbia University. In 1917, Columbia started awarding Pulitzer Prizes for outstanding achievement in journalism[48]. The Pulitzer Prizes have been expanded to now include annual awards in literature, poetry, history, music, and drama.

Historian Michael Barone noted how the Civil War was followed by increased, rather than lessened, differences between the North and the South. The South remained largely rural, while the North saw increased industrialization. Very few Northerners moved to the South and vice versa. Almost all new immigrants settled in the North. Barone noted that the foreign-born percentage of the Southern population peaked at 3.5% in 1860; by 1890, it was down to 2.6%. In contrast, the foreign-born percentage of the population in the North was 18% in 1860; by 1890, it was up to 20%[49].

1 Don H. Doyle. *The Cause of All Nations: An International History of the American Civil War*, Basic Books, New York, 2015, 159.

2 Doyle, 159.

3 Doyle, 169.

4 Doyle, 170.

5 Benjamin Apthorp Gould. *Investigations in the Military and Anthropological Statistics of American Soldiers*, Hurd and Houghton, New York, 1869, 4.

6 Doyle, 160-161.

7 *The New York Times*. "Adopted Citizens and the War," August 12, 1861.

8 Doyle, 171.

9 Barone, 129.

10 Barone, 130.

11 Sowell, 63.

12 Doyle, 173.

13 Doyle, 166.

14 Walter D. Kamphoefner and Wolfgang Johanne Helbich, eds. *Germans in the Civil War: The Letters They Wrote Home*, University of North Carolina Press, Chapel Hill, 2006, 267-8.

15 Kamphoefner, 317.

16 James G. Barber. *A Short History of the Civil War*, Smithsonian-Penguin Random House, New York, 2020, 260-261.

17 Sowell, 63.

18 Barone, 130-2.

19 Doyle, 174.

20 Doyle, 175.

21 Peter Welsh. *Irish Green and Union Blue: The Civil War Letters of Peter Welsh, Color Sergeant, 28th Regiment, Massachusetts Volunteers*, Fordham University Press, New York, 1986, 100-103.

22 Egan, *Irishman*, 25.

23 Egan, Irishman, 53.

24 Egan, Irishman, 77.

25 Egan, Irishman, 137.

26 Egan, Irishman, 137.

27 Egan, Irishman, 142.

28 Michael Cavanagh. *Memoirs of Gen. Thomas Francis Meagher*, Messenger, Worcester, MA, 1892, 368-9.

29 Egan, Irishman, 176.

30 Egan, Irishman, 192.

31 Egan, Irishman, 194.

32 Egan, Irishman, 215.

33 Egan, Irishman, 250.

34 Egan, Irishman, 256.

35 Egan, Irishman, 263.

36 Doyle, 175-6.

37 Daniels, 232.

38 Doyle, 173.

39 George B. McClellan. *The Armies of Europe*, J.P. Lippincott, Philadelphia, 1861.

40 Doyle, 176.

41 Doyle, 176.

42 William Seward. *Circular 19*, August 8, 1862, Foreign Relations of the United States 1861–1865, University of Wisconsin Digital Collections. uwdc.library.wisc.edu/collections/FRUS. 172.

43 John Bigelow. *Retrospections of an Active Life, 1817–1863*, Baker and Taylor, New York, 1909, 562-564.

44 Doyle, 214.

45 Kane, 81.

46 Daniels, 270.

47 Jessica Gunderson. *Immigrants Who Built an Empire.* Capstone Press, North Mankato, MN, 2021, 32-3.

48 Gunderson, 33-34.

49 Barone, 154.

87

Andrew Carnegie

Levi Strauss

CHAPTER 5

The Magnates

The years following the Civil War saw the development of mighty enterprises, the epitomes of successful capitalism. Many of those who built these companies were immigrants.

The flow of immigrants would continue. From 1860–70, another three million immigrants came to America, a third of whom were from the British Isles[1].

Andrew Carnegie immigrated as a boy in the company of his Scottish family to Pittsburgh in 1848. At age 14, Carnegie started working as a "bobbin-boy" in a cloth mill. Despite the family's poverty, conditions still seemed much better than in their homeland. He became a telegraph clerk, writing back to friends in Scotland, "Towns and cities spring up as if by magic ... our railroads extend 13,000 miles ... Pauperism is unknown ... Everything around us is in motion" [2]. Even as a youth, he desired "to become independent and then enjoy the luxuries which wealth can [and should] procure" [3].

His opportunity came when he accepted a job as a telegraphist and secretary to Thomas Scott, president of the Pennsylvania Railroad in Pittsburgh. Scott called the eighteen-year-old Carnegie his "white-haired Scotch devil" [4]. Carnegie soon became a division superintendent. Josephson wrote, "Carnegie advanced himself by breaking rules at opportune moments and boldly assuming responsibility in emergencies" [5]. Scott taught Carnegie about business and gave him a stock tip that led to his first successful investment, financed by mortgaging his mother's house. He borrowed $217.50, which he invested in a company making sleeping cars for railroads. Within two years, the stock was earning him $5,000 a year. He made more money investing in the newborn oil industry in western Pennsylvania.

Carnegie was pro-Union and anti-slavery, but his service during the Civil War focused on keeping the railroad working. When he was drafted, Carnegie, like many other wealthy men, hired a substitute to take his place in the Army[6].

Carnegie began to focus on iron production. In 1863, Carnegie, his brother Thomas, and two friends became minority partners with a German immigrant named Andrew Kloman, whose company produced iron axles for railroad cars. Within a few years, they had acquired a majority interest. Carnegie also bought or organized companies making iron bridges, iron rails, and locomotives. In 1865, Carnegie left the railroad to devote full-time to his iron companies. In December 1868, Carnegie wrote in his diary, "Thirty-three and an income of $50,000 per annum"[7].

Biographer David Nasaw wrote, "One of Carnegie's many gifts as a businessman was his capacity to generate enthusiasm for his projects ... Carnegie was not a 'dour Scotsman' or a cold, calculating capitalist, but a little man brimming with excitement for whatever business he was engaged in at that moment"[8].

In 1872, in London, Carnegie became aware of the Bessemer converter, which was a major advance in converting iron to stronger steel. Carnegie reportedly rushed home, exclaiming, "The age of Iron has passed—Steel is King"[9].

Carnegie was determined to dominate the market. Josephson wrote, "In an age that clamored for steel, Carnegie determined at last to supply it in monstrous quantities; and under conditions of natural economy, access to raw material, facilities of transport, and markets that would give him a crushing advantage over rivals in the field"[10].

Carnegie used downtimes, such as the crash of 1873, to purchase the properties of those less successful. In 1873, he bought out Kloman, who was facing financial problems. He admitted to "more pain than all the financial trials that I have been subjected to up to that time" when he refused to aid his first mentor, Thomas Scott, when the latter faced ruin[11].

In the 1870s, Carnegie periodically joined with other steel makers to divide up the market. He complained about having too small a share, telling his rivals, "I will then undersell you in the market and make good money doing it" [12]. Periodically, Carnegie would break away from the syndicate. His rivals felt that he was "always on alert to gather in business at lower prices than the others could afford" [13]. In 1883, Carnegie bought a massive, new, modern steel plant at Homestead from rivals for the cost of construction. The name Homestead would be heard again. Then, Carnegie recalled, as he wrote in his autobiography, "We could not get on without a supply of the fuel essential to the smelting of pig iron. The Frick Coke company had not only the best coal and coke property, but ... in Mr. Frick himself a man with a positive genius for its management" [14]. Carnegie and Frick's companies united in 1883; by 1889, Frick was appointed general manager of the combination allowing Carnegie to "retire."

Carnegie worked to pay the lowest wages possible to workers, which led to a preference for immigrants. A Pittsburgh social worker wrote, "Some employers of labor give the Slavs and Italians preference because of their docility, their habit of silent submission ... and their willingness to work long hours and overtime without a murmur. Foreigners, as a rule, earn the lowest wages" [15].

Carnegie, like most of the great industrialists of the time, was strongly opposed to labor unions. Carnegie professed opposition to hiring new workers to replace those striking, saying, "Thou shall not take thy neighbors' job" [16]. However, in the slump of 1884–5, he suddenly shut down his plant in Pittsburgh, blaming the workers' organization, the Amalgamated Association of Iron and Steel Workers, for "allowing other Bessemer mills to work at less wages than we pay" [17]. After a prolonged lockout, he forced his workers to come back on a non-union basis for lower wages.

The steel workers' union had won relatively favorable terms after a brief 1889 strike, with the contract expiring in July 1892. In the spring of 1892, Frick, although he knew the company was earning $4 million annually, claimed it was headed for bankruptcy unless a new non-union contract for lower wages was enacted. The union went on strike at the Homestead plant on July 1, 1892. Frick now sent a battalion of armed Pinkerton guards up the river to the plant on the night of July 6. The workers rose to resist the Pinkertons in one of the bloodiest struggles between labor and capital in American history. Historian John Fitch wrote, "A mob of men with guns coming to take their jobs ... to take away the chance to work, to break up their homes—that is what passed through the minds of the Homestead men that morning" [18]. The workers sent the Pinkertons fleeing and occupied the plant for five months before it was besieged and captured by the Army. Frick cabled Carnegie on November 21, "Strike officially declared off yesterday. Our victory is now complete and most gratifying. Do not think we will ever have serious labor trouble again" [19]. Carnegie, who pretended to be uninvolved in such conflicts, wired back, "Congratulations all around—life worth living again" [20].

Carnegie had moved with his mother to New York City in 1870. He increasingly left the business deals to underlings, instead turning to writing and friendships with the intellectual elite. He did not become a citizen until age 50 and did not marry until age 52.

In his *Gospel of Wealth* articles, Carnegie argued that the evolving economy required business leaders with a special talent for management and that they needed to be well rewarded for their achievements. However, his writing was not simply a self-congratulatory thanks to capitalists since it closed by arguing that their wealth was simply money in trust that they needed to manage for the common good. Thus, he argued for giving away all accumulated wealth during one's lifetime and set out to do just that.

Carnegie made multiple contributions but became best known for his contributions to libraries. He gave $5.2 million dollars that allowed the New York City library to create 65 branch libraries. He would give some $41 million to create almost 1,700 new public libraries across the United States[21]. The money he was not able to give away during his lifetime, the equivalent of $8 billion dollars in today's money, he gave to the Carnegie Corporation to donate afterward[22]. Initially, the Carnegie funds exceeded the endowment for basic research of all of the nation's universities combined[23].

Carnegie kept expanding, buying up iron ore mines and negotiating preferred rail shipping rates, sometimes battling with Rockefeller or J.P. Morgan for control. In 1899, Carnegie fell out with Frick, ousting the latter as chairman of the company. Finally, in 1901, Carnegie sold the Carnegie Steel Company for a price of $492 million to a syndicate organized by JP Morgan. The deal made Carnegie the richest man in the world, while Morgan proceeded to organize the "Steel Trust," combining Carnegie's and other companies as US Steel. Learning of the deal, Carnegie's friend Mark Twain wrote to him, "You seem to be in prosperity. Can you lend an admirer a dollar and a half to buy a hymn book with ... Don't send the hymn book, send the money; I want to make the selection myself" [24].

Carnegie also became a leader of those opposed to imperialism. He argued, in multiple forums, against the American annexation of the Philippines. He also tried to promote peace, pushing for countries to settle their disputes through binding arbitration rather than war. When *The New York Times* interviewed him for an article titled "Andrew Carnegie: Apostle of Peace," the reporter said that Carnegie's supreme ambition was "to see the dream of international arbitration come true"[25].

Carnegie was disappointed when nations, including the United States, refused to accept treaties of binding arbitration. Carnegie was stunned by the onset of World War I and the deaths that resulted from it. He died shortly after its end, on August 11, 1919.

A less wealthy immigrant, but one who also became immortal, was Levi Strauss. Levi, originally named Loeb Strauss, was born in Germany in 1829, the son of a Jewish peddler. Jews were forbidden most other occupations in Germany at that time. When his father died in 1845, two of Levi's half-brothers immigrated to America, becoming street peddlers in New York. Levi arrived two years later at age 18. In 1849, the world was convulsed by the discovery of gold in California. Levi, along with his sister Fanny and brother-in-law David Stern, decided to move to San Francisco to set up a business. Levi stocked up on supplies and sailed, with an overland leg through Panama, to San Francisco. He arrived on March 14, 1853, having just become an American citizen[26].

There were already over one hundred dry goods stores in the city, but Levi and Stern prospered due to their link to supplies from Levi's brothers in New York as well as their habit of being the first to meet arriving ships to bid on their cargo. Levi noted that the miners and other workers were clothed in ragged trousers, with one miner reportedly complaining, "Shoulda bought pants. Pants don't wear worth a hoot in the diggin's. Can't get a pair strong enough to last"[27].

Levi began selling tough blue denim, a durable twill-weave cotton, pants. The work pants caught on like wildfire, becoming the nexus of the business. Traveling salesmen brought the pants into mining camps, where they were eagerly snapped up.

Around this time, another Jewish immigrant, Jacob Davis (originally Jacob Youghes), was working as a tailor in Reno, Nevada. Davis, born in 1831 in Riga, had been much less successful until he hit upon the idea of making pants stronger by putting rivets into the pockets. Others soon asked for the riveted pants, and within 18 months, he had sold two hundred pairs. Yet, he did not have the resources to try to patent his invention. On July 2, 1872, Davis wrote to Levi, who had been supplying him with the material for the pants, proposing a partnership. Levi accepted. It would take until May 20, 1873, till their patent was approved. By then, Davis had sold out to Levi and went to work for him as head tailor and foreman of production in San Francisco[28].

Sales of the new pants, which Levi called "waist overalls," increased very quickly. By the end of the year, some 20,000 men would be wearing the pants, which became known as blue jeans. Levi lived with his widowed sister. At his factory, he would visit with people at all levels of the company, encouraging them to call him "Levi" instead of "Mr. Strauss." By 1876, sales had climbed to $200,000 a year and then, by 1880, to $2.4 million[29].

Levi became a multimillionaire, giving generously to charities. In his only known interview, in 1895, he told the *San Francisco Bulletin*, he said, "My happiness lies in my routine work ... I do not think large fortunes cause happiness to their owners, for immediately those who possess them become slaves to their wealth" [30].

Levi Strauss died in 1902, leaving the company to his nephews. The demand for jeans spread from the west across the country and abroad. By 1974, 75 million pairs of Levi's jeans were sold annually, in addition to being copied more than any other piece of clothing[31].

The rise of Jacob Schiff would not be based on anything as physical as steel or clothes. Schiff was born in Frankfurt, Germany, in 1847, the third child of a successful stockbroker. At the age of 16, Jacob went to work for his father. At age 18, he left, ostensibly to visit England. However, he had saved some $500, which he used to travel to New York City, where he was met by a fellow Frankfurter, William Bonn. Bonn, who worked in the financial industry, introduced Schiff to people on Wall Street. By 1867, Schiff formed a brokerage firm with two other immigrants from Frankfurt. He was technically too young to sign the partnership papers[32].

The partnership soon fell apart. After a brief spell back in Germany, in 1873, Schiff became a junior partner in the firm of Kuhn, Loeb, and Company. Schiff wrote to his mother, "The opportunity is enormous here" [33]. He began to try to learn as much as he could about railroads. A friend said, "He carries every railroad, every bit of rolling stock, every foot of track, and every man connected with each line—from the president to the last brakeman—inside his head." [34]. Using this knowledge, Schiff and the firm made themselves invaluable to the railroads when they sought more capital for growth and operations.

Schiff soon began to earn large amounts of money. Helping the Chicago and Northwestern Railroad with its finances would net him a check for $500,000 in 1877. Historian Stephen Birmingham wrote, "For the next thirty years, railroads would completely dominate the American financial scene, and Schiff from the beginning was determined that Kuhn, Loeb, and Company should dominate the field of railroad financing" [35].

In 1875, Schiff married the daughter of Solomon Loeb and became a full partner in the firm. The firm's main competitor was J.P. Morgan. Birmingham noted, "Jacob Schiff was the only German Jewish banker whom Morgan—at least occasionally and always begrudgingly—treated as a peer" [36].

The fabled Union Pacific Railroad company, which had built the first transcontinental railroad, had gone into bankruptcy. J.P. Morgan refused to become involved in its finances and called it "two streaks of rust across the plains" [37]. Schiff joined with railroad owner E. H. Harriman to resuscitate the Union Pacific, starting a decades-long collaboration. After the pair purchased the Union Pacific in 1897, Schiff raised large amounts of capital, including from Europe. Before long, the

Union Pacific had regained profitability while its actual operations were modernized and improved. By 1900, it had debt-free assets of over $200 million dollars[38].

"Schiff," stated biographer Naomi Cohen, "devoted hours to communal service. Schiff's devotion to individual Jews and Jewish causes won him the loyalty and admiration of the masses of Jews" [39]. He donated to both Jewish and non-Jewish causes but fought against the widespread private discrimination against Jews.

The end of the nineteenth century and the beginning of the twentieth saw horrific, increasing anti-Semitism in Russia, culminating in the deadly pogrom in Kishinev in 1903. These conditions caused three million Russian Jews to flee the country, two-thirds going to the United States. Thus, when the rising power Japan went to war with the Russian Empire, Schiff almost singlehandedly sought to raise enormous loans to Japan to allow them to win the war. Schiff, outraged by the pogroms, had called Russia "the enemy of mankind," while the Japanese envoy recalled that he had said, "A system of government ... capable of such cruelties and outrages ... [should be] taught an object lesson" [40].

Schiff, persuading Morgan and Rockefeller to join him, engineered three enormous loans to Japan that helped it emerge victorious in 1905. After the war, Schiff was invited to Japan to meet and dine with the emperor, a rare honor.

At home, Schiff worked on aiding the new Russian immigrants, although there would be distrust between the earlier German Jewish immigrants and the new Russian immigrants for many years. Schiff was unusually liberal for the very wealthy of that time. He supported the rights of Blacks, free public education, the abolition of child labor, and the trade unions. He urged radical banking reform to avoid panics, calling the American financial system "a disgrace to the civilized community" [41]. Schiff also thought that increased taxes on capitalists were reasonable[42].

Schiff argued against racial discrimination and for "justice for the Negro," but was unsuccessful in persuading President Wilson to remove segregation in government[43].

Schiff strongly argued against restrictions on immigration. He argued, "If we are going to reverse the immigration policy which has prevailed since times immemorial ... we had better proceed to Plymouth Rock and blast it into fragments" [44]. When a Columbia professor stated that unrestricted immigration of those from Eastern and Southern Europe would produce a "degenerate race," Schiff replied, "Are you aware that you are putting forward precisely the same arguments that were advanced by the so-called 'Know-Nothing' Party against German and Irish immigrants some five or six decades ago? ... You would draw a cordon around this country in order to preserve the comfort and self-indulgence of its people and shut your eyes to the woes of those who suffer either from persecution or oppression from unfortunate economic conditions" [45].

When WWI started, Schiff and his firm were accused of being pro-German, particularly when Schiff refused to back a large load to Britain and France unless they could guarantee that the money would not go to Russia. However, his partner Otto Kahn's efforts on behalf of the Allies would lead the firm to be denounced by the Kaiser as traitor[46].

Schiff had a long principle of giving 10% of his income to charity, regarding only contributions above that amount as being real charity. He would give away an estimated $50–100 million, only once allowing his name to be attached to a project[47]. *Forbes Magazine* commented, "Mr. Schiff spends almost as much time giving away money as making it" [48].

In 1906, Schiff helped found and fund the American Jewish Committee, which aimed to advocate for persecuted Jews across the world. The outbreak of WWI created mass migrations of peoples, particularly of eastern European Jews trying to escape the carnage. Schiff then helped found the Joint Distribution Committee, which was (and is) dedicated to supplying food and meeting the other needs of the refugees.

The Joint would end up donating up to $16 million annually. Historian Oscar Handlin wrote, "Its American insistence on 'giving all an equal opportunity for survival and creative life' was enriched by the 'Biblical concept of social obligation and mercy.' It could therefore rise above all factional divisions" [49].

Jacob Schiff died at home on September 25, 1920.

---

1 Isaac Asimov. *The Golden Door: The United States from 1865–1918*, Houghton Mifflin, Boston, 1977, 29-36.

2 Josephson, 42.

3 Josephson, 43.

4 Josephson, 43.

5 Josephson, 43.

6 David Nasaw. *Andrew Carnegie*, Penguin Books, New York, 2006.

7 Josephson, 105.

8 Nasaw, 148.

9 Josephson, 107.

10 Josephson, 109.

11 Josephson, 177.

12 Josephson, 258.

13 Josephson, 259.

14 Josephson, 263.

15 Josephson, 362.

16 Josephson, 369.

17 Josephson, 369.

18 Josephson, 371.

19 Josephson, 371.

20 Josephson, 372.

21 Nasaw, 590.

22 Nasaw 799.

23 Daniel Okrent. *The Guarded Gate*, Scribner, New York, 25.

24 Nasaw, 586-7.

25 William Griffith. "Andrew Carnegie, Apostle of Peace," *The New York Times*, November 6, 1904.

26 Evans, 110.

27 Evans, 110.

28 Evans, 112.

29 Evans, 112.

30 Evans, 113.

31 Evans, 113.

32 Stephen Birmingham. *Our Crowd: The Great Jewish Families of New York*, Dell Books, New York, 1967, 186-7.

33 Naomi W. Cohen. *Jacob Schiff: A Study in American Jewish Leadership*, Brandeis University Press, Hanover, 1999, 5.

34 Birmingham, 190.

35 Birmingham, 192.

36 Birmingham, 199.

37 Birmingham, 200.

38 Birmingham, 216.

39 Cohen, 45.

40 Birmingham, 334.

41 Birmingham, 371.

42 Cohen, 30.

43 Cohen, 71.

44 Cohen, 155.

45 Cohen, 158.

46 Birmingham, 380.

47 Birmingham, 385.

48 Cohen, 55-56.

49 Birmingham, 387.

Clara Lemlich

Mother Jones

CHAPTER 6

Protecting the Rights of Labor

Immigrants played a major role in fighting for labor, the workers who toiled for the various titans of industry. It would be impossible to discuss the American labor movement in the nineteenth century and the first half of the twentieth without immigrants. In this chapter, we will look at just a few of the immigrant labor leaders. Arguably, the four most important labor leaders of the nineteenth century were either immigrants such as Samuel Gompers, head of the American Federation of Labor, or children of immigrants, including Eugene Debs, president of the American Railway Union; John Mitchell, chief of the United Mine Workers; and Terence Powderly, head of the Knights of Labor.

Samuel Gompers was born in England in 1850 to a family of Dutch Jewish immigrants. At age ten, he left school to help support his family, first working at making shoes for the wage of six cents a week. After eight weeks, he became an apprentice cigarmaker, which was his father's trade. By the time he was 11, he was earning the equivalent of 24 cents a week. Gompers later wrote, "London seemed to offer no response to our efforts toward betterment. About this time, we began to hear more and more about America"[1]. Both Sam and his father belonged to the Cigarmakers' Society, a trade union[2].

In 1863, unable to find work, Sam Gompers' father moved

his family to New York City, where they had relatives. The family rented a four-room apartment where both parents and all four children worked in making cigars, which they sold at the price of $2 for one thousand cigars[3].

Having gone to work at 13, Sam Gompers joined the Cigar Makers' International Union (CMIU) at age 14. At age 16, with Gompers having gotten a job in a cigar shop, the other men in the shop chose him as their representative to talk to the owner about the working conditions. He was able to win improvements in their conditions because the shop owners needed skilled workers who could produce the expensive cigars. At age 17, he married Sophia Julian, with whom he would have ten children.

The invention of the cigar mold in 1869 meant that employers could hire unskilled labor to make cigars, posing severe competition to skilled workers[4]. Gompers began to read and learn about labor issues, being the most drawn to the socialist views of the International Workingmen's Association.

The people making the cheap cigars in the tenements had little bargaining power. Sam Gompers then organized all of the cigarmakers, skilled and unskilled, into the CMIU, striking for a ten-hour day and a minimum pay of $6 for one thousand cigars. The strike was broken. However, the Cigarmakers' Union went on to become one of the most successful unions, winning a salary of $15 a week for its workers[5]. While many unions struggled in the last quarter of the nineteenth century, the CMIU expanded from 1,016 members in 1877 to over 30,000 in 1901[6].

Gompers adopted a pragmatic attitude, which a mentor described by saying, "Study your union card, Sam, and if an idea doesn't square with it, it's not true" [7]. Gompers would judge everything going forward by whether it aided the unions or not.

The Cigarmakers union focused on improving their own working conditions. By 1875, Gompers was the leader of the largest local in the country. Gompers became an official organizer while still working a ten-hour day making cigars.

Following a large national rail strike in 1877, Gompers and over 10,000 cigarmakers went out in sympathy. Gompers was blacklisted for several months when the strike failed. Gompers, at the time, embraced a Marxist conception of class struggle, later writing, "I have been convinced … that the economic interests of the employing class and those of the working class are not harmonious" [8]. Gompers had to pawn almost everything, given his lack of money, and for a time, his family survived only on meals of flour soup [9].

Gompers tried to get the government to bolster working conditions. He argued for legislation to prohibit work in tenements, taking Theodore Roosevelt on a tour to show him the desperate conditions. After an extended effort, the New York legislature passed the law, only to have the courts strike it down as a restriction of personal liberty[10].

By age 30, Gompers was well known as an advocate for workers. In 1881, he attended a convention of various types of skilled workers in Pittsburgh. The delegates decided to join together, calling themselves the Federation of Organized Trades and Labor Unions of the United States and Canada (FOTLU). Their program included pushing for an eight-hour workday and the prohibition of child labor. Gompers urged for all workers to join a general strike to take place no later than May 1, 1886. On May 4 at the Haymarket Square in Chicago, several thousand workers were demonstrating in favor of an eight-hour day when a bomb was thrown at the police, resulting in gunfire. Four workers and seven policemen were killed. The event created a severe backlash against labor, particularly against anarchists, who were blamed.

In December 1886, FOTLU disbanded, creating instead a new organization, the American Federation of Labor (AFL). Sam Gompers was elected as its president. He spoke out for labor and tried to act as an intermediary between workers and employers. Gompers now advocated "pure and simple union-ism," in which the sole function of the union was to improve the lot of its members and not engage in any political activ-ity[11]. The AFL gave each of its member unions autonomy, allowing them to make their own rules.

Gompers was suspicious of anyone who claimed to act on behalf of labor other than actual workers. He was influenced by the violent suppression of a demonstration in Tompkins Square in New York City in 1874. Gompers later wrote, "I saw the dangers of entangling alliances with intellectuals who did not understand that to experiment with the labor movement was to experiment with human life ... leadership in the labor movement could be safely entrusted only to those whose hearts and minds had been woven the experience of earning their bread by daily labor" [12].

Gompers traveled widely, promoting unions. In 1893, the AFL created a journal, the *American Federationist*, for which Gompers served as reporter, columnist, editor, and proofreader. The AFL focused on organizing, at times spending a third of its income on organizing workers, funded by a half-cent-a-week tax on members[13].

The AFL was successful, in part because their unions of skilled workers could not be easily replaced. Over time, the workers won first a ten-hour and then an eight-hour day. By 1896, the AFL was the nation's largest union organization, with 447,000 members[14]. Biographer Donald Whisenhunt wrote, "From the first day of his presidency until his death thirty-eight years later, the AFL was Samuel Gompers' life" [15].

At the time, Gompers unsuccessfully urged the craft unions making up the AFL to organize unskilled workers. The AFL grew anyway, reaching 1.7 million workers in 1904.

Gompers tried to make the AFL apolitical, to shield it from the hatred of radicals and unions common to much of the upper classes. Still, he fell afoul of them anyway. Employers used the Sherman Anti-Trust Act against unions, finding sympathetic judges to issue injunctions against a range of union tactics. When the workers at the Buck Stove and Range Company went on strike, a court barred the AFL from putting the store on its unfair list. When Gompers did so anyway, he was held in contempt of court. Sentencing him to a year in jail, the judge called Gompers "the leader of the rabble who would unlaw the land, bringing hideous pestilence, and ... subordinate the law to anarchy and riot" [16]. Gompers only avoided jail when the president of the company died, and their successor dropped the case.

As the AFL grew more successful, Gompers grew more conservative. By 1903, Gompers was very antagonistic to socialism. In the 1870s, he had actively recruited women and unskilled workers for the CMIU. In the early days of the AFL, he refused to charter unions that barred African Americans and hired African American organizers to work in the South. Gompers wrote in 1892, "If we fail to organize and recognize the colored wage workers, we cannot blame them if they accept our challenge of enmity ... if common humanity will not prompt us to have their cooperation, an enlightened self-interest should" [17]. Yet, by 1896, he began to accept into the AFL unions that discriminated against African Americans, and gave up on trying to organize women or unskilled workers.

The defeat of labor efforts in the railroads in 1892 and steel mills in 1896 convinced Gompers that the AFL did not have the power to challenge business and would have to make themselves palatable to these powers in order to survive.

Gompers campaigned against child labor and for shorter working hours in individual contracts with employers but opposed legislation proposed by the Progressive movement for such things as national unemployment compensation and comprehensive health insurance. Gompers supported governmental regulations when they concerned such things that unions could not achieve, such as women's suffrage and prohibition of the sale of convict-made goods, but believed that fixing hours and wages should be left to the unions.

In his later years, Gompers was markedly hostile to social-ists and worker organizations that he saw as too political, such as the International Workers of the World (Wobblies). Biographer Harold Livesay wrote, "The Wobblies resembled Gompers in his younger, more militant days: radical talk fronting a practical program" [18].

Gompers attempted to work in the National Civic Federation with those business leaders who saw the acceptance of unions as cheaper than strikes. However, the mass of employers, as reflected by the National Association of Manufacturers, con-tinued to use aggressive legal tactics to break unions, claim-ing that collective bargaining infringed on employers' and employees' liberties.

Gompers and the AFL then turned back to politics. Finding the Republicans unsympathetic, they began to support the Democrats. From 1906–12, union efforts elected more pro-union legislators. When the Wilson Administration passed the Clayton Anti-Trust Act that stated, "Nothing contained in the antitrust laws shall be construed to forbid the existence of labor ... organizations," Wilson won Gompers complete loy-alty[19].

When Wilson led the United States into WWI, Gompers became a strong proponent of the war effort. Wilson lauded Gompers' support, noting his "patriotic courage, his large vision, his statesmanlike sense, and mind that knew how to pull in harness" [20].

The shortage of workers led to improved agreements for labor during the war in exchange for avoiding strikes. The AFL membership rose to 3.3 million in 1919 and then to a peak of four million in 1920.

However, the "Red Scare" and growing hostility to labor would reduce that number to 2.9 million in 1924. Gompers died in 1924, his last words being, "Say to the workers of America that I have kept the faith" [21].

Writing of Gompers, historian John Laslatt concluded, "It was true that Gompers was ambitious ... as well as being self-righteous, bigoted, and increasingly rigid in his later years. Yet he was also scrupulously honest, willing to drive himself to exhaustion in the cause of trade unionism as he saw it, and capable of great personal courage when a principle he believed in was at stake" [22].

Gompers built the first lasting organization to represent workers, but the AFL did nothing to represent the masses of unskilled workers. It would be far harder for them to successfully be organized in part because they could so easily be replaced.

The flow of immigrants to the United States continued unabated after the Civil War, peaking in 1880–1910 when eighteen million immigrants came to America[23]. Under these circumstances, protecting the rights of unskilled workers would be a monumental challenge, yet there were those who attempted this.

Mary Harris was born in Cork, Ireland, in 1837. Her family came to North America after the onset of the Irish potato famine in the late 1840s. She grew up in Toronto, Canada, where her father labored on building the railroads. Mary Harris attended school for prospective teachers, leaving before graduating to take a teaching job in Monroe, Michigan, in 1860[24].

Before the year was out, she moved to Memphis, Tennessee. Within a few months, she married George Jones, an iron molder and a member of the International Iron Molders Union. The Jones had four children over the next six years. Then, in 1867, Memphis was struck by an epidemic of yellow fever.

Yellow fever, transmitted by mosquitos, had caused periodic devastating epidemics throughout the nation. It was sometimes called the "Strangers' Disease" as it affected new immigrants worse than those who may have had some prior immunity. Outbreaks were sometimes blamed on immigrants; a yellow fever outbreak in Norfolk in 1855 led to a mob burning down the Irish section of the city[25].

The 1867 Memphis epidemic would devastate the city and the Jones family. First, George, and then all four of the Jones children, caught and died from the disease.

Mary Jones moved to Chicago, where she worked as a dressmaker. She later wrote, "We worked for the aristocrats of Chicago, and I had ample opportunity to observe the luxury and extravagance of their lives. Often while sewing for the lords and barons who lived in magnificent homes on Lake Shore Drive, I would look out of the plate glass windows and see the poor, shivering wretches, jobless and hungry, walking along the frozen lake front" [26].

Jones would suffer another devastating blow when the great Chicago Fire of 1871 cost her all of her belongings. It was at this point, she related, that she began to become involved in the labor movement. Like many, she was shaped by the events of 1877 when a financial panic led to a crisis for workers. When four railroads cut worker wages by 10%, the workers struck. The denouement came in Pittsburgh when workers who had shut down the trainyards were met by troops with bayonets. A general strike that was organized in sympathy in Chicago lasted three days, ending when troops fired into the crowds, killing thirty and wounding two hundred. Jones later wrote, "Then and there I learned in the early part of my career that labor must bear the cross for others' sins, must be the vicarious sufferer for the wrongs others do" [27].

Biographer Elliott Gorn wrote, "Chicago in the late nineteenth century was the most radical city in America, a hotbed of ideological ferment" [28]. It was here that a strike at the McCormick harvester plant led to a rally in Haymarket Square on May 4, 1886. When the police charged the crowd, someone threw a bomb, leaving several police officers dead. Eight anarchist leaders were arrested, largely on the strength of their rhetoric rather than any link to the actual bomb, and four were hanged. Jones was further radicalized by these events.

The exact date when Mary Jones became "Mother Jones"

is unclear, but the first public reference to her as such was in 1894 when she joined Coxey's "Army," thousands of unemployed workers who marched toward Washington [and] urged [the] creation of jobs for the unemployed." Gorn wrote, "Mary Jones was now on the road, where she would stay for thirty years" [29].

In 1894, Eugene Debs led the railway workers in a nationwide strike protesting cuts in wages. The strike was broken, and Debs was sent to prison. When he was released in 1896, Jones orchestrated a gathering of workers to welcome him, meeting him for the first time.

Coal mining helped power the Industrial Revolution in the United States, with production rising from two million tons in 1840 to 350 million tons in 1900, employing in 1900 some 677,000 men. By 1905, nearly half of the miners would be new immigrants[30]. Early attempts to organize the miners were largely unsuccessful, but in 1890, the United Mine Workers (UMW) was formed. It became the largest and most powerful union in the nation.

One of the factors in its success was its organizers, who sold the benefits of the union to the workers. One of the most successful was Mother Jones. Miner James Brophy recalled, "When she started to speak, she could carry an audience of miners with her every time ... she had a complete disregard for danger or hardship and would go in wherever she thought she was needed" [31].

With the UMW, Jones would persuade local farmers to donate food. She organized parades of children and brought women into the strike. She organized miners' wives into "mop and broom" brigades, shaming and intimidating strikebreakers from taking the miners' jobs. The coal companies complained that "foreigners" like Mother Jones had such an influence on the workers[32].

Jones had helped organize a strike in West Virginia in 1902. The coal companies persuaded a judge to issue an injunction against the strike and any demonstrations in favor of the miners. The result was the arrest of Mother Jones and most of the other local UMW organizers. Jones commented, "I have been served with injunctions in quantities sufficient to form a shroud for me when I am cold in death" [33].

At her trial, the prosecutor called her "the most dangerous woman in America" since she had persuaded thousands to strike[34]. She was given a suspended sentence.

Jones went to Colorado in 1903 to aid a strike by Western miners. After the strike was suppressed by the Colorado National Guard, Jones declared, "The generations as yet unborn will read with horror of the crimes committed by the mine owners of Colorado with their hired blood hounds aching to spill the blood of their slaves" [35]. By then, Jones had broken with the leadership of the UMW, which she felt was becoming too friendly to business. In 1905, she resigned from the union.

For several years, she had crusaded against child labor. In 1903, she threw herself into a strike at a Philadelphia textile mill. To publicize the battle, Jones announced a march of one hundred children along with textile workers and labor leaders from Philadelphia to New York. She declared, "What's the use of bringing a lot of children into the world to make more money for the plutocrats while little lives are being ground out in the mill and the workshop?" [36]. This "Children's Crusade" helped publicize the problem of child labor.

Jones explained her choice of life to a Congressional committee, stating, "I belong to a class which has been robbed, exploited, and plundered through many long centuries. And because I belong to that class, I have an impulse to go and help break the chains" [37].

From 1905–12, Jones spoke for the Socialist Party and raised money for different labor causes. In 1911, she broke with the Socialists and rejoined the UMW., campaigning for mine workers' rights in West Virginia. When violence broke out, Jones was among those arrested on charges of conspiracy to murder.

She told *The New York Times*, "Since I have to die, I would rather die for the cause to which I have given so much of my life" [38]. She was released after three months.

She went back to Colorado. She urged the miners to strike till they received better working conditions and pay, saying, "You are the biggest part of the population of the state. You create its wealth, so I say let the fight go on; if nobody else will keep on, I will" [39].

She was arrested again to prevent her from inciting "the more ignorant and criminally disposed to deeds of violence and crime" [40].

Protests came in from across the country. Pancho Villa wrote President Wilson, offering to swap one of his prisoners for her in an exchange of political prisoners. After three months, she was released.

When mine company guards massacred striking miners in Ludlow, Colorado, soon afterward, Jones secured a meeting with President Wilson, but he refused to intervene in the strike.

When the United States entered WWI, Jones supported it, telling a UMW convention, "If we are going to have freedom for the workers, we need to stand behind the nation" [41]. Jones continued to support labor's battles during the war.

She tried to continue her political activities in the 1920s but was increasingly crippled by arthritis. Mother Jones died on November 30, 1930.

Mother Jones was not the only woman whose courage inspired workers.

Clara Lemlich was born in 1886 in Ukraine, then a part of Russia. To divert attention from his regime's shortcomings, the ruling Czar Nicholas II encouraged pogroms, or mass attacks, against the region's Jews. When a pogrom in nearby Kishinev in April 1903 left 49 Jews dead and over five hundred injured, the Lemlich family left for America. At age 17, she arrived in New York City, where, within two weeks, she found a job in a clothing sweatshop. The workers had to pay the owner for the needle and thread they used. The workers, almost all girls, worked from 7 a.m.–7 p.m., hunched over footpedal-powered sewing machines. Lemlich recalled, "The shop we worked in had no central heating, no electric power. The hissing of the machines [and] the yelling of the foreman made life unbelievable" [42].

The apparel workers, few of whom spoke English, were often cheated of their wages. They were each searched to make sure they were not stealing any thread or garments. Lemlich noted all the signs at the factory saying, "Singing is Forbidden," "Laughing is Forbidden," and "Talking is Forbidden" [43]. Lemlich said, "To the bosses, the girls are part of the machines they are running" [44].

Lemlich took English classes and then, in 1906, was one of thirteen workers who founded Local 25 of the International Ladies Garment Workers Union (ILGWU). Its members were overwhelmingly Jewish or Italian immigrants. The garment trade was centered on the Lower East Side, where the eight hundred people per acre in some places made it the most densely populated neighborhood in the United States. *McClure's Magazine* called it "the lowest-paid, most degrading of American employment" [45].

By age 21, Lemlich had repeatedly led strikes, causing her to be repeatedly fired. She led strikes in 1907 and 1908. In 1909, the workers at Lemlich's employer, Leiserson's, went on strike. Lemlich would be arrested seventeen times during this walkout. Then, on September 10, 1909, she was beaten by thugs hired by the factory owners, leaving her bleeding on the sidewalk with six broken ribs. She did not tell her parents, with whom she lived. She later said, "Like rain, the blows fell on me. Unions aren't built easily" [46].

The next month, workers walked out at the Triangle Waist Company, New York's largest blouse factory. Workers protesting the use of scabs (i.e., replacement workers) were beaten up by hired guards. Newspapers ignored both strikes until Mary Dreier, a prominent reformer, was arrested while supporting the strikers.

The ILGWU called a meeting to discuss whether to call an industry-wide strike to support the striking workers. Samuel Gompers spoke, showing doubt about whether such a strike would succeed. Lemlich called out from the crowd that she wanted to speak. The *New York Call* wrote, "Willing hands lifted the frail little girl with flashing black eyes to the stage" [47].

Speaking in Yiddish, Lemlich said, "I have listened to all the speakers, and I have no further patience for talk. I am a working girl, one of those striking against intolerable conditions. I am tired of listening to speakers who talk in generalities ... I offer a resolution that a general strike be declared now" [48].

Two thousand workers jumped up in support, taking an oath: "If I turn traitor to the cause I now pledge, may this hand wither from the hand I now raise" [49]. The next morning, 15,000 workers, 90% of them women, walked out. Five thousand more joined them the next day, making it the largest strike by women in US history. The press called it "the uprising of the 20,000," while *Colliers* described it as a show of women's power "such as has not been known since woman entered the Garden of Eden" [50].

The workers asked for a 52-hour workweek, a 20% raise, paid holidays, an end to paying for needle and thread, and the recognition of the ILGWU. Within two days, 70 smaller factories accepted these terms. However, one hundred others vowed to resist. The police and judges were hostile to the workers, with the *New York Tribune* quoting a police officer as saying, "We ain't here to protect the strikers or anyone belonging to them. We're here to protect the scabs" [51].

The New York Sun reported, "The girls, headed by teenage Clara Lemlich, described by union organizers as a 'pint of trouble for the bosses' began singing Italian and Russian working-class songs as they paced in twos before the factory door.

Of a sudden, around the corner came a dozen rough-looking customers for whom the union label 'gorillas' seemed well chosen" [52]. The thugs proceeded to knock down the line of protesting women to let scabs slip into the factory. The police then arrested Lemlich and two other badly beaten girls.

Frances Perkins, later the Secretary of Labor, reported, "The brutality of the police was terrible. They would take these young Jewish girls and bang them over the head with a nightstick" [53]. In sentencing another teenage striker to prison, a judge said, "You are on strike against God and Nature," leading British playwright George Bernard Shaw to cable, "Delightful. Medieval America is always in the most intimate personal confidence of the Almighty" [54].

Appalled by the conflict, a group of society women nicknamed the "mink brigade" threw their vocal and financial support behind the strikers. The factories gradually surrendered. The Triangle Waist Company agreed to the pay increases but refused to recognize the ILGWU.

Five months later, the New York cloakmakers went on strike, putting 60,000 workers on strike. A board of arbitration made up of powerful Jewish leaders, including Jacob Schiff and future Supreme Court Justice Louis Brandeis, along with Samuel Gompers, persuaded the two sides to settle in what was called the Protocol of Peace. The union won official recognition along with improved wages and working conditions. The employers agreed to the "preferential shop," which meant that if competing job applicants were equal, preference would go to the union member. It would be one of the greatest victories for organized labor up to that time.

Ironically, the Triangle Waist plant later would be the site of one of the worst industrial accidents in American history. When a fire started in the factory on March 25, 1911, 146 workers would die, many because the exit door was locked to prevent worker theft. The two owners were found not guilty of manslaughter, a verdict that enraged the public.

Rose Schneiderman, a Polish immigrant and former garment worker, spoke at a meeting at the Metropolitan Opera House to honor the dead workers, saying, "I would be a traitor to these poor burned bodies if I came to talk good fellowship ... The life of men and women is so cheap, and property is so sacred" [55].

Lemlich was blacklisted by the textile industry. She refused an offer of free tuition to Columbia, saying, "It was too late. I was swallowed up by the trade union movement" [56]. The ILGWU hired her as a factory inspector, and she later became an organizer for the Women's Trade Union League. In the 1920s, Lemlich became a Communist. She unsuccessfully ran for City Council and led hunger marches during the Great Depression. When her husband became ill in the 1940s, she found a job back in the garment industry. When she was in a nursing home in her late seventies, she helped persuade the workers to unionize. She died on July 12, 1982.

Yet another immigrant would rise through the garment industry to become a confidant of presidents. Sidney Hillman was born in Russia in 1887 to a family with a long tradition of producing rabbis. Hillman ignored his father's wishes to study instead books about society, including those of Marx and John Stuart Mill. At age 15, in 1903, Hillman joined the Bund, the General Jewish Workers Organization. He was arrested in 1904 for leading a Bund demonstration and served time in prison before being released. In 1905, a revolt broke out in Russia. When a Bund-organized insurrection in his hometown of Zagare failed in 1906, Hillman was forced to flee to England, where he had an uncle[57].

In 1907, Hillman arrived in the United States. By 1909, he had become an apprentice cutter in the Chicago factory of HSM, one of the nation's largest clothing manufacturers. A strike of the entire Chicago garment industry, the third largest employer in the city, broke out in September 1910. Progressive leader George Creel later wrote, "The trouble was peculiar in that the workers ... presented only vague demands ... They were wretched without being able to state exactly the cause of their wretchedness" [58].

After four months, the United Garment Workers (UGW), a branch of the AFL, came to an arrangement that conceded to the manufacturer on every disputed issue. At a mass meeting to discuss the agreement, Hillman, using a combination of broken English and Yiddish, denounced the agreement and persuaded the workers to continue the strike. Biographer Steven Fraser wrote, "The moment immediately transformed him into a popular leader, a commanding moral presence" [59].

Hillman, working with Clarence Darrow and Jane Addams, then worked out an agreement that arranged for impartial arbitration of workers' issues. Hillman then prevailed over a militant minority who opposed the agreement as too much of a compromise. One of the clothing manufacturers, Joseph Schaffner, concluded that Hillman was less a rebel but instead was a man of "sweet reasonableness" [60].

Hillman began organizing a new local of the UGW, becoming a full-time labor organizer. He was able to prevent a recurrent strike in 1913, winning acceptance of the "preferential shop" that would give preference in hiring to union members. The management labor negotiator said of Hillman, "We learned to like him for his intelligence, his moderation, and his attractive personality ... his criticism was often found to be justified" [61].

Hillman would ally progressive reformers with immigrant garment workers and convince many employers in the field that a strong union could help prevent the development of economic anarchy and inefficiency. In 1914, Hillman moved to New York, where he was soon drafted to become the first president of the Amalgamated Clothing Workers of America (ACWA), formed by workers who had revolted against the conservative management of the UGW. Over the next few years, the ACWA organized nearly 90,000 workers and managed multiple strikes and organizing campaigns [62].

When American involvement in WWI loomed, the fear of labor unrest led to crackdowns on more militant workers. Into this breach, Hillman argued that collective bargaining and a positive union-business relationship could offer a better alternative. The ACWA agreed to a non-strike pledge. In exchange, it negotiated actions against sweatshops, poor working conditions, and child labor. The membership of the ACWA tripled from 1916 to 1919. Hillman developed lasting relationships with leading progressives such as Florence Kelley, secretary of the National Consumers League, and two future Supreme Court justices, Louis Brandeis and Felix Frankfurter. The liberal magazine *The New Republic* concluded that democracy's future "depends on the capacity of employers and workers to harmonize democratic ideals of freedom with the voluntary self-discipline essential to efficient production ... no group of men in America has a keener appreciation of this fact that Sidney Hillman and the ACWA" [63].

The ACWA pioneered educational and cultural programs for its members, who came from at least 26 nationalities, offering instruction in English and encouraging workers to become citizens. The ACWA also pioneered unemployment insurance, low-cost worker housing, and cooperative labor banking for its members. The conservative trend after WWI blocked efforts to spread these reforms [64].

The 1920s saw the ACWA unsuccessfully being sued by a manufacturer as an "illegal conspiracy," trying to maintain peaceful relations with other unions as well as socialists and communists and fighting the AFL, which opposed attempts to organize unskilled workers. Hillman argued that labor needed to organize the unskilled, stating, "We are a movement of those who have been oppressed ... it is our obligation to help those who are still suffering under the iron heel of oppression" [65].

The onset of the Great Depression led to a search for new solutions. Hillman saw the key to be the revival of mass purchasing power and for national planning to avoid the cycles of bust and boom. Hillman argued, "If we are to avoid the cycles of depression ... we must plan a more equitable distribution of our national income" [66].

President Roosevelt appointed Hillman to the National Industrial Recovery Board, which was charged with running the National Recovery Act (NRA). Hillman tried to push its legitimizing of labor organizing while defending it against liberal critics who considered it too business-friendly.

Hillman was attacked as a Russian and a radical. Hillman, who had become an American citizen before WWI, answered at a Congressional hearing, "At least I can say, Senator, that this country is not with me merely a matter of accident, but it is the country of my choice" [67].

When the NRA was declared unconstitutional, Hillman turned to expanding labor strength. In a split with the AFL, Hillman helped found the CIO, the Congress of Industrial Organizations, which represented unions trying to organize large industries filled with unskilled workers, and became its vice president. Hillman remained loyal to Roosevelt and the New Deal program of reforms, "convinced that there was no option for labor outside the Democratic Party" [68].

When Hillman was struck down by severe pneumonia in 1938, FDR wrote to him, "To be deprived of your counsel even very briefly at a time like this is a serious loss to the labor movement and the people of this country" [69].

Hillman, appointed to the National Defense Advisory Committee in 1940, persuaded the Committee to announce a policy that any business receiving defense contracts must obey labor laws, including a 40-hour week. Unfortunately, many violators of the policy continued to receive contracts.

Hillman would be attacked by the right for being too solicitous of workers and by the left for giving in to industry, for his service in the several government organizations during WWII aimed at keeping the war industry going. He had the thankless job of trying to prevent strikes while having little power to get workers a share of the money flowing to defense manufacturers.

Increasing anti-labor attacks before and during the war led Hillman and the CIO to create a political action committee that successfully helped increase the vote for pro-labor candidates. In 1944, the Republicans struck back, spreading the rumor that in the matter of the Democratic choosing a vice presidential candidate, President Roosevelt had said, "Clear it with Sidney" [70].

Republicans attacked Hillman as a foreigner and Jew, running billboards asking, "It's your country—Why let Sidney Hillman run it?" [71]. Nevertheless, Roosevelt won his fourth term as President. He wrote to Hillman, "Nobody knows better than I do how much you contributed to its [the campaign's] success" [72]. CIO President Phillip Murray declared, "I don't know of any individual in our movement that has suffered more real, filthy, scandalous, lying personal abuse than Sidney Hillman has during the course of the campaign" [73].

Speaking at his last Amalgamated convention, Hillman declared their goals, "We want a better America ... so that no child will cry for food in the midst of plenty ... An America that will have no sense of insecurity and which will make it possible for all groups, regardless of race, creed or color, to live in friendship" [74].

The stress of the multiple battles would prove too much for Hillman. On July 10, 1946, he suffered his fourth heart attack and died at the age of 59.

While Hillman was vice president of the CIO, the president was yet another immigrant. Phillip Murray was born in Scotland to an Irish Catholic family in 1886. At age seven, Murray collected food for the striking miners and then, at age ten, started working in the coal mines in Britain.

He arrived in the United States on December 25, 1902, in the company of his father, a coal miner and the secretary of his local union branch. Murray and his father settled in

Pennsylvania. Within a year, they had earned enough from coal mining to bring the rest of the family over.

At the time, coal miners were paid the weight of the coal they produced. When Murray protested to the manager that his production had been undercounted, the two got into a brawl. Murray was fired, resulting in an unsuccessful strike by the other workers. Murray later testified, "The day after the strike, my father and his eight children, including myself, were thrown from their home out into the street" [75]. Forced to leave town, Murray decided to dedicate his life to unions. Murray later explained, "The coal miner has no money. He is alone. He has no organization to defend him" [76].

Murray worked in a variety of mines in southwestern Pennsylvania and became head of a United Mine Workers (UMW) local in 1905. He became a citizen in 1911. In 1912, he was appointed to the UMW international executive board, then became District 5 president with the help of another union official, John L. Lewis. Murray repaid the favor by supporting Lewis for UMW vice president in 1917. In 1919, Murray supported Lewis' bid to become UMW president. When Lewis became president in January 1920, he appointed Murray vice president. Biographer Ronald Schatz wrote, "For the next twenty years, Philip Murray was John L. Lewis's right-hand man, handling such major responsibilities as negotiations for the anthracite fields; always he demonstrated complete loyalty to Lewis and his policies. Only in the arena of national politics did Lewis and Murray disagree, and until 1940, their differences seemed insignificant" [77].

An observer noted how they complemented each other in negotiations, saying that Lewis would "thunder and bluster and threaten the coal operators, then Philip Murray would move in with his solid array of facts. A first-rate negotiator, it was Murray who consolidated the gains won by Lewis" [78].

Murray felt that the union's success in coal mining depended on working with, rather than against, the federal government. In 1918, he defended an agreement the UMW had made with the federal government in which the miners received a wage increase in exchange for agreeing not to strike and to fines for those who did strike. In 1919, the UMW capitulated in a strike in the face of federal troops. In 1921, President Harding asked Murray to try to persuade 20,000 miners in West Virginia to call off a battle with the coal company guards and state police. Murray persuaded the workers to return home, noting that the presence of federal troops was prepared to crush the strike otherwise. Lewis and Murray pushed for the federal government to compel the employers and unions to reach an agreement. Murray testified to the Senate, "During the period of the [1919] strike, the government did not hesitate to use its great authority, under the war powers, against the United Mine Workers, even to the extent of placing its members in jail. Is there any reason why it should not have used its authority under the same war powers, to make non-union operators observe the terms of a decision by a governmental tribunal?" [79].

While Lewis, a lifelong Republican, mistrusted the expansion of government power under the New Deal, Murray endorsed it. Stung by the government's lack of support during a 1937 steel strike, Lewis endorsed Roosevelt's 1940 Republican foe, announcing that he would resign the presidency of the CIO if Roosevelt were reelected.

Murray, in contrast, was a close supporter of Roosevelt. In 1932, he had led a delegation of UMW leaders to Albany to meet with then New York Governor Roosevelt. Murray recalled, "The miners in 1932 were eating garbage, yes, garbage, and getting $1.50 a day for a ten-hour day ... but one day they found a friend. He was sitting on the end of a divan in his library in the Executive Mansion in Albany, New York. He knew the miners and their problems, and he said he would help them" [80].

A Murray advisor recalled, "Philip Murray was immensely

grateful to the New Deal, and he was not the type of person to repudiate friends ever" [81]. In addition, Murray, at Lewis' request, had taken over the CIO's effort to organize the steel mills. The CIO sought government help in its efforts to organize the steelworkers.

Murray and the CIO's efforts to organize the industry led to the formation of the United Steelworkers union and their eventual success in representing the workers in the steel industry.

When Lewis resigned as president of the CIO after Roosevelt's 1940 victory, he supported Murray to become the new president. After some soul-searching, Murray accepted the job.

As president, Murray led the CIO to fully support the Roosevelt administration's war efforts, telling the November 1941 CIO convention that he fully supported the Commander in Chief (Roosevelt) and that the war effort was paramount. Lewis saw Murray's support for Roosevelt and the war effort as a personal betrayal. At a May 1942 UMW meeting, Lewis excoriated Murray, accusing him of betrayal of the UMW. The UMW board soon declared that the vice presidency, though still held by Murray, was vacant.

Murray committed the CIO to a no-strike policy during the war. The Republican recapture of the Congress following the war would result in the radically anti-union Taft-Hartley Act. Murray, now president of the United Steelworkers as well as the CIO, would rely on intervention by the Truman administration in 1946, 1949, and 1952 strikes to achieve contracts closer to the union position.

Following the onset of the Cold War, Murray moved to oust Communist-dominated unions from the CIO. At a 1946 CIO executive board meeting, Murray commented, "There are some of our unions ... [who] permit their judgments to be substantially influenced by the Communist Party" [82]. Within a few years, the CIO had expelled the far-left unions.

In 1952, Murray saw the union movement threatened by

a possible Republican takeover of the presidency. He campaigned hard against the Republican candidate Eisenhower. When Eisenhower won a landslide victory in November 1952, Murray was crushed. His son Joseph recalled, "That was hard. I think it broke his heart" [83]. Murray died a few days after the election.

1 Samuel Gompers. *Seventy Years of Life and Labor: An Autobiography*, E.F. Dutton and Company, Inc, New York, 1925, volume 1, 19.

2 Craig Phelan. *Samuel Gompers*, in *American Portraits: History Through Biography: Volume II from 1865*. Donald W. Whisenhunt, ed. Kendall-Hunt Publishing, Dubuque, IA, 1967, 45.

3 Bailey, 172.

4 Phelan, 45.

5 Phelan, 46.

6 Phelan, 48.

7 Harold C. Livesay. *Samuel Gompers and Organized Labor in America*, Little, Brown and Company, Boston, 1978, 407.

8 John H. M. Laslett. *Samuel Gompers and the Rise of American Business Unionism*, in *Labor Leaders in America*, ed. Melvyn Dubofsky and Warren Van Tine, University of Illinois Press, Urbana, IL, 1987, 69.

9 Livesay, 50.

10 Livesay, 60.

11 Phelan, 49.

12 Phelan, 49.

13 Livesay, 90.

14 Laslett, 71.

15 Bailey, 175.

16 Walter Lord. *The Good Years*, Bantam Books, New York, 1960, 149.

17 Laslett, 76.

18 Livesay, 161.

19 Livesay, 168.

20 Annie E. S. Beard. *Our Foreign-Born Citizens*, Thomas Y. Crowell Company, New York, 1955, 84-5.

21 Livesay, 181.

22 Laslett, 63.

23 Lord, 150.

24 Elliott J. Gorn. *Mother Jones: The Most Dangerous Woman in America*, Hill and Wang, New York, 2001, 31.

25 Gregg Coodley and David Sarasohn. *Taming Infection: The American Response to Disease from Smallpox to Covid*, Atmosphere Press, 2022, 85.

26 Mother Jones. *The Autobiography of Mother Jones*, eds. Mary Field Parson, Charles H. Kerr, and Company, Chicago, 1925, 12-13.

27 Jones, 14-16.

28 Gorn, 54.

29 Gorn, 63.

30 Gorn, 69-70.

31 Gorn, 74.

32 Gorn, 80.

33 Phillip Foner. *Mother Jones Speaks*, Monad Press, New York, 1983, 481-3.

34 Gorn, 96-97.

35 Gorn, 112-3.

36 Gorn, 134.

37 Terry Golway. *The Organizer: Mary "Mother" Jones*, in *Nine Irish Lives: The Fighters, Thinkers and Artists Who Helped Build America*, ed. Mark Bailey, Algonquin Books, Chapel Hill, 2018, 49.

38 "Mother Jones Defiant, *The New York Times*, March 11, 1913, 1.

39 Golway, 48.

40 Gorn, 211.

41 Gorn, 246.

42 Steven Greenhouse. *Beaten Down, Worked Up: The Past, Present and Future of American Labor*, Alfred A. Knopf, New York, 2019, 49.

43 Greenhouse, 50.

44 Deborah Heligman. *Clara Lemlich*, Philomel Books, New York, 2021, 24.

45 Greenhouse, 51.

46 Greenhouse, 52.

47 Greenhouse, 53-54.

48 Greenhouse, 54.

49 Greenhouse, 54.

50 Greenhouse, 54.

51 Greenhouse, 55.

52 Greenhouse, 55.

53 Greenhouse, 56.

54 Greenhouse, 56.

55 Greenhouse, 55.

56 Greenhouse, 66.

57 Steven Fraser. *Sidney Hillman: Labor's Machiavelli*, in *Labor Leaders in America*, ed. Melvyn Dubofsky and Warren Van Tine, University of Illinois Press, Urbana, IL, 1987, 208.

58 George Creel. "A Way to Industrial Peace," *Century Magazine*, July 1915.

59 Fraser, *Machiavelli* 211.

60 Fraser, *Machiavelli*, 211.

61 Steven Fraser. *Labor Will Rule: Sidney Hillman and the Rise of American Labor*, Free Press, New York, 1991, 73.

62 Fraser, *Labor*, 96.

63 Fraser, *Machiavelli*, 214.

64 Fraser, *Machiavelli*, 215-6.

65 Fraser, *Labor*, 197.

66 Fraser, *Machiavelli*, 217.

67 Fraser, *Labor*, 317.

68 Fraser, *Machiavelli*, 222.

69 Fraser, *Labor*, 433.

70 Fraser, *Machiavelli*, 228.

71 Fraser, *Machiavelli*, 229.

72 Fraser, *Labor*, 535.

73 Fraser, *Labor*, 539.

74 Fraser, *Labor*, 574.

75 Ronald Schatz. *Philip Murray and the Subordination of the Industrial Unions to the United States Government*, in *Labor Leaders in America*, ed Melvyn Dubofsky and Warren Van Tine, University of Illinois Press, Urbana, IL, 1987, 236.

76 Schatz, 236.

77 Schatz, 238.

78 Bailey, 186.

79 Schatz, 241-2.

80 Schatz, 244-5.

81 Schatz, 245.

82 Schatz, 252.

83 Schatz, 256.

Anti-Chinese Cartoon Contrasting Western and Eastern Immigration

Asian Immigrants Arriving at Angel Island

CHAPTER 7

The Anti-Asian Hysteria

Many groups of immigrants ran into bigotry. The second half of the nineteenth century through the first half of the twentieth century was a time of particular hostility to Chinese and Japanese immigrants.

The Chinese, mainly men, began arriving on the West Coast starting in 1848. They took jobs Whites refused, plus other jobs for less money than White workers. By 1865, there were 50,000 Chinese in California, of whom over 90% were young men. Many were miners who faced special discrimination. Chinese miners paid a special tax and were restricted to working on tailings, mines that had already been worked[1].

The discrimination against the Chinese extended further than that. They were refused the option of citizenship, could not testify in court, and were barred from certain professions. In 1858, the California legislature prohibited them from entering the state, although this was not well enforced. 1858 also saw anti-Chinese riots in California[2].

Nevertheless, for many Chinese, conditions were still better than in China, which was wracked by the Taiping rebellion from 1851–64, in which millions died, plus cycles of famine and overpopulation. The years from 1700–1850 saw a tripling of the population in China, from 150 to 450 million[3]. The emperor legalized the recruitment of Chinese workers for

America in 1859, leading to a further swell of Chinese immigrants to the West Coast.

Most Chinese immigrants came from Southern China, from around Canton or Hong Kong. Chinese brokers would pay for the cost of passage as well as an advance of about forty dollars per man. The workers would pay off this debt and the interest on it over several years. Upon arriving in California, the immigrants relied on the Chinese Consolidated Benevolent Association (the Chinese Six Companies), which offered them banking, legal, and medical services. Although these were run by merchants rather than criminals, these companies aroused the suspicion of the White Californians. The Chinese community started two bilingual newspapers, beginning in 1855[4]

In 1862, the Pacific Railroad Act picked two companies to build a railroad across the continent. The Union Pacific would work westward from Iowa, while the Central Pacific would go east from San Francisco. The Central Pacific was formed by four wealthy Californians: Collis Huntington, Leland Stanford, Mark Hopkins, and Charles Crocker, who each put in only $1500 apiece. The four then demanded increasing government subsidies[5].

Yet the Central Pacific found it hard to find workers who were willing to do the backbreaking work for relatively little money. White workers increasingly quit, drawn to new silver and gold strikes.

In February 1865, Charlie Crocker met with the railroad construction foreman, James Strobridge, proposing the use of Chinese labor. Strobridge objected, "I will not boss Chinese," to which Crocker replied, "But who said laborers had to be White to build a railroad?" [6].

They agreed to try 50 Chinese workers for a month. The Chinese worked hard, without complaints, and with an efficiency often exceeding that of the White workers. The Central Pacific began to hire as many Chinese as possible to take the place of the unavailable White workers.

Historian Kevin Baker wrote, "They were replaced by 10,000 Chinese. Despised by White Californians, subjected to special 'permission' taxes and regularly attacked and lynched, the 'Celestials' were usually paid half the amount of White laborers on the railroad and had much of the rest of their pay seized by the Chinese 'trading companies' that had smuggled them into the United States in the first place. They averaged just four foot-ten and 120 pounds, but they proved to be wiry, tireless men who worked carefully and well" [7]. The railroad had to traverse the towering Sierra Nevadas with the labor mainly being done by hand and sometimes with the use of dynamite. Eventually 80% of the 13,500 workers for the Central Pacific would be Chinese. Some 1,500 workers would die building this section of the railroad[8].

The Chinese workers, who had a more varied diet than the other workers, were also healthier. They drank tea with boiled water, avoiding the suspect water consumed by the White workers. Historian John Hoyt Williams wrote of them, "The Celestials had few vices. They almost never drank whiskey, they rarely quarreled or fought—at least with outsiders—and they were scrupulously honest and religiously clean" [9].

The Chinese workers did like to gamble, leading Mark Twain to write, based on his observations, that "almost every third Chinaman runs a lottery" [10]. Twain also wrote about the Chinese that "a lazy one does not exist" [11].

Nevertheless, the prejudice against the Chinese did not abate. Editor Horace Greeley would write, after a trip to California, that the average Chinese was "an inveterate gambler, an opium smoker, a habitual rum drinker, and a devotee to every sensual vice" [12].

The unstinting, uncomplaining work by the Chinese workers did have one interruption. On June 24, 1867, three thousand Chinese workers laid down their tools and sat by the track. They demanded a raise to $40 a month from their current $33 and an eight-hour day, equal to the Whites. The Central

Pacific refused to budge. After a few days, the strikers went back to work, having gained only a two-dollar-a-month pay raise[13].

Hatred of the Chinese was not confined to California. Several anti-Chinese riots occurred in Nevada from 1867–69. Estimates were that up to a hundred Chinese were murdered in California and Nevada in the late 1860s, but only two of the murderers would be hung[14].

In the end, the companies competed to lay down the most miles in a day. The Union Pacific led with a day of 7.5 miles. Then, on April 28, 1869, the Central Pacific team, comprised of 848 Chinese and eight Irishmen, would complete over ten miles, winning Crocker a bet of $10,000[15].

Eventually, the railroad was completed on May 10, 1869. The two railroad companies would receive grants of almost 280 million acres of land as part of the payment for their services.

Many of the Chinese chose to stay in the United States afterward, where they would be joined by new Chinese immigrants.

The Union Pacific also employed Chinese as coal miners but always insisted that they were really employees of a contractor, A. G. Beckwith, Quinn, and Co. Beckwith subtracted various fees before turning over the wages to the Chinese workers but did offer credit against future wages. The Chinese Six Companies supplied the Chinese workers to Beckwith and others, being paid for their costs out of the workers' wages. The Six Companies made most of their money selling provisions and other supplies to the Chinese workers[16].

Chinese would continue to be a major part of the labor force in building other Western railroads over the next two decades.

In total, some 300,000 Chinese would enter the United States from 1848–1882, although many would return to China. Ninety percent of the immigrants would come from the Canton area or the Pearl River delta in Southern China. The censuses in 1880 and 1890 showed that Chinese males outnumbered females by more than 20 to 1[17].

As the Chinese population grew, there was an explosion of resentment against the Chinese immigrants. In 1871 and 1877, there were anti-Chinese riots in California. Still, like other immigrants, the Chinese were lured by the better economic opportunities in America. Roughly 180,000 Chinese permanently immigrated to the United States from 1849–1882[18].

Some saw political opportunity in opposing the Chinese. In the late 1870s, Denis Kearney started the New Workingman's Party in San Francisco, whose slogan was, "The Chinese must go"[19].

The California legislature set up a Special Committee on Chinese Immigration, which concluded in an 1878 report that the Chinese "were the most debased people on the face of the earth ... justice to our race demands that they should not be allowed to settle on our soil"[20].

One of the few leaders who spoke out against the anti-Chinese prejudice was Andrew Carnegie, who labeled the anti-Chinese agitation in California as "the usual prejudice of the ignorant races next to them in the social scale"[21].

In 1870, Congress passed the Naturalization Act of 1870. While the Act made Blacks eligible for citizenship, Asians were excluded from this option. Chinese would remain ineligible for citizenship until 1941[22].

Opposition from the railroads and a treaty with China prevented the passage of bills eliminating Chinese immigration through the 1870s, but the anti-Chinese fervor did not abate. Anti-Chinese leagues were started in many California cities, while the new 1879 California Constitution denied Chinese the vote and banned their employment on public works[23].

In 1879, Congress passed a law limiting Chinese immigration, but it was vetoed by President Hayes. The Chinese immigration continued, growing to 40,000 immigrants in 1882. As a result, Congress passed a bill in 1882 to exclude Chinese immigrant workers for ten years. An initial bill was vetoed by President Arthur, but he signed a somewhat weaker version of the Chinese Exclusion Act on May 6, 1882. Only certain exempt classes of Chinese, including merchants, students, and travelers, were allowed to enter the nation[24]. Chinese immigration dropped to only eight thousand in 1883. The law particularly limited the immigration of Chinese women, for few fitted into one of the exempt categories.

In 1885, Congress went further, passing the Foran Act, banning all contracts "to import alien workers for labor and service"[25].

1885 also saw one of the worst anti-Chinese riots, occurring in the coal mining town of Rocks Springs, Wyoming. A dispute between a Chinese and a White worker turned to violent conflict. An armed mob of Whites, ironically mainly European immigrants, marched on the Chinese section of town. When the riot was over, at least 28 Chinese were confirmed dead. Charles Francis Adams wrote that Rock Springs was "the most atrocious, cold-blooded, systemic ... massacre anywhere in the country"[26].

There were multiple other acts of violence against Chinese immigrants, including the lynching of 17 Chinese in Los Angeles after a policeman was shot by a Chinese suspect. Mobs forced all the Chinese to leave town in Eureka, California, as well as in Tacoma and Seattle, Washington[27].

Labor also often opposed Chinese workers. In 1886, John Cooke, Secretary of the Oregon Knights of Labor, demanded that the local railroad dismiss all Chinese workers, attacking "their complete monopoly of the various branches of unskilled labor on the Pacific Coast," while claiming the Knights were acting, "to protect our interests, our country, and our race"[28].

Sadly, even many national labor leaders were not immune from this prejudice. Samuel Gompers wrote in his autobiography that, during strikes, "we had to meet the threats of employers to import Chinese strikebreakers"[29]. Gompers and other unions supported the Chinese Exclusion Act of 1882. Gompers had once written that the Chinese "as a race were cruel and treacherous," prone to "gambling halls, opium joints, and dens of iniquity and vice" [30]. Mother Jones supported the UMW stance in favor of excluding Chinese immigrants[31].

The Chinese Exclusion Act was renewed for an additional ten years in 1892, and then in 1902, it was renewed indefinitely[32].

Those Chinese who had immigrated to the United States would increasingly live in urban areas, most often in ethnic enclaves known as "Chinatown." Others, particularly in California, were farmers. In the Sacramento and San Joaquin delta area, 95% of the Chinese population worked as farmers, with historian Carey McWilliams calling them "the vital factor" in the growth of California agriculture[33].

Two Chinese horticulturalists made special contributions. Ah Bing developed the Bing cherry in Oregon, while Lue Gim Gong created new strains of oranges and grapefruit in Florida[34].

The Exclusion Act, by freezing the Chinese population in a skewed male-to-female ratio, would result in a declining Chinese population until the 1920s[35]. In 1900, only 5% of the Chinese in the United States were women[36].

In urban areas, Chinese immigrants often opened restaurants or laundries, two businesses that did not require professional degrees or English fluency and that could be run by individuals or families[37].

Despite the laws, an estimated 300,000 Chinese would enter the United States from 1882–1943, most by falsely claiming membership in one of the excluded groups[38].

There was minimal Japanese immigration to the mainland of the United States before 1890. A larger number of Japanese came to Hawaii as plantation workers. However, the period 1890–1900 saw 26,000 Japanese immigrants arrive, many from Hawaii, settling almost completely on the West Coast. This was enough to stir up antipathy for them among White

Californians. In part, they were brought in to take the place of the no-longer-available Chinese.

Japanese emigration was the result of both rapid population growth in Japan in the last quarter of the nineteenth century and the modernization and pro-Western attitudes that followed the Meiji Restoration in 1868. The latter was followed by the teaching of English in Japanese schools starting in 1876, along with the legalization of Christianity. Japanese intellectuals and the government extolled the virtues of America[39].

Japanese immigrants to the United States represented neither the poorest Japanese nor the upper classes but instead consisted of men of limited means who could obtain family or village support for the travel to the States. Most were able to send substantial money back to their home villages. The initial welcome by California farmers faded when the hard work of the Japanese allowed them to become tenant farmers or landowners. In 1913, California passed the Alien Land Law, prohibiting ownership of land by those not eligible to be citizens (such as all Asians). Californians also pushed to stop Japanese immigration[40].

However, whereas the Chinese could be excluded without worry about offending what was a very weak Chinese government, the Japanese came from a growing power. As a result, the United States and Japan reached a "Gentleman's Agreement" in August 1900. The United States would not pass a law barring Japanese immigrants, but the Japanese government would make sure that not too many emigrated from Japan to America. Nevertheless, there was increasing hostility to the Chinese and Japanese in California. The Hearst chain of newspapers warned of "the Yellow Peril," while anti-Asian "Exclusion Leagues" sprung up in California. San Francisco segregated the Asian children in the city schools[41].

President Theodore Roosevelt complained in private about "the foolish offensiveness" of the "idiots" in the California legislature for their actions against the Japanese immigrants.

Complaining about anti-Japanese protests in San Francisco, he publicly pointed out that the "mob of a single city may at any time perform acts of lawless violence that would plunge us into war" [42].

When the Japanese government strongly protested, the Japanese, but not the other Asian children, were allowed to go to school with Whites.

The Japanese population was originally almost all men, with just 985 women out of 24,325 Japanese immigrants in 1900. The "Gentleman's Agreement" with Japan did allow for family members of Japanese already in the United States to enter, which helped reduce the gender disparity.

This further changed to a degree over the next 20 years as many Japanese immigrants acquired "picture brides," where marriages were arranged after an exchange of pictures. By 1920, a fifth of 100,000 Japanese immigrants were women. Yet the idea of remote marriage was seized on by those opposed to the Japanese immigrants being in the United States as a heinous arrangement, and the Japanese government ended the practice in 1920[43]. The 1920 Census showed a two-to-one male-to-female ratio in a total population of 111,000[44].

The Japanese immigrants were heavily involved in agriculture, again particularly in California where they took the place of now-excluded Chinese. By 1919, Japanese immigrants would be farming 450,000 acres in California. While this was only 1% of the farmland in the state, the Japanese immigrants produced about 10% of the total value of crops in California[45].

Japanese immigrants were noted for their hard work and enterprise, with many branching out into contract gardening and starting small businesses. The Japanese were also noted for their stable families, well-behaved children, and low crime rates[46].

The most famous Japanese immigrant farmer would be George Shima (1863–1926). Born Kinji Ushijima, he immigrated to the United States in 1889. Within twenty years, the newspapers would be calling him the "Potato King" for the potato crop he introduced in the Sacramento delta. By 1913, he employed over five hundred workers on his farms[47].

The center of Japanese life in the continental United States was the city of Los Angeles, where the Japanese dominated the production of fresh vegetables and some fruit crops. By 1930, 35,000 Japanese, a quarter of their population in the nation, would live in Los Angeles[48].

The majority of the Japanese immigrants went to Hawaii, where they were heavily involved in agriculture, helping to create the sugar industry in Hawaii. In 1909, some seven thousand Japanese workers in the industry went on strike against being paid less than other workers. Although the strike was broken, it did result in the Japanese gaining wage parity[49].

Korean immigration to the United States began following an 1882 treaty allowing Korean immigration. Korean immigrants mostly worked in agriculture in Hawaii. A growing population in India, along with the huge need for workers on the West Coast of the United States, drew the first immigrants from India. The first Sikh temple in the United States was opened in Stockton, California, in 1912[50].

Prejudice extended to other Asian immigrants. On September 4, 1907, hundreds of White men attacked South Asian migrant workers in Bellingham, Washington, crying, "Drive out the Hindus" [51]. The workers, who were mainly Sikhs, left town.

Indians were viewed as the least able to assimilate of all the Asian immigrants, with a 1911 United States Immigration Commission viewing them as "universally regarded as the least desirable race of immigrants thus far admitted to the United States" [52].

Congress went on to pass legislation creating the Asiatic Barred Zone in 1917 that eliminated immigration from southern and southeastern Asia.

American law had always viewed those born in America as being American citizens, yet some felt this should not apply to

Asians. In 1898, the Supreme Court ruled that all persons born in the United States, regardless of race, were full citizens[53].

The law forbidding citizenship for Japanese immigrants would be tested when a Japanese immigrant named Takao Ozawa applied for US citizenship in Honolulu in 1914. Ozawa had arrived in America in 1894. His application challenged the 1790 naturalization law mandating that only free Whites were eligible for citizenship. After an extended case, the judge ruled against Ozawa, stating that he was "in every way eminently qualified under that statute to become an American citizen" but that he was not eligible because he was not White[54]. Ozawa appealed the decision, which went up to the Supreme Court. On November 13, 1922, the Supreme Court ruled against him, noting that he was "well qualified by character and education" but that the law only allowed citizenship for immigrants who were White[55].

The 1924 Immigration Act would go further, blocking all immigration of Asians into the United States. Yale zoologist and author Madison Grant wrote, "There is immediate danger that the White stocks may be swamped by Asiatic blood" [56]. There were enough who agreed to pass the laws' further limits on Asian immigration.

Filipinos were in a special category, for the United States had taken sovereignty over the Philippines following the Spanish-American War. Filipinos were regarded as "US nationals" but not citizens. Some 150,000 Filipinos migrated to the United States, the majority to Hawaii, where they found work in agriculture. Others worked as migrant farmworkers in California and cannery workers in Alaska. The Filipino Labor Union would lead a strike of six thousand Filipino lettuce pickers in 1934 California, winning wage hikes and union recognition[57].

Filipinos, barred from many neighborhoods, formed their own neighborhoods, with Stockton's "Little Manila" becoming the largest Filipino community outside the Philippines from 1920–70[58]. Prejudice against Filipinos grew in the 1920s and '30s, with frequent violence against them on the West Coast. Monterey Judge D.W. Rohrback described Filipinos as "little brown men about ten years removed from a bolo and breechcloth" [59].

In 1934, the Philippine Independence Act promised the Philippines independence after ten years, but it also changed Filipinos from US nationals to aliens, leading to Filipino immigration being limited to an annual quota of fifty[60].

Ironically, it would take WWII to end the Chinese and Filipino exclusions. With China being an ally, it became too embarrassing to block the entry of Chinese into the country. In addition, up to 15,000 Chinese Americans, nearly 20% of the adult male Chinese population in the US, would serve in its military[61]. In 1943, Congress repealed the Chinese Exclusion Act, setting up a limited quota for Chinese immigration, with a larger loophole for wives from China[62].

Congress made small gestures to other Asian allies. In 1946, a one-hundred-person annual quota for Indians and Filipinos was passed, also giving them the right to become citizens[63].

While WWII resulted in token gains for other Asians, it would prove a disaster for Americans of Japanese descent. The sudden attack on Pearl Harbor on December 7, 1941, by Japan led many Californians and other Westerners to argue that the Japanese immigrants in their midst would be a "fifth column," secretly aiding a Japanese invasion. Many US military leaders agreed. Faced with this intense lobbying, President Franklin Roosevelt signed Executive Order 9066 on February 19, 1942, allowing the Secretary of War to remove "any or all persons" from designated military areas. The military, arguing that they could not tell which Japanese Americans were loyal or disloyal, proceeded to remove 120,000 Japanese Americans from the West Coast. They were placed in internment camps surrounded by barbed wire and guards. No roundup was made of the 150,000 Japanese in Hawaii, where the Pearl Harbor attack occurred. These immigrants subsequently demonstrated that Japanese immigrants were not a threat.

Some of those interned were bitter enough to leave the country after the war. However, others argued that their best weapon was to demonstrate their American patriotism. Michael Masaoka, a member of the Japanese American Citizens League, argued, "There are politicians even now who are trying to pass laws in Congress to strip us of our citizenship and ship us to Japan when the war is over. The most effective weapon against this kind of persecution is a record of having fought valiantly for our country side by side with Americans of other racial extractions" [64].

Masaoka successfully lobbied the government to establish a regiment made up entirely of second-generation Japanese Americans. The resulting 442nd regiment fought in Europe, becoming one of the most decorated units. The 18,000 Japanese Americans who served in the regiment earned more than three thousand Purple Hearts, three hundred Silver Stars, eight hundred Bronze Stars, and one Congressional Medal of Honor[65].

In December 1944, the Supreme Court ruled that "citizens who are concededly loyal" could not be held in the internment camps. The day before, the Roosevelt administration had announced the end of the exclusion orders, allowing Japanese Americans to return home beginning In January 1945[66].

In 1948, the Court struck down the provision in the California Alien Land Law that prohibited Japanese from owning property[67].

In 1952, the otherwise regressive McCarran-Walter Act would end the bar on Japanese immigration and allow them to become citizens. Still, the immigration quotas for Asians would remain tiny.

---

1 John Hoyt Williams. *A Great and Shining Road: The Epic Story of the Transcontinental Railroad*, University of Nebraska Press, Lincoln, 1988, 95.

2 Williams, 95.

3 Erika Lee. *The Making of Asian America*, Simon and Schuster, New York, 2015, 46.

4 Williams, 95-6.

5 Baker, 49.

6 Williams, 96.

7 Baker, 49.

8 Baker, 52.

9 Williams, 98.

10 Mark Twain. *Roughing It*, New York, 1882, 65.

11 Twain, 105.

12 Horace Greeley. *An Overland Journey from New York to San Francisco in the Summer of 1859*, New York, 1860, 289.

13 Williams, 181.

14 Williams, 210.

15 Evans, 147.

16 Richard White. *Railroaded: The Transcontinentals and the Making of Modern America*, W.W. Norton and Company, New York, 2011, 294-5.

17 Daniels, 239, 241.

18 White, 296.

19 White, 299.

20 White, 300.

21 Nasaw, 191.

22 Daniels, 245.

23 White, 299.

24 Lee, 60.

25 Asimov, 64.

26 White, 303.

27 Lee, 93-4.

28 White, 312.

29 White, 298.

30 Greenhouse, 179.

31 Greenhouse, 179.

32 Gorn, 357.

33 Lee, 75.

34 Lee, 75.

35 Asimov, 162.

36 Lee, 68.

37 Lee, 76.

38 Lee, 95.

39 Daniels, 246.

40 Sowell, 156.

41 Sowell, 162-3.

42 Asimov, 162-3.

43 Daniels, 254-255.

44 Gee.

45 Daniels, 252.

46 Daniels, 253.

47 Sowell, 168.

48 Daniels, 253.

49 Lee, 116.

50 Lee, 160.

51 Daniels, 254.

52 Lee, 163.

53 Lee, 85.

54 Jia Lynn Yang. *A Mighty and Irresistible* Tide, W. W. Norton and Company, New York, 2020, 27.

55 Yang, 52.

56 Lee, 134.

57 Lee, 182.

58 Lee, 184.

59 Lee, 185.

60 Lee, 188.

61 Lee, 255.

62 Yang, 53-54.

63 Yang, 87.

64 Yang, 162.

65 Yang, 162-3.

66 Lee, 240-1.

67 Lee, 248.

Immigrants Arriving at Ellis Island

CHAPTER 8

The Other Europeans

The years after 1880 saw the immigration of almost thirty million Europeans into the United States. While the earlier arrivals were predominantly from western and northern Europe, i.e., Britain, Germany, and Scandinavia, the immigrants after 1880 would be mostly from the southern and eastern parts of the continent, namely Italy, Russia, the Austro-Hungarian Empire and Greece[1].

The migration was driven by a large rise in the populations of and a worsening of economic conditions in the areas from whence the migrants came. For example, the Jews of Eastern Europe saw a fivefold growth in their population during the nineteenth century[2].

While the new immigrants were predominantly from parts of Europe that had not had many emigrants leave for the US, it is worth noting that large-scale immigration continued from Britain, Ireland, Germany, and Scandinavia. While in the heaviest decade of immigration, 1900–10, 6.5 million came from Southern and Eastern Europe, there would still be 1.5 million immigrants from the traditional sources listed above[3].

The immigrants increasingly went to the growing cities of the United States, which in 1920 housed three-quarters of the foreign-born compared to a bare majority of the total population[4].

4.2 million Italian immigrants arrived in the United States between 1880 and 1920. Overpopulation and the poverty of

Southern Italy drove most of those immigrants to America. Some 30–50% of the mainly male Italian immigrants would return to Italy, driven largely by family ties[5].

Immigration from Russia would be galvanized by the assassination of Czar Alexander II in 1881. The Russian government responded by blaming Russian Jews for the problems of society. Hundreds of pogroms, the massacres of Jews, took place, injuring or killing thousands. As a result, the Jewish population, whenever they could, tried to flee Russia. Four million Jews left from 1880 to 1924, of which three million came to the United States[6].

The Russian Jewish immigrants tended not to be either the most religiously orthodox or the more affluent and assimilated people. A survey concluded that "the Jewish immigrant community in the United States is by and large a concentration of one social psychological type, which is the enterprising, activistic person with a strong individualistic attitude" [7].

Another source of immigrants was the vast Austro-Hungarian Empire. The growing population and the inequities in land ownership resulted in growing hardship for the poor. One writer reported, "Their standard way of life was one of slow starvation" [8]. About 1.5 million people living in the Empire would immigrate to the United States in the forty years before WWI[9].

Some 600,000 Greeks immigrated to the United States from 1890–1924, again driven by poverty at home. They predominantly settled in the cities[10].

Finally, there would be immigrants from other parts of the Balkans and from Syria, Lebanon, and Armenia.

Almost all immigrants arrived after a voyage in steerage, the lowest priced tickets. Morris Cohen, one such immigrant, described the voyage: "We were huddled together in the steerage literally like cattle—my mother, my sister, and I sleeping in the middle tier, people being above us and below us as well as on the same level" [11].

Another immigrant noted, "Our greatest suffering was due to a scarcity of water. We all provided ourselves with a tin can to hold the water distributed every evening. It was all you could get until the following evening. After a few days out, the quantity that each one received was cut down" [12].

Another immigrant wrote, "Who can depict the feeling of desolation, homesickness, uncertainty and anxiety with which an emigrant makes his voyage across the ocean ... And echoing through it all were the heart-lashing words, 'Are you crazy?'" [13].

Yet, in relative terms, conditions had improved greatly. Earlier, in the middle of the century, some 10% would die on the voyage, mainly from a variety of diseases as well as shipwrecks. In addition, the length of the voyage fell from about forty days in the 1830s–1840s to a little over a week in 1900[14].

In addition, the cost of the voyage decreased. A ticket from Liverpool, one of the four major ports of embarkation, might cost as little as $10, which represented ten days' pay for a laborer in America at the time[15].

Many immigrants were fearful of being turned away for medical or other reasons, although these fears turned out to be overstated. Ninety-eight percent of those who passed through Ellis Island were ultimately admitted. Author David Laskin wrote, "Ellis Island was a form of purgatory—but for most, it was a swift, transient purgatory. For all the dread, the average time of processing was just five hours" [16].

The immigrants were often overwhelmed by their first experience of America. Maurice Hindus, arriving in 1905, wrote of his first experience of New York, saying, "Proudly I walked the streets, but inwardly I felt bewildering[ly] alien, for no two worlds could have been more stupendously unlike than the mud-sodden village from which I had been uprooted and the towering New York into which I was flung" [17].

The new immigrants were far more often urban than their earlier predecessors. At the same time, the overall urban percentage of the population went from one in three Americans in 1900 to a majority of Americans by 1920. New York doubled in size, with over a third of the population being foreign-born, while three-quarters of Chicago's population had been born abroad[18].

The growth meant that some of the slums, particularly in New York City, were the most crowded in the world, outstripping London and the cities of India and China. The Tenth Ward on the Lower East Side was the most crowded, with over 523 inhabitants per acre, compared to an average of sixty for the whole city[19].

The Jews who left Russia were not typical of the population, being younger and more likely to have skills. They were also far more likely to stay in the United States than other immigrants, with less than 1 in 20 returning to Europe (many of whom later came back to the United States). The high percentage of women among Jewish immigrants, some 45%, also correlated with a lower tendency to return to Europe[20]. In all, one-third of the Jewish population in Eastern Europe would immigrate to the United States from 1880–1920[21].

Prior to immigrating, almost half of Russian Jews worked in some aspect of clothes production[22]. Not surprisingly, then, the Jewish immigrants found the most work in the growing garment industry, which employed some 150,000 Jewish immigrants in 1900. Jacob Riis commented in 1890, "The Jewish needle made America the best-dressed nation in the world" [23].

Despite being packed into the slums, particularly on the Lower East Side, the Russian Jewish immigrants had lower death rates than others in similar circumstances, which has been attributed to a traditional emphasis on cleanliness as well as lower rates of alcoholism. By 1897, over one-half of public bathhouses in New York City were Jewish[24].

A few appreciated the strides the new immigrants were making. Muckraking journalist Burton J. Hendrick wrote in

McClure's in 1907 about the Russian Jews, noting that "No people had a more inadequate preparation, educational and economic, for American citizenship ... Their only capital stock is an intellect which has not been stunted by centuries of privation, and an industry that falters at no task, however poorly paid. In spite of all these drawbacks, the Russian Jews have advanced in practically every direction. His economic improvement is paralleled by that of no other immigrating race" [25].

Yet for every Riis or Hendrick who appreciated the new immigrants, there were many more who looked askance. The Jewish immigrants would appall many cultured men of old wealth. The novelist Henry James said he was disgusted by the "swarming" Jews in the Lower East Side, saying they reminded him of "small, strange animals ... snakes or worms" [26]. Historian Henry Adams said," The Jew makes me creep" [27].

The Jewish immigrants overwhelmingly settled in the cities of the Northeast and Midwest, with seven of ten staying in New York City[28]. Over half earned a living doing manual labor[29]. While the Russian Jews felt looked down upon by the earlier Jewish arrivals from Germany, they also benefited from extensive assistance from the earlier immigrants. The newcomers also tended to be less religious than those who had stayed behind. Most importantly, they rushed to embrace American education. Daniels wrote, "Even by the 1920s, Jewish academic success was so pronounced that Harvard, Yale, and other elite institutions were establishing quotas to keep the number of Jewish students below a certain level[30].

The biggest voice for the new Russian immigrants arrived in New York himself in 1882. Abraham Cahan, a member of the revolutionary underground, had fled Russia to avoid arrest. In 1897, he founded *The Forward*, a Jewish socialist newspaper. After several years of working for the regular newspapers, he returned to *The Forward* in 1902, where he would serve as editor for almost fifty years. Cahan built up the circulation from

6,000 in 1902 to 250,000 in the 1920s. While the paper supported labor unions and socialism, it also appealed to non-socialists, teaching the cultural basics of being an American. A popular feature was encouraging readers to write to him for advice. *The Forward* would be the biggest of some one hundred Yiddish newspapers that started from 1885–1900[31]. Cahan also wrote *The Rise of David* Levinsky in 1917, one of the most important novels about immigrants[32].

Increasingly entrenched wealth began to shut out Jews, barring them from joining clubs, staying in certain hotels, or refusing to hire them. Academic institutions began to limit Jewish students to a small quota. The first organized anti-Jewish violence would begin in the 1890s, the same decade that featured lynchings of Italians and, of course, most of all, Blacks.

Prejudice was almost as strong against others from southern and eastern Europe. Historians and other scholars regarded as progressives for the day, such as John R. Commons, Edward A. Ross, and Henry Pratt, despised the new immigrants. Fairchild held that the superiority of American democracy was due to the superiority of Anglo-Saxons, regarding the Southern and Eastern European immigrants as ignorant and inferior. These scholars argued that adding these new people to the old American stock would mean national decline. It should be noted that prejudice against Blacks was even greater[33].

Economics professor William Z. Ripley, who boosted ancestors going back to Plymouth Rock, published *The Races of Europe* in 1899 to glowing reviews. Ripley argued that the new immigrants would fatally injure those Americans of Anglo-Saxon descent, warning that immigration was bringing "a great horde of Slavs, Huns, and Jews and drawing large numbers of Greeks, Armenians, and Syrians. No people is too mean or too slow to seek an asylum on our shores" [34]. Historian Nell Irwin Painter noted that Ripley "delivered racist notions in scholarly tones" [35].

Historian Oscar Handlin, in his Pulitzer Prize-winning book *The Uprooted*, wrote of the two college presidents who argued that "the immigrants were beaten men from beaten races, biologically incapable of rising, either now or through their descendants, above the mentality of a twelve-year-old child" [36].

One of the few scholars to argue against the academic consensus about the superiority of the Anglo-Saxons was a German Jewish immigrant named Franz Boas. Born in Germany in 1858, Boas earned a doctorate at Kiel University in 1881. In two years of fieldwork among the Inuit peoples, Boas came to the heretical conclusion that "We [civilized people] have no right to look down on them" [37].

Moving to the United States, Boas took a faculty position in Anthropology at Columbia University. Boas approached the US Immigration Commission with a proposal to study whether immigrants from Southern and Eastern Europe could adjust to their environment. With this funding, Boas found that rather than the physical differences in the new immigrants being immutable, they changed quickly in the new environment. Boas concluded that "the adaptability of the immigrant seems to be very much greater than we had a right to suppose before our investigations were instituted" [38].

Boas' conclusions, contrary to the scholarly consensus, would be ignored by the Immigration Commission.

Ironically, immigrants, contrary to the prejudice of the day, committed fewer crimes than native-born citizens[39].

Facing such sentiment, it is not surprising that the immigrants tended to support local leaders who seemed interested in their welfare. Immigrant support for city machines such as Tammany Hall would be strong, rewarding the bosses' interests in the immigrants' welfare. Handlin wrote, "The reformers never understood that most of the people they addressed did not want government to be a business. Efficiency too often expressed itself in an inhuman disregard for the individual ...

To the immigrants, the abstract principle was not worth the suffering it entailed" [40].

In pure numbers, the greatest number of these "new" immigrants were Italian. There had been scattered Italian immigration into the United States before 1820, with the federal government only keeping records after 1820. Approximately 17,000 Italians would enter the United States between 1820–1865. Far more would move to South America during this time[41]. In 1850, New Orleans claimed more Italians than any other American city[42].

These early Italian immigrants boasted many artisans and musicians, including Lorenzo da Ponte, who supervised the building of the first American opera house, and Constantino Brumidi, who painted the frescos in the dome of the U.S. Capitol, as well as other frescos throughout the building[43]. There were also scholars such as Philip Mazzei (1730–1816), a physician who settled near Thomas Jefferson and served as an American agent in Europe during the Revolution. Guiseppe Vigo (1747–1836) became one of explorer George Rogers Clark's chief lieutenants[44].

The Italian unification of 1861 would change the flow of immigrants coming from mainly the north of the country to coming from the south. Unification removed prior laws prohibiting emigration in Southern Italy, while the relative prosperity of the North reduced emigration from there. Some 60,000 Italians would immigrate to the United States between 1865–1879. These numbers rapidly accelerated; close to two million would come between 1880–1900, and another two million would immigrate from 1900–1910. Most would enter through New York. One Italian immigrant wrote, "In this country, immigrants of the same town stick together like a swarm of bees from the same hive" [45]. While the majority clustered in the Northeast, a portion would spread out throughout the nation. Describing the tendency of the Italian immigrants to follow where others had gone before, immigrant Robert Severo commented, "Always, I was told, they went because they had a friend, but surely there was somebody at one point who went and had no friend" [46].

Like the Russians and those from Austria-Hungary, most Italian immigrants found work as manual laborers in the growing industries of the time. Disdain for the Italians, at times, went beyond the intellectuals' scorn. The 1890s and the start of the following century saw many lynchings of Italians for alleged crimes.

One of the most sensational cases took place in 1890 when twelve Italian immigrants were arrested in New Orleans in 1890 for the murder of the chief of police. When they were acquitted, an angry mob broke into the jail on March 14, 1891, and lynched the men. The Italian government broke off relations with the United States over the incident, yet most American newspapers declared that the victims were members of the Mafia who deserved what happened to them. The State of Louisiana refused to cooperate in identifying the leaders of the mob, but the federal government eventually gave money to the victims' families[47].

Like other immigrants, some of the Italians found their way to riches. Amedeo Obici created the Planters Peanut Company, while the three Vaccaro brothers, along with Salvatore D'Antoni, began a banana importation business that became the Standard Fruit and Steamship Company. John Riccardi founded the Roman Cleanser Company, which introduced household bleach to the nation[48].

Other Italians established farms near big cities that specialized in fruit and vegetables , leading an observer to comment in 1905, "There is not a single of one of the cities of this country yet reached by the Italians, where there is available market land nearby, that is not now receiving vegetables and fruit and the produce of Italian labor" [49].

The Italians settled mostly in the East and Midwest, with the 400,000 Italian immigrants in New York City in 1920 comprising a quarter of all Italian immigrants. Another large concentration of Italian immigrants settled in California, where they made up the largest foreign-born group in 1920, comprising one-tenth of the population[50].

Some 97% of Italian immigrants came through Ellis Island, with 84% of those arriving in the years 1890–1910 being from Southern Italy. While there was some diffusion of Italian immigrants, as discussed above, by as late as 1970, over half of Italian Americans lived within one hundred miles of Ellis Island[51].

The Italian immigrants tended to get along well with other ethnic groups. For the years of peak immigration, a particular feature was the existence of "padrones," who recruited and supervised work crews, helping the workers and employers in exchange for a fee. Family structure was all-important for most immigrants, leading many Italian women, like the Jewish women, to shun work as domestic servants for the wealthy, which would have taken them away from their own children. Italian immigrants were notable for lower crime rates than other groups and much lower rates of divorce or family separation[52].

The third great source of immigrants during these times originated from the polyglot Austro-Hungarian Empire. Since only the nationality was reported, it is difficult to know how many of each ethnic group immigrated. During the 1910 census, immigrants were asked about their mother tongue. Over 900,000 answered Polish, with Polish immigrants originating from Russia, Austria, and Germany, as no Polish nation existed at that time[53]. Other data suggests a total of 2–2.5 million Polish immigrants, of whom about a third returned to Europe[54].

Poles largely settled in large cities, with the greatest concentration in Chicago. The largely Catholic Poles were also marked by a strong link to the church, with the majority of children going to parochial schools, and a strong sense of Polish nationalism[55]. A 1910 report about Polish immigrants in Buffalo noted, "They have their own churches, their own stores and business places, their own newspapers. They are content to live alone, and the rest of the population generally knows little about them and cares less" [56].

Hungarian immigration in America peaked from the late 1890s to the outbreak of WWI. During this time, 450,000 Hungarians arrived, mainly driven by worsening economic factors at home. They settled mostly in the Midwest, with Cleveland, Ohio, being the epicenter. Most initially found jobs in heavy industry[57].

One notable Hungarian immigrant, Charles L. Fleischmann, arrived in the United States earlier in 1865 at age 30. Dissatisfied with the local bread, Fleischmann and his brother Max formed the first American company to commercially produce yeast. The Fleischmann company became the world's largest producer of yeast.

Slavic immigrants from the Austro-Hungarian Empire, except for the Czechs, tended to settle in cities in the industrial regions of the East and Midwest. Many Czechs settled on Midwest farms in the years after the Civil War, although by 1890, most Czechs headed to cities, especially Chicago[58].

Over half a million Greek immigrants came to the United States, mostly in the 1890s and later. Many of the ethnic Greeks came from Turkish-controlled regions. The Greek emigrants were mainly male and had a relatively high rate of return migration to Europe. They also settled mostly in the East, in the Midwest, and in California. In addition to manual labor, many started small businesses, particularly restaurants. Greeks were also heavily involved in the new movie industry. Spyros Skouras and his brothers, for example, controlled the 20th Century Fox studios[59].

Loukas Kyriakides was born of Greek parents in Turkey in 1884. Following school graduation in 1902, he emigrated from Turkey to the United States, where he shortened his name to Kyrides. He obtained his Ph.D. in chemistry from the University of Michigan in 1909. In his career as an industrial chemist, he would create over one hundred inventions, ranging from a drug for syphilis to the first synthetic rubber tire. He commented, "The laboratory is my life, and happiness comes to me only when my hands are doing things that may someday prove of lasting benefit to mankind" [60].

Two other groups that immigrated in relatively large numbers during the 1880s–1924 were Arabs, particularly from Lebanon, and Armenians. Both groups were heavily Christian, making them minorities in their home countries. The Arab diaspora was most concentrated around Detroit, while the largest center of the Armenian immigrants was in California's Central Valley near Fresno[61].

One of the most famous Lebanese immigrants was Kahlil Gibran. He was born in Lebanon in 1883 and immigrated to the United States in 1895 with his family. His first book in English, *The Madman*, was published in 1911. His most famous work, *The Prophet*, was published in 1923. Translated into over one hundred languages, it has been one of the world's best-selling books. Gibran was called "the single most important influence on Arabic poetry and literature during the first half of [the twentieth] century" [62]. Gibran would die in 1931 at the age of 48 due to liver failure.

One of the common factors among the immigrants discussed in this chapter was their lesser status in their countries of origin. Barone wrote, "When we look at the Ellis Island immigrants, what we see are people who were second-class or second-caste citizens of large multiethnic empires. We see that the vast majority of Italian immigrants were from Southern Italy ... Similarly, we see that the vast majority of immigrants from the tsarist empire of Russia were Poles and Jews, with smaller numbers of Ukrainians and Lithuanians" [63]. Similarly, immigrants from the Austro-Hungarian Empire were mainly Slavs, with relatively few Austrians or Hungarians. Even among the immigrants from Britain, a disproportionate number came from Wales or Scotland during the nineteenth century.

Barone continued, "The empires of pre-World War I Europe were giving the United States their second-class citizens, their subject peoples, their disfavored ethnic groups ... The language barrier in the United States must have seemed not much higher than the language barrier in Italy, Austria-Hungary, or Russia for those not fluent in the governing language or dialect. The possibility of becoming full-status citizens in a democratic republic was an option that did not seem open to them in their native lands" [64].

There was another group of immigrants that would encounter prejudice. These were French Canadians who immigrated to the New England area in large numbers after the Civil War until the end of that century. Several hundred thousand would immigrate to the United States, particularly supplying labor for New England's textile mills. In 1881, Carroll Wright, the Massachusetts Commissioner of Labor Statistics, stated, "The Canadian French are the Chinese of the Eastern States. They care nothing for our institutions, civil, political, or educational ... They are a horde of industrial invaders" [65]. Wright would later temper his remarks, but hostility to the French-Canadian immigrants persisted

Among the working classes, particularly the foreign language presses of the immigrants, many disputed the supposed racial superiority of the earlier American immigrants. Painter wrote that in America, "the so-called beaten men from beaten races were doing most of the work. In the garment, iron, and steel industries, in the mines and mills that kept the amazing American economy running, immigrants supplied the necessary brawn" [66].

It was not simply the parents that worked. In 1911, some two million children under age 16 worked full time, ten hours a day, for a fraction of the pay of adults[67].

Still, the essential contribution of the immigrants to the growth of American industry and the overall economy mattered little to some. The American Protective Association, founded in 1887, focused on anti-Catholicism, and by the early 1890s, it had half a million members[68].

The prejudice against the Russian Jews, Italians, Greeks, Slavs, and other new immigrants would later culminate in new laws effectively prohibiting their entry into the country.

---

1 Milton Meltzer. *Taking Root: Jewish Immigrants in America,* Farrar, Strauss, and Giroux, New York, 1976, 12.

2 Meltzer, *Taking Root,* 19-20.

3 Daniels, 188.

4 Daniels, 185.

5 Meltzer, *Bound for America,* 53-54.

6 Meltzer, *Bound for America,* 47.

7 Meltzer, *Taking Root,* 21.

8 Meltzer, *bound for America,* 48.

9 Meltzer, *Bound for America,* 51.

10 Meltzer, *Bound for America,* 61.

11 Meltzer, *Taking Root,* 36.

12 Meltzer, *Taking Root, 36.*

13 David Laskin. *The Long Way Home: An American Journey from Ellis Island in the Great War,* Harper Perennial, New York, 2010, 34.

14 Handlin, 46, 48.

15 Daniels, 187.

16 Laskin, 38-9.

17 Meltzer, *Taking Root,* 48.

18 Meltzer, *Taking Root,* 2.

19 Meltzer, *Taking Root,* 65.

20 Daniels, 225.

21 Sowell, 69.

22 Sowell, 79.

23 Meltzer, *Taking Root,* 85, 98.

24 Sowell, 85-6.

25 Meltzer, *Taking Root*, 134.

26 Meltzer, *Taking Root*, 242.

27 Meltzer, *Taking Root*, 242.

28 Daniels, 226.

29 Laskin, 51.

30 Daniels, 230.

31 Meltzer, *Taking Root*, 194.

32 Daniels, 230.

33 Meltzer, *Taking Root*, 239-40.

34 Painter, 225.

35 Painter, 225.

36 Handlin, 248.

37 Painter, 230.

38 Painter, 240.

39 Handlin, 145.

40 Handlin, 197-8.

41 Vincenza Scarpaci. *The Journey of the Italians in America*, Pelican Publishing Company, Gretna, LA, 2009, 11.

42 Scarpaci, 67.

43 Daniels, 191.

44 Daniels, 190.

45 Laskin, 51.

46 Scarpaci, 13.

47 Scarpaci, 267.

48 Scarpaci, 80.

49 Scarpaci, 133.

50 Daniels, 195.

51 Barone, 166-8.

52 Sowell, 118-9.

53 Daniels, 213.

54 Daniels, 219.

55 Daniels, 222.

56 Daniels, 233.

57 Daniels, 203-4.

58 Barone, 169.

59 Daniels, 208, 210.

60 Andrea Sella. "Kyrides' Seal," *Chemistry World*, July 30, 2021.

61 Daniels, 258.

62 Barone, 163.

63 Salma Khadra Jayyusi. *Modern Arabic Poetry: An Anthology*, Columbia University Press, New York, 1987, 4.

64 Barone, 164.

65 Laskin, 61-62.

66 Painter, 253.

67 Laskin, 45.

68 Daniels, 273.

John Muir

Emma Goldman

Jacob Riis

CHAPTER 9

Reformers, Muckrakers, and Revolutionaries

The last part of the nineteenth century and the beginning of the twentieth saw many reformers who sought to change America and correct the ills they observed in society. Many of the most influential were new immigrants.

There were almost five million immigrants to the United States from 1880–1900, some 3.7 million of these in the 1890s. Immigration would peak in the first decade of the 1900s, with over one million immigrants coming each year in 1905, 1906, and 1907.

As noted earlier, the immigrants were increasingly from Southern and Eastern Europe. From 1901–5, there would be nearly one million from Italy, another million from Austria-Hungary, and 700,000 from Russia. In comparison, only a half million would come from western and northern Europe[1].

One immigrant of the latter category was instrumental in the creation of National Parks in America to conserve the best of the remaining nature. John Muir was born in 1838 in Scotland. At age 11, John, the family's oldest son, accompanied his father when he moved to Wisconsin to farm. While his father needed his labor on the farm, Muir wanted to go to school and explore the natural world outside the farm. In his spare time, he read widely and invented new gadgets. At age 21, he exhibited and started selling his gadgets, including a clock that woke people by tipping over the bed. Muir attended the University of Wisconsin, focusing on science. He then traveled through Canada and the Midwest, suggesting improvements in factory processes. At one factory, he suffered an accident that threatened his sight.

After he recovered, he began roaming through the United States while writing a journal about the plants, animals, and people he encountered. By the 1860s, he had made his way to California, where he settled in the Yosemite Valley. He worked as a sheepherder and then a carpenter while spending his spare time exploring the Valley. In 1871, he authored an article on how glaciers had dug out the Valley that was published in the *New York Herald Tribune*[2].

Muir would write many more articles about Yosemite and other aspects of nature. Scientists began to accept his theories about glacial changes. Muir got married and then lived on a ranch in central California, crossbreeding fruits while continuing to write scientific articles that made him famous[3].

Muir was roused to action when lumbering and mining companies threatened to exploit Yosemite. Muir organized others into a group called the Sierra Club to lobby to protect Yosemite and other natural wonders. Muir traveled the nation, lobbying for federal protection for Yosemite. Secretary of the Interior Stewart Udall wrote that Muir "was thirty when he first saw the Golden Gate and set eyes on the summits of the Sierra Nevada [range]. It was the spring of 1868, and he knew at once that he had found his homeland. Muir, a city hater, came down from the mountains, time after time, to do battle for his wild lands"[4].

After President McKinley's assassination catapulted Theodore Roosevelt into the presidency, Roosevelt traveled to Yosemite to spend two weeks camping with Muir. Roosevelt, convinced that natural wonders should be saved for future generations, would increase the lands of the national parks and forests almost fivefold during his time in office[5]. Muir's efforts led to the creation of the national parks of Sequoia, Yosemite, Mount Rainier, Crater Lake, and Mesa Verde, plus two national monuments, Grand Canyon and Olympia, which became national parks[6].

During the Roosevelt years, Roosevelt's most important environmental advisor was Gifford Pinchot. Originally allies, Pinchot and Muir would fall out, starting with the issue of sheep grazing in the national forests. Pinchot argued a utilitarian view that the forests were there for the use of man, adding, "We were faced with this simple choice: Shut out the grazing and lose the forest reserves, or let stock in under control and save the Reserves for the Nation" [7]. Muir instead argued that wilderness was important for its own sake and that Pinchot had given up too much under political pressure.

After his wife died, Muir traveled the world to see its mountains and rivers. Muir would receive honorary degrees from the University of Wisconsin, Harvard, and Yale but is probably best memorialized by the trails and woods that bear his name. Muir proclaimed, "People are beginning to find out that going to the mountains is going home, that wilderness is a necessity and that mountain parks and reservations are useful not only as foundations of timber and irrigating rivers but as foundations of life" [8].

While John Muir was associated with the wilderness, another reformer, Jacob Riis, would make his mark in the cities, most notably America's biggest, New York City.

Riis was born on May 3, 1849, in Denmark, the third of 14 children. His father was a teacher, but Riis was an indifferent student. At age 15, he decided to become a carpenter. Tough economic times that left him unemployed and an unsuccessful marriage proposal led him to seek his fortune in the United States. He arrived in New York City in May 1870, expecting to find the city overrun by Indians and buffalo[9]. Riis traveled across the eastern United States, working as everything from a coal miner to farmhand to salesman. He returned to New York City, where he described joining "the great army of tramps, wandering around the streets in daytime with the one aim of somehow stilling the hunger that gnawed at my vitals" [10].

After three years, Riis took a job as a news reporter, specializing in human interest stories. In 1874, he secured a loan with which he bought the *South Brooklyn News*, where he worked as its publisher, editor, advertising agent, and reporter. After five months, he was able to pay off the loan. He then persuaded the woman who had rejected him in Denmark to reconsider. He sold the paper, sailed to Denmark, and returned, bringing his bride to America.

Riis then secured a job as the police reporter for the *New York Tribune*. Yet, as he later wrote, it was in the surrounding tenement district that "I was to find my lifework" [11]. Riis became an American citizen in 1885.

In 1887, he learned of advances in photography that would allow pictures to be taken in areas with little light. He then started taking pictures of the slum district to accompany his writing. He first found little interest from magazines, but eventually, an editor from *Scribner's* saw a presentation Riis was giving at a church. Subsequently, Riis wrote an 18-page article accompanied by 19 of his photographs that appeared in the December 1889 issue of the magazine under the title "How the Other Half Lives." Soon after, Riis was asked to enlarge the article into a book.

How the Other Half Lives was published in November 1890. The book was a critical success, going through five printings, with critics saying it deserved as wide a reading as the famous expose of slavery, *Uncle Tom's Cabin*[12]. Riis found himself in great demand as a lecturer. His second book, *The Children of the Poor*, focused on child labor.

Riis continued to work as a reporter. His story revealing pollution of the city water supply forced the city to safeguard the supply, helping prevent an epidemic. Riis became friends with other reformers and writers, including Jane Adams, Stephen Crane, and Lincoln Steffens. Riis' most important friendship was with Theodore Roosevelt, who sought Riis out after reading *How the Other Half Lives*. When Roosevelt became police commissioner, the two would explore New York City at night, often discovering policemen asleep, absent from their posts, or exhibiting brutality and/or corruption.

As Roosevelt rapidly ascended the political ladder, he often sought Riis' counsel. Riis repeatedly turned down Roosevelt's offer of government jobs. Riis fought to create parks in the slums, to create playgrounds at the schools, and to push for minimum standards in the tenements. He wrote multiple books, mostly dealing with conditions in the slums. He was active in the movements to create the Boy Scouts and Big Brothers organizations. He kept writing and campaigning for reforms despite declining health. Jacob Riis died on May 26, 1914. Historian Peter L. Petersen concluded of Riis, "He did more than any other person to awaken the American people to the problems of the new industrial city ... He contributed greatly to the growing realization that the poor often were more the victims of poverty than its creators" [13].

Samuel S. McClure was called the father of investigative journalism, what was disparagingly called muckraking. McClure was born in Ireland to an impoverished Protestant family in 1857. His father died in a shipyard accident when he was nine. His mother took her four sons to America, where she had relatives in Indiana. McClure's grades in school were impressive enough to win him entry to attend Knox College, starting at age 14. He was full of energy, telling a college friend, "I feel like a chained tiger. I fret against my chains" [14].

He married the daughter of a professor against her father's opposition. They moved to Boston, where McClure edited a bicycling magazine. McClure then took a job at a printing house in New York. McClure achieved financial success by creating a system that syndicated the work of writers to hundreds of newspapers across the county.

By 1893, McClure launched *McClure's Magazine*. Despite starting in a time of economic hardship, the magazine prospered. It was known as a place to read good fiction and biographies featuring writers, including Mark Twain, Willa Cather, Stephen Crane, Emile Zola, and Jack London in early issues. By 1899, its circulation reached 400,000, making it one of the most popular magazines in the nation[15].

The magazine then began to examine some of the deep social issues of society. McClure said the magazine's accomplishments were "the result of merely taking up in the magazine some of the problems that were beginning to interest the people a little bit before the newspapers and other magazines took them up" [16].

McClure's was also unusual in being priced at a low rate, 15 cents an issue, which allowed working-class people to afford it. The January 1903 issue of *McClure's* would mark a watershed in muckraking. Lincoln Steffens revealed vast corruption in "The Shame of Minneapolis," while the issue also featured the third of nineteen segments by Ida Tarbell about the oil monopoly in "The History of Standard Oil." The public's outrage forced the government to act to break up Standard Oil. The editorial in the issue read, "Capitalists, workers, politicians, citizens—all breaking the law or letting it be broken. Who is left to uphold it? There is no one left; none but all of us" [17].

Michael Moore wrote, "McClure moved on to his next mission: finding solutions to improve the government and arguing for them ... McClure did another crazy thing: he publicly started pushing Americans to consider ideas that were working well in Europe" [18].

McClure traveled widely and spoke in support of reforms. At Stanford University in 1912, he stated, "Why are the fire losses in our great cities seven times as great as those of Europe—in structures of absolutely the same material? Why? Because our building inspectors are bribe seekers and takers ... In the countries of despots, young girls may be burned at the stake in the marketplace, but in America, they are burned to death in the factories through insufficient fire protection" [19].

McClure inspired other magazines to follow his lead. An estimated two thousand examples of muckraking, investigative journalism, would be produced in the first two decades of the twentieth century[20].

Immigrants would be prominent among the ranks of the radicals and revolutionaries, those who considered reform too weak a solution for the problems of American society. One of the most prominent radicals was Emma Goldman.

Goldman was born in Lithuania in 1869. After living for a time in Germany, she arrived in America as a teenager. She worked for a time in a clothing factory, working for ten and a half hours a day for a salary of $2.50 a week[21].

Goldman became famous for her espousal of anarchism. Anarchists argued for the abolition of all forms of government. The anarchist movement was also associated with violence, for while the leaders did not always advocate it, their followers too often adopted violence as the best way to achieve the new society.

In 1890, the exiled German anarchist leader Johann Most addressed an audience at a memorial meeting for the Haymarket martyrs. Attending the meeting were 23-year-old Emma Goldman and Alexander Berkman, a fellow Russian Jewish immigrant. They were both won over to the cause of anarchism, while Goldman became lover with both Most and Berkman. Then in 1892, the steelworker strike at Homestead, Pennsylvania, was crushed by Henry Frick, resulting in significant loss of life. Berkman, with Goldman's support, resolved to kill Frick in revenge, saying, "Homestead. I must go to Homestead" [22].

Berkman succeeded in wounding but not killing Frick. After Berkman was arrested and sentenced to 16 years in prison, Most stunned a meeting of anarchists by denouncing Berkman. Goldman then sprang out of the audience, repeatedly striking Most with a horsewhip.

In July 1900, a Polish immigrant named Leon Czolgosz read of the killing of the Italian king. He had heard Goldman lecture. On September 6, 1901, he killed President McKinley, noting that he had heard Emma Goldman argue "that all rulers should be exterminated" [23]. The outcry against anarchism led to an amendment to the Immigration Act in 1903, barring entrance to persons "teaching disbelief in or opposition to all governments" [24]. Alexander Berkman later would write Goldman from prison that individual acts of violence were futile. Goldman took longer to come to that position.

By 1915, Goldman claimed to have renounced violence but still argued for anarchism. Goldman would write, "I believe that Anarchism is the only philosophy of peace, the only theory of the social relationship that values life above all else. I know that some Anarchists have committed acts of violence, but it is the terrible economic inequality and political injustice that prompts such acts, not Anarchism" [25]. She was a popular and forceful speaker, giving frequent lectures to large crowds. In 1915, she gave 321 lectures, appearing, in the words of historian Adam Hochschild, "before audiences everywhere from Carnegie Hall to the Jewish Consumptive Sanitarium in Edgewater, Colorado" [26]. Able to talk about everything from her own experiences in factories to Shaw and Freud, she shocked many with her frank discussion about the erotic lives of women and homosexuality, leading Hochschild to conclude, "Arguably, Goldman enraged the country's establishment more than any other American of her time" [27].

Goldman was not a stranger to jail. She spent a year in prison for "inciting workers to riot" by urging them to demand jobs or bread and seize it if it was not given to them. In 1916, she would be jailed for two weeks for giving out literature on birth control, which was then illegal.

However, the onset of WWI and, specifically, the American entrance into the war would reduce official tolerance for dissenting opinions to almost zero. In June 1917, the Espionage

Act was passed, making a crime of almost any statement opposing the war. Goldman opposed the war and the draft, creating the No-Conscription League, which denounced the draft. Goldman wrote, "I, for one, will speak against the war as long as my voice will last" [28].

The government worried about her influence, with one Federal agent reporting, "She is doing tremendous damage. She is womanly, a remarkable orator, tremendously sincere, and carries conviction" [29]. Goldman and her longtime collaborator and former lover Alexander Berkman would be arrested on the day the Espionage Act went into effect, charged with "conspiracy to interfere with the draft."

Their trial opened two weeks later, with newspapers covering it like a sporting event, *The New York Sun*, for one, offering the headline, "Reds vs. US Game Stands as a Draw" [30]. The prosecutor argued that Goldman could hold "spellbound ... the minds of ignorant, weaker, and emotional people" [31].

Goldman told the jury, "It is my mission in life to ascertain the cause of our social evils and our social difficulties ... It is organized violence on top which creates organized violence at the bottom ... May there not be different kinds of patriotism as there are different kinds of liberty ... We say that if America has entered the war to make the world safe for democracy, she must first make democracy safe in America ... shall free speech and free assemblage, shall criticism and opinion—which even the espionage bill did not include—be destroyed?" [32].

Goldman and Berkman were each sentenced to two years in prison.

Goldman and Berkman were released from prison in September 1919. He had spent seven months in solitary confinement in a tiny punishment cell for protesting the killing of a Black convict shot in the back. Goldman noted, "The large sums of money raised while we were in prison ... had gone for appeals in cases of conscientious objectors, in the political amnesty activities, and in other work. We had nothing left, neither literature, money, or even a home. The war tornado had swept the field clean" [33].

The government was not finished with them, moving to deport them the following month. Even though Goldman, her mother, and her sisters had lived most of their lives in the United States, she had never become a citizen. The driving force behind their deportations was a new, 24-year-old official, J. Edgar Hoover. On December 19, 1919, Goldman, Berkman, and 247 other "undesirable" immigrants were deported on the *Buford*, a rundown troopship.

As the ship prepared to leave, Hoover asked Goldman, "Haven't I given you a square deal, Miss Goldman?" Goldman replied, "Oh, I suppose you've given me as square a deal as you could. We shouldn't expect from any person something beyond his capacity" [34].

The federal government was not done. In what would be called the "Palmer Raids," after Attorney General Palmer, perhaps some thousands of immigrants were jailed to be subsequently deported. Then, the acting Secretary of Labor, Louis S. Post, intervened. A former prosecutor and liberal journalist, Post found that many of the arrests had been made without warrants and that the accused had not been given access to lawyers or informed of their rights. Post blocked the deportation of 80% of the 2,435 arrested.

Post told the press of some of the injustices, highlighting the case of Thomas Truss, a Polish American cleaning worker with no police record, who had been arrested because a Communist party had mailed him a membership card, which he never acted upon. He was arrested without a warrant and was not told the reason for his arrest or given access to a lawyer. Post's defense of free speech and knowledge of immigration law at a Congressional hearing, plus the failure of a threatened "Red Uprising" to occur on May 1, helped deflate the deportation movement. The conservative Republican presidential candidate, Warren Harding, commented, "Too much has been said about bolshevism in America" [35]. Harding, during his term, would gradually free most of the imprisoned radicals.

Goldman spent two years in Russia but then, disillusioned, left for Europe and Canada. She was never allowed to live again in America.

The anti-immigrant movement that had pushed for the deportation of radicals at the end of WWI had been temporarily defeated, but it would return in a few years to enact the most anti-immigrant legislation in American history.

1 Asimov, 163.

2 John Muir. "Yosemite Glaciers," *New York Herald Tribune*, December 5, 1871.

3 Bailey, 140.

4 Steward Udall. *The Quiet Crisis and the Next Generation*, Gibbs Smith, Layton, UT, 1988, 115.

5 Bailey, 141.

6 Gregg Coodley and David Sarasohn. *The Green Years: When Democrats and Republicans United to Repair the Earth*. University Press of Kansas, Lawrence, KS, 2021, 20.

7 Udall, 118.

8 John Muir. *Our National Parks*, (Houghton Mifflin, Boston, 1901), quoted in Benjamin Kline, *First Along the River: A Brief History of the US Environmental Movement*, Acada Books, San Francisco, 1997, 21.

9 Peter L. Petersen. *Jacob A. Riis*, in *American Portraits: History through Biography: Volume II from 1865*, Donald W. Whisenhunt, Editor, Kendall Hunt, Dubuque, IA, 1993, 77.

10 Petersen, 78.

11 Petersen, 79.

12 Petersen, 81.

13 Petersen, 83.

14 Michael Moore. *The Muckraker: Samuel S. McClure*, in *Nine Irish Lives: The Fighters, Thinkers and Artists Who Helped Build America*, ed. Mark Bailey, Algonquin Books, Chapel Hill, 2018, 103.

15 Moore, 106.

16 Moore, 107.

17 Moore, 110.

18 Emma Goldman. *Red Emma Speaks*, Third edition, ed. Alix Kates Shulman, Humanity Books, Lanham, MD, 1995, 59.

19 Moore, 112.

20 Moore, 114.

21 Moore, 119.

22 Barbara Tuchman. *The Proud Tower*, The MacMillan Company, New York, 1962, 94.

23 Tuchman, 95.

24 Tuchman, 123.

25 Goldman, 363-4, 369-70.

26 Tuchman, 125-6.

27 Adam Hochschild. *American Midnight: The Great War, A Violent Peace and Democracy's Forgotten Crisis*, Mariner Books, New York, 2022, 75.

28 Hochschild, 75-76.

29 Hochschild, 76.

30 Hochschild, 76-77.

31 Hochschild, 78.

32 Hochschild, 79.

33 Hochschild, 277.

34 Hochschild, 293.

Gerty and Carl Cori, Nobel Prize-Winning Immigrants

CHAPTER 10

The Scientists: The Civil War Through WWII

America was not considered the center of science in the nineteenth century; this honor was reserved for several nations in Europe. It would be the contributions of multiple immigrant scientists who would begin to change this estimation.

Leo Baekeland was born in Belgium in 1863, growing up in Ghent as the son of a shoemaker. The boy started to learn his father's trade until he won a scholarship from the City of Ghent. He went to the government high school, the Royal Athenaeum, and then spent the evenings at a vocational high school. He particularly became interested in photography and chemicals. Baekeland was outstanding at school. By age 21, he won a summa cum laude doctorate from Ghent University, and by 24, he was an associate professor of physics and chemistry at Bruges University[1].

Baekeland married Celine Swarts, daughter of his boss, Professor Theodore Swarts, and moved to Ghent University. Awarded a traveling scholarship, he sailed for America. Arriving in New York City, he decided to give up his professorship to stay in America to work for a company focused on photography. Just previously, George Eastman brought out the first easy-to-use Kodak camera in 1889.

Baekeland, facing financial difficulties, became ill. He recalled, "While I was hovering twixt life and death, with all my cash gone and the uncomfortable sentiment of rapidly growing debts ... it dawned on me that instead of keeping too many irons in the fire, I should concentrate my attention upon the one thing which would give me the best chance of the quickest possible result" [2].

After recovering, he focused on photography, inventing a superior photographic paper, which he sold under the name Nepera Chemical. Soon afterward, Eastman bought Nepera for $750,000, the equivalent of $25 million in the twenty-first century. Baekeland's share made him rich. Baekeland took up a life of apparently wealthy leisure. In fact, he spent most of his time working in the lab in his home[3].

At this time, one of the biggest scientific quests was to find a substitute for shellac. Shellac, produced by the female *Laccifer lacca* beetle, was essential as an insulator of electricity. However, 15,000 beetles were needed to make a pound of shellac, making it too expensive for widespread use. Baekeland took up the quest for an alternative in 1902. By 1907, Baekeland tried a new approach. Instead of creating a mixture and then applying it, he would "attempt to carry out the reaction so as to produce the substance right on the spot where I wanted it" [4].

After a series of experiments, Baekeland created a compound he named Bakelite. As historian Harold Evans wrote, "Bakelite would not catch fire, melt, or break, it would not conduct electricity, and it was quick and cheap to make. It was the first thermoset plastic ... it was the harbinger of the Synthetic Century" [5].

Baekeland began marketing Bakelite for a variety of uses. It served as an essential insulator for a growing number of electrical devices, including toasters, washing machines, and vacuum cleaners, and as the insulator for the third rail on subways and in elevator shafts. Bakelite was used for a number of crucial processes in automobiles, from steering wheels and radiator caps to magneto couplings and timing gears. It would be used in cigarette holders, radios, and telephones[6].

Baekeland set up the Bakelite Corporation. He sold 700,000 pounds of Bakelite in 1913. By 1922, sales were up to 8.8 million pounds. He fought off many patent challenges, then often offered partnerships to those inventors with ideas he thought worthwhile. When his patents began to expire in 1926, a number of large companies began offering new plastics. Baekeland, at the age of 75, sold his company in 1939 for stock valued at $16.5 million. He died in 1944, having won the designation as the "father of plastics"[7].

Michael Pupin made a number of crucial discoveries that made many devices usable. Pupin was born to Serbian parents in Hungary in 1863. He left his school in Prague before he could be conscripted into the army and immigrated to the United States in 1874. He sold his watch, books, and all his clothes to buy passage, arriving with five cents to his name. When the American immigration officials asked if he had any friends in the country, he replied, "Yes—Abraham Lincoln and Benjamin Franklin," to which the official replied, "You have chosen your friends wisely"[8].

Pupin worked for a farmer, as a photographer, and in a cracker factory, all the while improving his English. He decided to go back to school in science and started taking classes at night. At age 20, he received a scholarship to Columbia University. Pupin graduated in 1883, then studied at Cambridge University in Britain and the University of Berlin, from which he received a Ph.D. in 1889. He returned home to Columbia University, where he secured a series of positions, becoming a professor of electronics in 1902[9].

Pupin would undertake a series of investigations in physics that led to practical improvements. He commented, "There is no worthwhile purely scientific problem, the correct solution of which will not someday have a practical value"[10].

Pupin developed selective tuning to separate electrical operations, allowing for the reception of messages of different lengths when Marconi invented the wireless two years later. He also invented a device to eliminate static interference with wireless. Pupin invented "Pupin's Coil," a device that greatly eliminated interference and static on long-distance phone calls. After Roentgen created X-rays, Pupin developed a process that shortened the time needed to do an X-ray from hours to minutes, increasing its practical value[11].

Pupin won renown for his work and fame as a teacher. His 1922 autobiography, *From Immigrant to Inventor,* won a Pulitzer Prize. Pupin wrote, "The main object of my narrative was, and still is, to describe the rise of idealism in American science ... occasionally an immigrant can see things which escape the attention of the native[-born]" [12].

Pupin died on March 12, 1935, at the age of seventy-seven.

When Hideyo Noguchi was born to a poor peasant girl in Japan in 1876, the idea that he would become a renowned American scientist would have been preposterous. Soon after his birth, his father abandoned the family. At age three, Noguchi was badly burned. He survived but with the loss of all the fingers of his left hand. Realizing that he could not be a good farmer, given his disability, he threw himself into his studies, finishing at the top of his class in secondary school. When a doctor in a nearby city was able to partially repair his left hand, he decided to become a doctor. He was apprenticed to and stayed with the doctor. Noguchi graduated from the Tokyo Medical School in 1897[13].

Noguchi wanted to go into research. He joined the staff at the Government Institute of Infectious Diseases. He wrote books and traveled to China to manage an outbreak of plague. He met visiting American scientists, including Dr. Simon Flexner of the University of Pennsylvania. The next year, Noguchi traveled to America uninvited. Flexner found him a job with Dr. Silas Mitchell, an expert on snake venom. Noguchi wrote back to friends, "I have entered the sweet realm of science" [14].

Noguchi received recognition for his venom research.

After a year's fellowship in Denmark, he returned to a position at the new Rockefeller Institute for Medical Research. There, he would compile an enviable record of achievement. In October 1910, he became the first person to grow in culture the spirochete that caused syphilis. He then grew the spirochetes responsible for other diseases, such as European and African relapsing fevers. Noguchi discovered the syphilis organism in the brains of patients who had what was called "the general paralysis of the insane," proving that syphilis was the cause.

Noguchi married an American in 1912, but the immigration law of the time prevented him from becoming a citizen. He mastered multiple languages and learned to paint and fish. He continued his research, discovering a serum for Rocky Mountain spotted fever and other viral infections. Starting in 1918, Noguchi began to research yellow fever. In 1928, he was researching yellow fever in South Africa when he caught the disease and, like several researchers before him, died from it[15].

Nikolai Tesla was born July 9, 1856, to Serbian parents living under Austro-Hungarian rule. He began tinkering in childhood. His older brother was killed at age 12, which may have contributed to his later phobias. He later wrote about how he invented things, noting, "My method is different. I do not rush into actual work. When I get an idea, I start at once building it up in my imagination"[16].

He excelled in school but suffered from recurrent bouts of malaria and almost died of cholera. He enrolled in the Austrian Polytechnic in 1875 in Gratz, Austria, but had to drop out after one year due to lack of money. In 1881, Tesla devised the first usable alternating current (AC) motor, building the first actual motor in 1883. Biographer Margaret Cheney wrote, "Practically all electricity in the world in time would be generated, transmitted, distributed, and turned into mechanical power by means of the Tesla Polyphase System"[17].

Tesla moved to Paris in 1882, where he got a job with the

Continental Edison Company. He was disappointed when they were not interested in his motor. The manager gave him a letter of introduction to Thomas Edison. Tesla immigrated to the United States in 1884. Edison recognized his talent but was not interested in his alternating current, having been committed to direct current (DC). Edison promised him a $50,000 bonus to redesign his company's dynamos but reneged once the job was done, leading Tesla to resign.

The two men of genius were not compatible; Edison rejected the idea of alternating current, saying, "Spare me that nonsense. It's dangerous. We're set up for direct current in America. People like it, and it's all I'll ever fool with" [18].

Tesla formed his own company with the aid of investors interested in alternating current. After opening in 1887, he would file forty new patents in four years. Tesla would find his best supporter in George Westinghouse, the inventor of the railroad air brake. However, when Westinghouse faced financial difficulties, he could only raise the needed money if Tesla gave away the patents. Tesla did so, assuring that alternating current would be developed but leaving Tesla financially insecure thereafter[19].

Tesla would greatly advance scientific understanding in multiple areas, developing ideas about cosmic rays and laying the foundation for the electron microscope. He demonstrated the principles of radio before Marconi. However, he frequently was unable to connect his inventions to commercial success. Cheney wrote, "Potentially valuable inventions were often put aside without the final time-consuming perfection required for commercial success ... Once he understood exactly how an invention worked [in his mind], he tended to lose interest, for there were always exciting new challenges just over the horizon" [20].

Nevertheless, Tesla advanced the cause of alternating current despite Edison's attacks, demonstrating its use at the 1893 Chicago World Fair to the 25 million people, one-third of the country's population, who visited the Fair, and then built an AC power station at Niagara Falls in 1895. Cheney wrote, "The New Year 1898 found Edison and Tesla in a neck-and-neck race to see who could boggle the minds of lesser mortals with more outrageous claims" [21]. Tesla's claim was for solar energy as a source of power, an idea that would be increasingly widespread 120 years later.

Tesla continued to develop new ideas, even as he continued to struggle financially. He never married or apparently had any intimate relationships but inspired many with his ideas. He developed the principles that lay behind radar and vertical takeoff planes, two inventions that would come to later fruition. Cheney noted, "Tesla was more an originator of broad concepts than of discrete innovations. His lectures radiated ideas that many others took in hand, applied practically, and subsequently patented" [22]. Nikolai Tesla died on January 7, 1943, at age 88, in New York City.

Ottmar Mergenthaler is another immigrant whose inventions would revolutionize the world. Mergenthaler was born in Germany in 1854. At age 14, he refused to follow in his father's footsteps as a teacher, instead taking a four-year apprenticeship to the local clockmaker. When he finished in 1872, economic problems in Germany led him to decide to emigrate. He borrowed money from the son of his late employer for the voyage in exchange for working in the latter's electric instrument shop in Washington, DC. Following his arrival in the United States in 1872, Mergenthaler went to work in the shop and, in two years, became a foreman[23].

At the time, the process of printing was slow and laborious, requiring the setting of type by hand. By 1884, Mergenthaler devised a machine that used type bars to create a matrix, after which liquid metal would be applied to create a finished printed page. This was the ancestor of the typewriter as well as large-scale printing that could be done in a fraction of the time of existing methods. Mergenthaler devised an improved machine by 1885 and a further improved copy by 1886. It was named a linotype[24].

Soon, many newspapers were using the linotype to print more quickly and for less money. Mergenthaler continued to make improvements. The linotype became used for printing most books, newspapers, and magazines, allowing more work to be published, again at less cost.

Mergenthaler would contract tuberculosis in 1894 and died from it five years later at age 45[25].

One immigrant whose fame has endured is Alexander Graham Bell, the inventor of the telephone. Bell was born on March 1, 1847, in Scotland. He came from an unusual family in which his grandfather, father, uncle, and two brothers had all studied sound and speech. At age 21, Bell began teaching elocution in London. Tragedy struck when Bell's two brothers died from tuberculosis and he himself was infected. He left with his parents for Canada, where his disease became quiescent. He taught a group of Mohawk Indians a sign language invented by his father. The Board of Education of Boston then offered him $500 to introduce the system in a school for deaf mutes. His success won him a professorship at Boston University[26].

Bell would give this up to pursue his experiments in trying to create a machine that would convey the sound of the human voice. He was financially supported by the fathers of two deaf-and-mute boys he had taught. He would marry the daughter of one of them a few years later[27].

Bell produced the idea of a telephone composed of two discs that would function like ear drums, connected by an electrified wire to catch the vibrations of sound at one end and reproduce them at the other end. In June 1875, Bell first heard a faint sound from the device. He would work on improving the device. On March 10, 1876, Bell spoke to his assistant, Thomas Watson, three floors below, via the device. Watson clearly heard the words, "Watson, come here, I want you" [28].

Bell secured a patent as the inventor of the telephone.

Most people still regarded it as a toy. Bell, confident in his invention, said in a speech in 1878, "It is conceivable that cables of telephone wire could be laid ... connecting up by branch wires private dwellings, country homes, shops, manufacturing establishments, etc., and also connecting cities and towns ... I am aware that such ideas may appear to you utopian and out of place, but I believe that such scheme will be the ultimate result of the introduction of the telephone to the public" [29].

October 9, 1876, saw the first conversation between two places over the two-mile distance from Boston to Cambridge. By 1880, there was speech over forty miles, then from New York to Philadelphia by 1885, and from New York to Chicago by 1893. Along the way, Western Union claimed to have invented the telephone and began to lay phone lines. Bell engaged in an 11-year struggle, but at last, Western Union admitted that Bell was the inventor and that his patents were valid[30].

Bell and his investors sold their interests in the telephone for large sums, becoming very wealthy. Bell continued his research, creating other inventions, including a telephone probe to look for the location of bullets in wounded soldiers. He also founded and gave large sums to the American Association to Promote the Teaching of Speech to the Deaf.

The function of the telephone would be improved by Thomas Edison and Charles Batchelor, who invented a carbon button transmitter that allowed telephone users to use it without having to shout. Bell would, in turn, improve Edison's phonograph by developing a version that played wax cylinder records[31].

Bell's improvement would be developed further by Emile Berliner, a German-Jewish immigrant working at Volta Labs, a research institute created by Bell. Berliner came up with the idea of recording on a flat disc in 1887. Berliner's invention would allow the mass production of recordings[32].

The use of the telephone spread quickly. By 1888, there were a million calls each day. By 1921, there would be 12 billion calls in that year. By 1951, there would be some 75 million phones in use in the world, with calls in the United States alone of over 200 million a day[33].

In 1880, Bell won the Volta Prize, which honored scientific inventions. Bell used the prize money to establish the Volta Bureau to promote the teaching of speech to the deaf and Volta Labs to promote new scientific developments and inventions. Volta Labs would lead to Bell Labs, founded in 1925, which would develop a host of groundbreaking inventions in the next hundred years[34].

Alexander Graham Bell died in 1922, but his invention of the telephone continues to revolutionize the world.

Ironically, there is strong evidence that the telephone was invented earlier by another immigrant, Antonio Meucci. Meucci was born in Florence, Italy, in 1808. He first moved to Cuba. While developing a system for treating illnesses with electric shocks, he was able to hear a friend's voice in the next room via the copper wire running between them. In 1830, Meucci moved to New York. In 1836, when his wife became ill, Meucci created a device that allowed him to speak to her in the bedroom from his workshop. He called this the "telettrofono" [35].

Meucci was unable to find the money to promote his invention. He went bankrupt and then was seriously injured when the ferry he was riding on exploded. His wife had to sell his *telettrofono* models and designs to a pawnshop for $6 to pay for his medical expenses.

Meucci rebuilt and improved the *telettrofono*. However, lacking the $250 to file a patent, he could only pay $10 to file a notice of an impending patent in 1870, renewing it for the next three years. Meucci failed to renew the impending patent notice in 1874. In 1876, Bell filed his patent for the telephone. Meucci tried to sue to get credit for the discovery. After 13 years, while the case was still pending, Meucci died penniless in 1889[36].

Charles Steinmetz was born in Germany in 1865 and was broadly educated, including in engineering. He was forced to flee after arousing the ire of the government for his socialist leanings. After arriving in the United States in 1889, he took engineering jobs, becoming the Consulting Engineer for the new General Electric Company. He also became a professor of electrical engineering. Steinmetz invented safe methods for high-voltage transmission, allowing electric transmission from large power plants. His invention of several motors helped make possible improved cars and street lighting, as well as quicker elevators. Small in size at only four feet tall, he was lauded as "the little cripple with a giant mind" [37]. Steinmetz died in 1923 at age 58.

Igor Sikorsky was yet another immigrant whose work was of cardinal importance, in his case, in the development of modern aviation. Sikorsky was born in Russia in 1889. Early on, he began to tinker with mechanical objects, developing objects such as a stream-driven motorcycle. He graduated from St. Petersburg Naval College in 1906. Refusing a naval commission, he returned to Kyiv to enter the Polytechnic Institute, intending to become an engineer. Bored with the academic focus, as opposed to the practical, he left the Institute for Paris, which was then the center for aeronautical experimentation.

On his return home, Sikorsky made two unsuccessful attempts to build a helicopter before turning to conventional aircraft. On June 3, 1910, his plane, the S-2, flew for the first time. When it crashed later in the month, Sikorsky was almost killed, but he persevered in his attempts to develop better planes. By 1911, his S-5 remained aloft for a half hour at one thousand feet. Sikorsky then set a world record for flying at 75 mph while carrying three passengers[38].

Sikorsky pioneered the development of planes with more than one engine, allowing for greater speeds and for greater safety should one engine fail. In 1913, his plane set another world record, staying aloft for one hour and fifty-four minutes with eight passengers. In World War I, Sikorsky built multi-engine bombers for Russia, becoming wealthy from the sales. The onset of the Russian Revolution led Sikorsky to flee the country, arriving in the United States in 1919. Unable to find work in the aircraft industry, Sikorsky taught Russian immigrants at the settlement house where he also met his wife.

In 1923, Sikorsky began working on his first American plane. On a farm on Long Island, Sikorsky built a multi-engine plane capable of carrying 14 passengers. The success of the plane allowed Sikorsky to win more investment in his Sikorsky Manufacturing Company. He built the first tri-motor plane in America and then the first amphibian, the S-38. Pan American Airlines used thirty S-38s to pioneer air travel to South America. In 1929, Sikorsky sold his company to United Airlines, allowing him to pursue a variety of hobbies[39].

Sikorsky continued to design new aircraft. In 1934, he built the S-42, an amphibian able to carry 32 passengers, breaking more world records for speed, altitude, and payload. Sikorsky then designed and built the world's first helicopter by September 14, 1939. After further modifications, helicopters began to be used in WWII for reconnaissance and aerial rescue. By the Korean War, helicopters would rescue over one thousand crashed pilots and evacuate over 20,000 casualties[40].

Sikorsky retired in 1957 but remained active as a consultant. Sikorsky died in 1972.

Gerty Radnitz Cori was born in Czechoslovakia in 1896. She met her husband, Carl, in an anatomy class in medical school. They would work together as colleagues even before their marriage in 1920. In 1922, they moved to the United States, obtaining positions at the Roswell Park Cancer Institute in Buffalo. The Coris became American citizens in 1928. In 1931, Carl was offered multiple university positions, but the same institutions had no place for Gerty. They took positions at Washington University in St. Louis, which was willing to hire them both, although Gerty was given a lower position and lower pay.

During their nine years in Buffalo, the couple published some fifty papers on the mechanism of metabolism in the body. They continued their research, showing how glycogen is broken down and resynthesized in the body to serve as a store of energy. In 1947, Carl and Gerty Cori shared the Nobel Prize "for their discovery of the course of the catalytic conversion of glycogen," which was named the Cori Cycle[41].

In 1947, Gerty Cori was also diagnosed with a fatal disorder of the bone marrow. She would die from this disorder in 1957.

---

1 Evans, 172.

2 Evans, 174.

3 Evans, 174-5.

4 Evans, 176.

5 Evans, 177.

6 Evans, 177-178.

7 Evans, 179.

8 Beard, 106.

9 Beard. 107-8.

10 Beard, 108.

11 Beard, 108-9.

12 Beard, 110.

13 Beard, 125.

14 Beard, 127.

15 Beard, 131.

16 Margaret Cheney. *Tesla: Man out of Time*, Touchstone, New York, 1981, 32.

17 Cheney, 45-6.

18 Cheney, 53.

19 Cheney, 74.

20 Cheney, 33.

21 Cheney, 155.

22 Cheney, 233.

23 Beard, 98-100.

24 Beard, 101-102.

25 Beard, 104.

26 Beard, 49.

27 Beard, 50.

28 Beard, 51.

29 Beard, 51.

30 Beard, 53.

31 Baker, 76.

32 Baker, 219-220.

33 Beard, 55.

34 Baker, 76-77.

35 Ella Schwartz. *Stolen Science*, Bloomsbury Children's Books, New York, 2021, 26.

36 Schwartz, 28-9.

37 Beard, 117.

38 Beard, 223.

39 Beard, 229-230.

40 Beard, 233.

41 Rachel Swaby. *Headstrong: 52 Women Who Changed Science—and the World*, Broadway Books, New York, 2015, 18.

AMERICA OF THE MELTING POT COMES TO END

Effects of New Immigration Legislation Described by Senate Sponsor of Bill—Chief Aim, He States, Is to Preserve Racial Type as It Exists Here Today

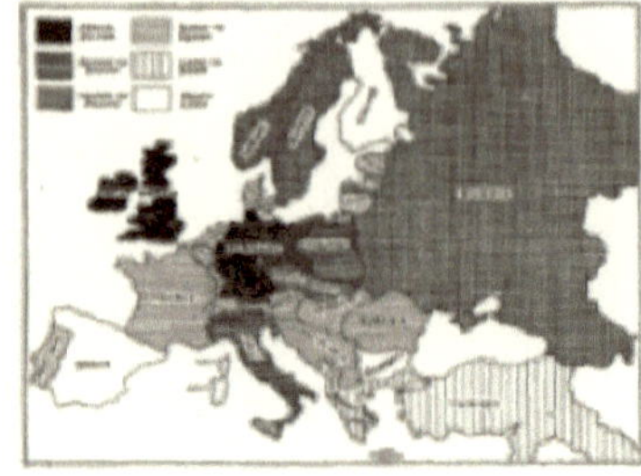

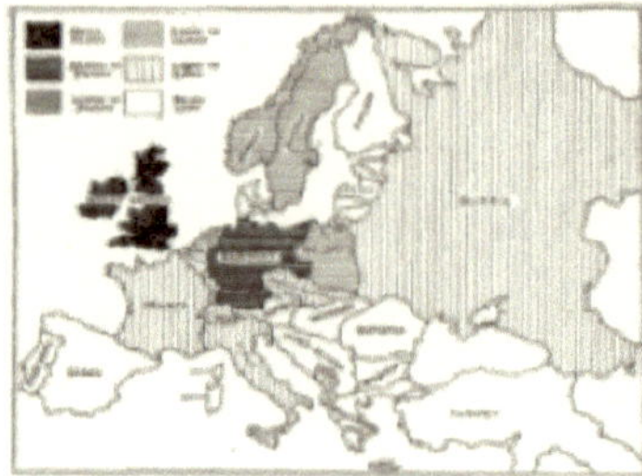

Cartoon Depicting Italian Immigrants as Rats

CHAPTER 11

The Evil That Men Do: The 1924 Immigration Act

Throughout American history, from the Federalists to Donald Trump, there have been those who sought to limit immigration into America. The common theme has been to limit those who were different, most notably by not being White Protestants of British descent.

Their efforts would be largely unsuccessful for years except with regard to Asian immigrants. Despite the ongoing clamor against these new immigrants, from Irish to Jews and Italians, etc., the country was felt to be big enough and the need for labor so great that attempts to limit immigration were unsuccessful. As described earlier, the bias against Asian immigrants would be powerful enough to result in laws limiting early Chinese and Japanese immigration.

Yet the haters and those who feared immigrants for all sorts of reasons would finally succeed in slamming shut the doors to most new immigrants in 1924. There would be a confluence of factors that led to this.

The preceding period would be a high point of the eugenics movement that sought to limit the number of those deemed inferior. Well-credentialed men would lend intellectual credence to hateful theories. Madison Grant, a Yale-educated zoologist, claimed, in a book titled *The Passing of the Great Race*, that Southern Europeans were lesser humans than those from the North, providing inspiration to those opposed to new immigrants in the United States and later to Hitler. Grant wrote, "The altruistic ideas which controlled our social development ... and the maudlin sentimentalism that has made America 'an asylum for the oppressed' are sweeping the nation towards a racial abyss" [1].

Iowa livestock breeder Dr. Harry Laughlin argued that cross-breeding between Americans of different backgrounds would weaken the nation. Testifying to Congress in 1920, Laughlin stated, "The character of a nation is determined primarily by its racial qualities" [2]. Eugenicist Charles Davenport argued that if the average American was "darker in pigmentation," they would become "smaller in stature, more mercurial, more attached to music and art, and more given to crimes of larceny, kidnapping, assault, murder, rape, and sex—immorality" [3].

The eugenicists would eventually lend "scientific credence" to those campaigning against the immigration of those seen as inferior. The Immigration Restriction League was formed on May 31, 1894. The League's long-time leader, Prescott Farnsworth Hall, wrote of the League's goals in a letter to the *Boston Herald* in June 1894, stating, "Should we permit these inferior races to dilute the thrifty, capable Yankee blood ... of the earlier immigrants?" [4].

With rare exceptions, both the eugenics movement and the anti-immigration movement would be dominated by upper-class Protestants whose families had immigrated to the United States generations previously.

Republican Senator Henry Cabot Lodge had tried to limit immigration since the 1890s. No one would rank higher on the Boston class scale than Lodge, to which the saying, "The Cabots only talk to the Lodges, and the Lodges only talk to God," was well deserved. A prominent member of the Immigration Restriction League, Lodge argued for a literacy test for immigrants, telling the Senate, "The races most affected by the illiteracy test are those ... with which the English-speaking peoples have never hitherto assimilated, (and) are alien to the great body of the people of the United States" [5].

Lodge persuaded Congress to pass laws requiring literacy tests for immigrants in 1896, 1913, and 1915, but each was vetoed by the president at the time. In 1897, President Grove Cleveland, in vetoing one such bill, praised the new immigrants as "a hardy, laboring class, accustomed and able to earn a living" [6]. President Taft would veto a similar measure in 1913.

President Woodrow Wilson, who was prejudiced against Blacks and viewed immigrants from Southern and Eastern Europe with suspicion, nonetheless vetoed the bill, saying, "The bill embodies a radical departure from the traditional and long-established policy of this country ... it seeks to close entirely the gates of asylum which have always been open to those who could find nowhere else" [7]. Finally, the bill would be passed over Wilson's veto in 1917, but it failed to decrease immigration significantly, with the new immigrants proving more educated than opponents had suspected. In the year following, some 800,000 immigrants entered the country, while only 1,450 were barred by failing the literacy test [8].

As the number of immigrants from southern and eastern Europe grew starting at the end of the nineteenth century, so did antagonism. The increased anti-Semitism that accompanied the increased immigration of Russian Jews would be matched by increased hostility to Italians, who made up the largest group among the newer immigrants. Stanford University President David Starr Jordan said, "There is not one in a thousand from Naples or Sicily that is not a burden on America" [9]. In 1906, a *Washington Post* column claimed that 90% of the Italian immigrants were "the degenerated spawn of the Asiatic hordes [that], long centuries ago, overran the shores of the Mediterranean" [10].

Leading the fight against immigration restrictions was the National Liberal Immigration League, which drew support from wealthy German Jews and other immigrant groups, as well as figures as diverse as Congressman James Michael Curley, descendent of Irish immigrants, Andrew Carnegie, and Harvard President Charles W. Eliot. The League and their allies had earlier helped defeat earlier attempts to pass a literacy test for immigrants.

The first two decades of the twentieth century saw repeated efforts by well-educated upper-class men to use questionable research to halt the immigration of Southern and Eastern Europeans. Madison Grant managed to combine his twin antipathies to Jews and Catholics in a letter where he warned against the threat posed by "the Catholic Church under Jewish leadership"[11]. Professor Edward Ross, president of the American Sociological Society, wrote, "That the Mediterranean people are morally below the races of Northern Europe is as certain as any social fact" [12].

The Protestant elite campaign to limit immigration of "inferior race" would be joined by a popular groundswell of bigotry. The post-WWI period saw the revival of the Klu Klux Klan, whose creed burned with hatred of Catholics, Jews, and Blacks. The original Klu Klux Klan was set up after the Civil War to suppress Blacks. It would be largely broken by President Ulysses S. Grant.

The post-Civil War period would be marked by attempts to reverse the results of the war, at least in terms of Black freedom. In the South, Jim Crow laws segregated the races, while other laws prevented Blacks from voting. While 50% of Blacks in the South voted in 1880, that figure was below 1% by 1920[13]. Revisionist literature, most notably the film *Birth of the Nation*, cast Blacks as lazy or evil, while the Klu Klux Klan became heroes.

Inspired in part by *Birth of a Nation*, the Klan would be revived in 1915. The new Klan would preach hatred of Catholics and Jews while retaining their ill will against Black Americans. The new Klan took off, most notably in certain Northern states whose populations were almost entirely White Protestants.

In 1920, Klan membership soared from 3,000 to 100,000; by 1922, the numbers grew by over one million[14].

The Klan soon began to elect governors, senators, congressmen, and other leaders. Its influence grew great enough to have an anti-Klan resolution voted down at the 1924 Democratic convention. The Klan had become equal opportunity haters, as one Klan pamphlet declared, "The Jews control the moving pictures, jewelry, and clothing industries and own us financially. The Greeks control the restaurant and confectionary business, the Italians the fruit and produce business," while another read, "The Irish Catholics control us politically and are trying to control us religiously. The public press is controlled by Irish Catholics and Jews" [15].

After WWI, immigration from devastated Europe increased again. In 1921, Congress passed a one-year emergency measure limiting immigration to 355,000 a year. Introduced by William Dillingham, who had headed the United States Immigration Commission of 1909–11, the bill set a national quota for immigrants of 3% of their number in the 1910 census while limiting total immigration to 355,000 (compared to an average of over one million in the five years before WW1). The law would cut immigration dramatically—from Poland by 70% and from Italy by 82%[16]. Immigration would be made even more difficult in that there would be quotas set for each month, leading ships containing immigrants to rush to arrive in the first days of each month[17].

Congress would extend the measure two more times. However, by 1924, the forces opposing new immigrants were ready to push stronger restrictions. They would be led by Congressman Albert Johnson (R-WA), who had become the chair of the House Immigration Committee. Johnson had written earlier, "The greatest menace to the republic today is the open door it affords to the ignorant hordes from Eastern and Southern Europe" [18].

There were many others who wanted to restrict immigration, particularly of Jews, Italians, and others deemed inferior.

Secretary of Labor James Davis, himself a Welsh immigrant, had commented, "The people that came to this country in the early days were of the beaver type, and they built up America because it was in their nature to build. Then the rat people began coming here" [19]. *The Saturday Evening Post* commented, "If America doesn't keep out the queer, alien, mongrelized people of Southeastern Europe, her crop of citizens will eventually be dwarfed and mongrelized as well" [20].

The Saturday Evening Post, under its longtime editor George H. Lorimer, was one of the nation's most popular periodicals by the 1920s. Historian Painter wrote that it became "an excellent platform for a well-illustrated, coldhearted, nativist campaign against immigrants from Eastern and Southern Europe" [21]. The *Post* writer Kenneth Roberts combined virulent anti-Semitism with hysteria over immigrants, whom he called "a matter of life or death for the American people" [22]. Roberts described the Jews as "unassimilable human parasites [and] a poisoned emigration from Europe" [23].

Forgotten in these smears was the fact that immigrants made up 18–20% of the American soldiers in WWI. A huge number of these were Italians, Jews, and Slavs. While only 3.27% of the American population in 1917, Jews made up 5.73% of the Army, while 72% served in combat units[24]. A historian wrote, "Even though glory consisted of getting maimed or killed (and having your name misspelled in the newspapers), more than 300,000 Polish immigrants and Americans of Polish descent served before the conflict terminated" [25]. The smears ignored the Italian immigrant soldier and the Slovenian Marine who won the Congressional Medal of Honor. Historian David Lakin wrote, "Medals, military honors, and loyal service counted for nothing if you spoke with an accent, held a union card, [or] dared to advocate the brotherhood of man" [26].

Johnson now proposed limiting immigration to 2% of those originating from each nation in the United States, based on the 1890 Census. Picking that year would cripple the new immigration of Southern and Eastern Europeans, which had largely started immigrating to the States after 1890.

Opposition to the restrictions came from big businesses and cities with large numbers of immigrants. Adolph Sabath (D-IL), a Czech-born Congressman, stated that the bill "would be the first instance in our modern legislative history for writing into our laws the hateful doctrine of inequality between the various component parts of our population" [27]. Congressman Fiorello La Guardia commented, "The mathematics of the bill disclose the international discrimination against the Jews and Italians" [28].

Johnson answered that the use of the 1890 census "was an attempt to preserve, as nearly as possible, the racial status quo in the United States" [29]. Ironically, in terms of future events, the bill did not limit immigration from Mexico or anywhere in the Western Hemisphere, as Southwestern agricultural interests wanted their immigrant labor to harvest their crops. Starting in the 1930s, federal law defined Mexicans as White, allowing them to vote without restrictions and serve in White units in the military[30].

Supporters of immigration restriction also moved to end Asian immigration. Johnson also included in the bill a provision that barred the admission of any "alien ineligible for citizenship," effectively ending all Japanese immigration. Despite complaints from Japan, the measure would remain in the final bill, generating outrage in Japan. The Japanese government declared the day of the bill's passage a day of mourning while one Japanese committed suicide after writing the American ambassador, "We are now humiliated by your country in the eyes of the world without any justification" [31]. The antagonism between Japan and the United States that would culminate at Pearl Harbor was given a big boost by this measure.

The Johnson-Reed National Origins Act of 1924 passed by overwhelming margins. Immigration was to be based on quotas, based on the census of 1890, before most Southern and Eastern Europeans had arrived. The numbers allowed for these groups thereafter would be minuscule. On May 24, 1924, President Coolidge, who had proclaimed in his message to Congress that "America must be kept American," signed the bill into law[32].

To complaints that the bill was discriminatory, the Senate sponsor, Senator David Reed, remarked, "I think the American people want us to discriminate" [33].

The effect would be immediate. While nearly 250,000 Italians immigrated in 1921, the number in 1925 was reduced by 90%. While 200,000 Russian Jews arrived in 1921, the number in 1925 was down to seven hundred. Greek immigration dropped in one year from 46,000 to a few hundred[34].

Reed commented, "The new immigration legislation marks a complete reversal of our previous policy ... We no longer are to be a haven, a refuge for the oppressed the whole world over ... America will cease to be the melting pot" [35].

Indeed, immigration dropped dramatically. More immigrants arrived in the first decade of the twentieth century than would come from 1931–71[36]. The 1924 Act was tightened further in 1929 when quotas were cut from 3% to 2%[37].

In fact, the State Department went beyond the limits of the quotas to create further barriers to entry. In 1930, President Herbert Hoover ordered the State Department to more widely apply a provision, from the 1882 immigration law, barring foreigners who might become a public charge, changing it from applying only to those with mental or physical disability to anyone who might not get a job during what was the Great Depression[38].

The Great Depression was marked by four years, 1932–36, when people emigrating from the United States actually outnumbered new immigrants to the country[39].

As the Nazis applied increasingly stronger anti-Semitic measures during the 1930s, advisors urged President Franklin Roosevelt to liberalize the criteria. However, the State Department, many of whom were openly anti-Semitic, strongly opposed allowing more German Jews to immigrate. The German quota of roughly 25,000 immigrants annually from 1933–38 went unfilled. In 1936, State Department files recorded 97,000 Germans requesting immigration permits, yet only 6,300 came to the United States[40].

Nor were Germans the only ones whose immigration was hampered. Italy had a quota of 5,800 a year, but the process of applying and trying to get a visa made sure that the number of immigrants never reached that level[41].

Despite the liberalization of the requirements in 1937, the State Department, whose American consuls could make these decisions about any immigrant, continued to find ways to deny immigration permits.

In 1939, the first attempt was made to liberalize the law when legislation was proposed to allow the entry of 20,000 refugee children above the quotas. Fierce opposition scuttled the proposals.

The State Department continued to bar the door to immigrants from Europe during most of the War. It would not be until 1944, when the mass murders of Jews by the Nazis could not be denied, that FDR created the War Refugee Board to deliver supplies to refugees and help them leave Nazi-occupied countries.

When WWII ended, Harry Truman had become president upon the death of FDR in April 1945. Pressed to do something to aid seven million displaced persons in Europe, Truman sent a team to survey the situation. The report outlined the desperate situation of the refugees, many still stuck in concentration camps. Earl Harrison, the dean of the University of Pennsylvania Law School and leader of the survey team, reported back, "As matters now stand, we appear to be treating the Jews as the Nazis treated them except that we do not exterminate them" [42].

Yet despite the Holocaust and the suffering of millions of survivors of many nationalities, public opinion remained largely antagonistic to allowing increased immigration. When Americans were polled about how many people from Europe the country should admit relative to before the war, only 5% answered more, while 51% wanted fewer or none[43].

In December 1946, President Truman issued an executive order that displaced persons should receive preferential treatment within the immigration quotas and adjusted the rules barring people who might be "public charges" to say that social welfare groups could sponsor immigrants. Truman also urged Congress to pass a law to allow more refugees to immigrate about the quotas[44].

In 1948, Congress passed a bill allowing for the admission of 200,000 refugees over two years, but with provisions designed to limit the number of Jewish immigrants, giving priority to agricultural workers and those in certain areas by a cutoff date of December 22, 1945. Truman signed the bill with "very great reluctance," noting that "in its present form, the bill is flagrantly discriminatory" and that the cutoff date "discriminates in callous fashion against displaced persons of the Jewish faith" [45].

After much conflict, a revised displaced persons bill would pass in 1950, increasing the total of those allowed to enter to 400,000 and eliminating much of the discriminatory language. Truman signed the bill, saying, "I have every confidence that the new Americans who will come to our country under the provisions of the present bill will also make a substantial contribution to our national well-being" [46].

This would be the last grasp at reform for a while. Instead, Congress passed the McCarran-Walter Immigration and Nationality Act of 1952. The bill raised the total number of immigrants slightly to 154,000 but retained the discriminatory quota system. Truman vetoed the bill, stating, "The basis of this quota system was false and unworthy in 1924. It is even worse now. At the present time, this quota system keeps out the very people we want to bring in. It is incredible to me that, in this year of 1952, we should again be enacting into law such a slur on the patriotism, the capacity, and decency of a large part of our citizenry" [47]. Congress overrode the veto to enact the measure into law. The gates of entry remained shut.

Handlin found that the restrictions had an effect beyond blocking new immigrants, noting, "Restriction involved a rejection of the foreign-born who aspired to come to the United States. It also involved a condemnatory judgment of the foreign-born already long established in the country" [48]. The Italians, Poles, and Russians already here received the clear message that they were judged as second-class and unwanted.

The Literacy Act of 1917 had not blocked the flow of immigrants from Southern and Eastern Europe because, contrary to the expectations of the Act's proponents, these immigrants learned to read if that was necessary to enter the country. Yet this result, which should have prompted a rethinking of the view of these immigrants as inferior, did not. Logic did not enter into the analysis, for the immigrants were attacked for the logical step of being self-congregating when they were under attack. The new immigrants were attacked for being poor, rather than this being seen as the usual condition of most immigrants on initial arrival to the country. It is impossible to escape the conclusion that the driving factor of the immigration restrictions was hatred and prejudice.

Ironically, these battles would become less and less relevant. While the quota system would have allowed around two million immigrants in the 1950s, there were actually 3.5 million immigrants, only one-third of whom came under the quotas. In addition, the proportion of European immigrants would drop dramatically over time. While Europeans made up 52.7% of immigrants in the 1950s, they were only a third of immigrants in the 1960s, and by the 1980s, just over a tenth of immigrants[49]. As prosperity returned to Western Europe after

WWII, few wanted to emigrate to the United States, while immigration from Eastern Europe and Russia would be closed by the Iron Curtain. Those Southern and Eastern Europeans the nativists wanted to keep out had either died in the war or were no longer able to come to America.

---

1 Ja Lynn Yang. *One Mighty and Irresistible Tide*, W.W. Norton and Company, New York, 2020, 23.

2 Yang, 33.

3 Timothy Egan. *A Fever in the Heartland*, Viking, New York, 2023, 107.

4 Okrent, 58.

5 Okrent, 62.

6 Okrent, 66.

7 Yang, 30.

8 Daniels, 278-9.

9 Okrent, 98-9.

10 Okrent, 99.

11 Okrent, 208.

12 Okrent, 188.

13 Egan, *Fever*, 19.

14 Egan, *Fever*, 24, 34.

15 Egan, *Fever*, 250.

16 Okrent, 288.

17 Okrent, 294.

18 Yang, 28.

19 Yang, 15.

20 Yang, 41.

21 Painter, 301.

22 Panter, 303.

23 Painter, 304

24 Laskin, 332.

25 Laskin, 128.

26 Laskin, 314.

27 Yang, 42.

28 Yang, 9.

29 Yang, 43.

30 Painter, 360.

31 Yang, 39.

32 Yang, 58.

33 Okrent, 331.

34 Egan, *Fever*, 171-2.

35 Yang, 3.

36 Yang, 2.

37 Daniels, 283.

38 Yang, 73.

39 Daniels, 295.

40 Yang, 74.

41 Handlin, 261.

42 Yang, 97.

43 Yang, 103.

44 Yang, 104-107.

45 Yang, 114.

46 Yang, 139.

47 Yang, 171-2.

48 Handlin, 262.

49 Daniels, 333.

The Warner Brothers

Hedy Lamarr

CHAPTER 12

The Movies

Few industries owe as much to immigrants as that of the movies.

When one thinks of American movies, the word Hollywood comes to mind. Yet Hollywood came into being almost by accident. One filmmaker in New Jersey flipped a coin between moving to Florida and California and ended up in Hollywood in 1911. In 1913, Cecil DeMille, the famous director, had intended to make a movie in Flagstaff, Arizona, but when he arrived, rain spurred him to continue on to California[1]. The sunny climate, particularly important for early cameras, drew others. By 1919, 80% of all the films in the world were made in Southern California, most in Hollywood[2].

One of the first movie stars, Florence Lawrence, was born in Ontario, Canada in 1886. She started out in vaudeville with her mother. In 1906, Lawrence was hired by Edison Studios to star in *Daniel Boone*, a movie about the frontiersman. She soon began to appear in a host of movies. In 1908, she appeared in over fifty films[3]. Her face became well known to millions, but not her name because, in those days, the movies did not list the names of the actors, figuring that it would make them ask for more money. In 1908, Lawrence's name was revealed to the press, followed by the first ad featuring a movie star.

Lawrence's career would be cut short by a back injury while filming in 1914. Her career never recovered. On December 28, 1938, Florence Lawrence committed suicide, writing in her note, "I hope this works ... they can't cure me, so let it go at that" [4].

When Rudolph Valentino died in 1926 from an abdominal infection, an estimated 100,000 people lined the streets of New York City, hoping to get a view of his casket. Valentino had moved from Italy to the United States in 1913. He had roles as an extra in films in New York until he moved to Hollywood in 1917. After a series of small roles, he starred in the 1921 film *The Four Horsemen of the Apocalypse,* after which the *Los Angeles Times* stated that Valentino "had assumed a place among the most dominant romantic actors on the screen"[5]. He made several other smash hits. Then, on August 14, 1926, he collapsed with what proved to be acute appendicitis. Valentino died shortly thereafter at 38 years old. The aftermath of his death led to a riot in which over one hundred of the grieving fans were injured.

Movie star Mary Pickford was dubbed "America's Sweetheart," yet she too was an immigrant, from Canada. Pickford was a gifted actress who often played children's roles well into her thirties. In 1916, she became the highest-paid star when she signed a contract worth over a million dollars. Pickford, after a divorce, would marry the actor Douglas Fairbanks in 1920. The pair, from their home in Beverly Hills, hosted visiting royalty, American presidents, scientists, writers, and other notables, leading their estate, Pickfair, to be labeled the "White House of Hollywood"[6].

Pickford successfully transitioned when movies began to have sound, winning an Academy Award for Best Actress in 1930. Fairbanks, unable to manage the transition, traveled abroad, leading the couple to divorce in 1936. Mary remarried in 1937. The estate hosed soldiers during WWII and disabled veterans afterward. Mary Pickford died on May 29, 1979.

Sessue Hayakawa became one of the biggest movie stars and sex symbols of the silent movie era, an astonishing feat for a non-White in a time of deep prejudice. Born in Japan in 1886, Hayakawa decided to move to the United States following his efforts to rescue the crew of an American ship that had crashed in 1907. Arriving in Los Angeles, he started acting in Japanese theater in the city, where he also met his wife. In 1914, he appeared in his first film, but he became a star in Cecil B. DeMille's 1914 film *The Cheat*. Other successes followed. Hayakawa commented, "Public acceptance of me in romantic roles was a blow of sorts against racial intolerance, even though I lost the girl in the last reel" [7]. Hayakawa would make his first film with sound in 1931, but the Motion Production Code of 1930, which prohibited interracial love scenes, plus a lawsuit about an affair, led him to move to Japan and later to France. He spent WWII in France, rejecting the requests of the Japanese government and Germany to act on their behalf. After the war, Humphrey Bogart lured him back to Hollywood to play in the movie *Tokyo Joe*. In 1956, Hayakawa was cast as the Japanese colonel in *The Bridge on the River Kwai*, for which he was nominated for an Academy Award. After several more movies, he retired, dying in 1973.

Frank Capra immigrated to California from Italy in 1903 at age six, joining his older brother. Frank Capra served in the US Army in WWI and was naturalized as a US citizen in 1920. By the 1930s, he had become a very successful movie director, directing a host of hits, including *It Happened One Night* (1934), *Mr. Deeds Goes to Town* (1936), *You Can't Take it With You* (1938), and *Mr. Smith Goes to Washington* (1939). Capra won two Academy Awards as Best Director. His films featured ordinary Americans, invariably non-ethnic Whites, fighting for justice. Painter wrote, "Omnipresent Nordicism characterized Hollywood films from the period even though most filmmakers—writers, directors, and producers—came from immigrant backgrounds, both Jewish and Catholic" [8].

Certainly, the dominance of immigrants in the men who built the great movie studios was overwhelming. Adolph Zukor was born in Hungary. Both parents died before he was eight. He lived with an uncle who adopted his older brother, but not Adolph. After serving a three-year apprenticeship in a dry goods store, he persuaded the Orphan's Board to pay for his passage to the United States. He later wrote, "No sooner did I put my foot on American soil than I was a newborn person"[9].

Zukor got a job as an apprentice at a furrier, attended night school, and began to box and play baseball. At age 19, he formed a partnership with a friend, tanning and selling furs. Zukor was successful in this partnership and in another in 1896 with a fur dealer, Morris Kohn, whose daughter Zukor married. Kohn and Company made Zukor a wealthy man[10].

In 1903, Zukor persuaded Kohn that they should invest in an arcade, which featured "thirty-second peepshow" movies and other diversions. Their company, Automatic Vaudeville, was so successful that they soon liquidated their fur business. Zukor had become interested in movies and opened a theater above the arcade. From there, he opened additional theaters. By 1908, Zukor began to look beyond the short films of the day to make longer, better movies. Within a few years, he formed a film production company, the Famous Players Company. In 1912, their first feature film, *Queen Elizabeth*, starring the actress Sarah Bernhardt, opened successfully. The *New York Clipper* stated, "Adolph Zukor, president of the Famous Players, is one of the seven wonders of the motion picture business ... The first to recognize the possibility of producing famous plays and introducing famous players cinematographically"[11].

By the summer of 1913, Zukor had completed five feature films. In 1916, he took over Paramount Pictures. When some exhibitors signed up actors away from Paramount, Zukor convinced Wall Street to invest money that allowed Paramount to take over many of the theaters. Asking for a $10 million loan, Zukor said, "I pointed out that if we got it, motion pictures would be regarded as an important industry"[12]. Historian Neal Gabler wrote, "Zukor had finally integrated the film industry, putting production, distribution, and exhibition in the same hands ... He had, in short, won respectability and legitimacy for the business of motion pictures" [13].

Carl Laemmle was born in Germany on January 17, 1867. He would wait to immigrate to America until his mother's death in 1883. In America, he worked variously as an errand boy, office boy, wheat farmer, clerk, and bookkeeper. He moved to Oshkosh in 1894, going from bookkeeper to manager of Continental Clothing's Oshkosh branch over the span of 12 years. Then, he was abruptly fired after asking the company's manager for a raise[14].

For reasons that are disputed, he decided to go into the movie business. He opened his first theater in Chicago in 1906. His success there allowed him to buy other theaters. When a film distributor reneged on delivering a film, Laemmle bought his own film to show and then added buying or renting films to his business. By 1909, he could claim to be the largest film distributor in the nation[15].

Laemmle then ran into problems with the Motion Pictures Patent Company, a trust or monopoly that owned all the patents of movie cameras and prohibited anyone from using them without paying for their permission. The Patent Company had also signed an agreement with Eastman-Kodak, the largest producer of film, prohibiting anyone from buying film without their permission.

To circumvent this monopoly, Laemmle began to produce his own movies in 1909. Laemmle began to steal away stars from the trust, starting with Florence Lawrence. Laemmle led the "Independent" producers in the revolt against the monopoly. He named his new company Universal and soon opened a new studio. When asked how he picked the name Universal, Laemmle explained, "I was looking down on the street as a covered truck went by. On the top was painted Universal Pipe Fittings" [16].

After years of success, things began to go downhill for Laemmle in 1919 when his wife died in the flu epidemic. In worsening health, Laemmle paid less attention to the business. When Universal became financially strapped during the

Great Depression, Laemmle was forced out.

Another champion of the "independents" was William Fox. Fox was brought to America as an infant from his birthplace in Hungary. Fox quit school at age 11. By age 13, he was a foreman at a clothing store. At age 20, he had saved enough to create his own clothing firm. In 1903 in Brooklyn, Fox created his first movie theater. Fox paired movies with vaudeville, selling tickets at prices low enough to make it affordable for working people. He soon became a millionaire. In 1907, Fox opened the Greater New York Rental Company to rent movies to theater owners. When the trust tried to shut him down, Fox filed an anti-trust suit against the Motion Pictures Patent Company. Fox used his political contacts to persuade the Justice Department in Washington to file an anti-trust action as well[17].

Fox began to make movies, saying that his aim "was to make a name that would stand for the finest in entertainment the world over" [18]. Fox was a workaholic. Gabler noted that while the establishment would do business with him, they would never invite this Jewish immigrant from the slums "to their inner circle of fashionable culture" [19].

Another immigrant turned mogul was Louis Mayer. Mayer's family had emigrated from Russia to Canada when he was three. At age 19, he left for the United States to Boston, where he soon met and married his wife. He had a variety of jobs, including helping in a local movie house. He then moved to Haverhill, Massachusetts, in 1907 to take over a local movie house. Quickly, he expanded to run several venues in the city, offering a variety of movies, vaudeville, and live performances. In 1912, he decided to focus on movies. A partner in his new film company said of him, "Louis was a worker—he never sleeps, you know, and he is always scheming up something" [20].

Mayer decided to produce, as well as distribute, films. His first film, *The Great Secret*, was made in the east. For his second film, he joined the move to Los Angeles in 1918. The main lure for all the producers was the weather, which allowed long shooting schedules. Los Angeles also lacked the same kind of social elite that, back East, would keep the doors shut to new immigrants. Mayer's biggest break would come when Marcus Loew, owner of a large chain of theaters, decided he needed better films for them. He purchased the Metro production company and then Goldwyn Pictures, which offered excellent facilities. Mayer persuaded Loew to put him in charge. In April 1924, Mayer took over as first vice president of Metro-Goldwyn, which became Metro-Goldwyn-Mayer, or MGM, in 1926. As Gabler wrote, "Mayer remained puritanical, using his life and films to purvey what he regarded as a virtue, stating, 'I worship good women, honorable men, and saintly mothers.'"[21]. By the early 1930s, MGM had become the predominant studio.

Some very different men would establish Warner Brothers Studios. Benjamin Warner immigrated to the United States in 1883, later sending for his wife and children, including his oldest son, Harry Warner. Another son, Jack, would be born when the family spent time in Canada. Eventually, the family, which would ultimately include nine living children, settled in Youngstown, Ohio. Another son, Sam Warner, would introduce the family to the movie business when he persuaded them to pool their savings to buy a movie projector. The Warners launched this new venture in 1903, setting up a tent in their yard to show movies. From there, they took the projector on the road until they rented a more permanent place in New Castle, Pennsylvania. There Harry rented the space, his brother Albert kept the books, Sam ran the projector, and Jack and his sister Rose would sing and dance[22].

After further successes and failures, the brothers moved to California in 1916. Their first large financial success was the film *My Four Years in Germany*, which allowed them to give up distribution to focus on producing movies. The Warners were regarded, including by themselves, as outsiders. Harry

Warner commented, "Warner brothers personally have always construed themselves as one" [23].

While Wall Street remained wary of the immigrant-dominated film industry, the industry drew support from the son of another immigrant. A.P. Giannini, the son of Italian immigrants, had successfully opened a bank in 1904, which he named the Bank of Italy. He successfully opened branches on both coasts while his brother Attilio became close to many of the film executives[24]. Eventually, the bank would be renamed Bank of America.

The Warner brothers' biggest coup came when they learned that Bell Lab engineers had synchronized sound with film. The Warners would purchase exclusive rights for the sound process while committing to buy 2,400 sound-linked film systems over the next four years. The first film with sound, *Don Juan*, was first shown on August 6, 1926. Although the audience was stunned, many movie theaters refused to install the sound equipment. After two more small films, the Warners produced *The Jazz Singer*, which starred one of the day's leading singers, Al Jolson. Opening on October 6, 1927, the movie won over everyone to movies with sound. The moment would be ruined for the Warners by the death of Sam Warner from an abscess on the day before the film debuted[25].

The next five years would bring financial success and personal tragedy to the Warner Brothers. By 1930, Warner Brothers had acquired over five hundred theaters, as well as buying record companies and radio shows and financing shows on Broadway. However, in 1932, Harry's son Lewis, the heir apparent to the studio, died of blood poisoning. Then Jack left his wife to live with and eventually marry another woman. The straitlaced Harry, as well as his sisters, ostracized the new wife. The split between Harry and Jack never healed. Gabler wrote, "Jack and Harry Warner, the two pillars of the Warner Brothers studio, loathed each other ... by the end of their lives, they barely spoke to one another" [26].

Each of the studios' films reflected the ethos of the studio heads. MGM movies were often testaments to glamour and wealth. Universal's most common movies were Westerns and horror pictures. Paramount radiated sophistication. In contrast, Gabler wrote, "Warner films, like the Warners themselves, were permeated with a vague underdog liberalism, and if their films lacked refinement and glamour, they did have a conscience—deliberately so ... [and] one could see the conscience at work, if less palpably, in the dozens of films that embraced the losers and loners" [27].

For years, MGM would feature an almost unbroken run of success. By the middle of the Great Depression, Louis Mayer was the highest-paid individual in the nation, earning over $1 million a year[28].

The last years of ownership for the immigrants were filled with controversy. In the late 1930s, the studio heads wrestled with whether to make films opposing the Nazis. Most would desist, at least until the United States entered WWII. Even Harry Warner hesitated before committing the studio to make anti-Nazi pictures, saying, "Are we making it because we're Jews or because it can make a good movie?" [29].

Soon after the war was over, Hollywood had to deal with an investigation by the House Committee on Un-American Activities (HUAC) looking into Communism in the film industry. In the face of threatened boycotts, the studios would "blacklist" anyone accused of being a communist. Gabler wrote that, for the studio heads, "the choice between abetting HUAC and unleashing anti-Semitic forces they believed might be aimed at them or opposing HUAC and risking charges of anti-Americanism posed a terrible dilemma" [30].

Meanwhile, one by one, the immigrants who had founded and ran the movie studios gave up the reins. Carl Laemmle had taken a permanent vacation in 1936 by selling his ownership in Universal. Willian Fox saw Fox wrestled away from him by Chase National Bank, who merged it with 20th Century. The

Warner Brothers, undercut by television and independent producers and an anti-trust action that forced them to sell theaters, was bought in 1956 by a bank-led syndicate. Louis Mayer resigned as head of MGM in 1951 under pressure from investors due to a run of financial losses. Adolph Zukor remained at Paramount, albeit in a reduced role. On January 7, 1973, Paramount celebrated his hundredth birthday. The chairman of Gulf and Western, which had acquired Paramount, said, "Mr. Zukor exemplified the American Dream" [31].

While William Fox lost control of his studio, he would soon be succeeded by another immigrant, Spyros Skouras. Skouras was born in a small town in Greece in 1893. In 1910, Spyros followed his older brother Charles to America. Skouras started as a bartender and waiter in St. Louis. Joined by their younger brother George, the Skouras brothers had by 1913 saved $3,500, which they used to purchase a nickelodeon, followed soon by a second theater. In WWI, Spyros, who was an American citizen by then, served in the Air Force.

After the war, the Skouras brothers began expanding their movie theater holdings. Briefly halted by the stock market crash in 1929, they again began to expand their theater ownership. Spyros helped with the reorganization of the newly merged 20th Century Fox. In 1942, he would be named president of 20th Century Fox, a position he would hold for the next twenty years. Antitrust action forced the brothers to separate their interests, with Charles and George each owning a chain of theaters while Spyros remained in control of the studio[32].

Spyros Skouras would also organize and direct the Greek War Relief fund after WWII, raising money for food, clothing, and medical supplies. When he said that a toast to Greece was going to be made at a charity luncheon, he stated, "Tell them I don't want it because I am American" [33].

In 1953, Skouras introduced wide-screen movies, which helped the industry compete better against television. Skouras was ousted as Fox president in 1963 due to a shareholder revolt against cost overruns. Skouras died in 1971.

Meanwhile, immigrants would become some of the most famous actors and directors. Greta Garbo from Sweden and Germany's Marlene Dietrich were just two in a series of famous actresses who immigrated to the United States. Some 1,500 German members of the film industry fled Nazi Germany, including Fritz Lang, Peter Lorre, Otto Preminger, and Douglas Sick. Director Billy Wilder came from Austria for the same reasons.

Samuel Wilder was born on June 22, 1906, in Austria, but his mother nicknamed him Billy after Buffalo Bill. Wilder became a freelance reporter and movie scriptwriter before moving to Berlin. There he found success in writing or co-writing twelve early sound films. When Hitler took power in January 1933, Wilder moved to Paris. There, he met movie director Joe May. In exchange for a story idea, May hired him for Columbia, offering a one-way ship ticket to the United States and $150 a week. Over his subsequent career in America, Wilder was nominated for 21 Academy Awards, including 12 for writing, eight for directing, and one for producing. Wilder won seven Academy Awards, including those for Best Director, Best Picture, and Best Screenplay[34]. In his obituary, *The New York Times* commented, "Mr. Wilder skeptically probed and exposed human weakness, particularly venality and greed. He had an inventive talent for making unpleasant situations hilarious, and he had the courage to deal with traditionally taboo sub-jects" [35]. Wilder himself said that "his goal ... was to have audiences stay awake" [36]. Billy Wilder died at age 95 from pneumonia.

Another Austrian immigrant was both a glamorous movie star and an inventor. Hedwig Kiesler was born in Vienna in 1914. At age 16, she left school to pursue acting. She later said that her father "made me understand that I must make my own decisions, mold my own character, think my own thoughts" [37].

She married a German munitions maker who forced her to give up acting. In 1937, she left him and traveled to London. There, she met Louis B. Mayer, who offered her a contract at $125 a week. She turned him down but arranged to travel across the Atlantic on the same line as Mayer and his wife. By the end of the voyage, she had a contract for $500 a week and a new name, Hedy Lamarr. She was cast in her first film seven months later[38].

Even as her career blossomed, Lamarr became alarmed by the actions of Nazi Germany, especially the sinking of two ocean liners carrying children in 1940. Lamarr decided to design something that would help the American war effort once the United States entered the war on December 7, 1941. American torpedoes were failing 60% of the time in 1942. Radio messages from submarines to torpedoes could be jammed. Lamarr, along with her friend composer George Antheil, produced the idea of varying the frequencies to foil radio jamming. The pair patented the idea and sent it to the National Inventors Council. Liking it, the Council leaked the concept to *The New York Times*, which wrote, "Hedy Lamarr, screen actress, was revealed today in a new role, that of inventor. So vital is her discovery to national defense that government officials would not allow publication of its details" [39].

The Navy, however, decided that they did not want to pursue a new system. The idea lay dormant for two decades, but the frequency-hopping communications technology later contributed to technology such as wireless cash registers, bar code readers, and home control systems[40]. In 1997, Lamarr would be awarded the Electronic Foundation Pioneer Award.

In the interim, Lamarr became successful and famous after the film *Algiers* in 1938. She would make an array of successful films over the next two decades. She became an American citizen in 1950. Lamarr died in 2000.

Another famous director came from England. Alfred Hitchcock was born outside of London in 1899. After an early

Catholic education at the Jesuit-run St. Ignatius College, he went to technical school, becoming a junior technician for a telegraph company. Hitchcock attended art school at night. At age 20, he got a movie job working in design and graphics. There, he met his future wife and collaborator, Alma Reville. In 1923, his role in movies increased when he managed to do the scriptwriting, set, and costumes, essentially being the assistant director, on the film *Woman to Woman*[41].

In 1925, Hitchcock made his directorial debut in Germany. Two years later, back in England, he had his first hit in *The Lodger*. Over the next decade, Hitchcock made many well-reviewed, successful movies. The *Sunday Times* movie critic wrote, "In *The 39 Steps*, the identity and mind of Alfred Hitchcock are continuously discernible, in fact, supreme. There is no doubt that Hitchcock is a genius. He is the real star of the film" [42].

By the late 1930s, Hitchcock had begun thinking about moving to the United States. After several visits, he finally moved to Los Angeles in March 1939. In 1940, Hitchcock's film *Rebecca* won the Academy Award for Best Picture. He continued to make hit films. In 1955, Hitchcock became an American citizen.

In addition to his films, Hitchcock became the host of *Alfred Hitchcock Presents*, a weekly series of stories shown on television. In 1965, hosting the inaugural gala for President Lyndon Johnson, Hitchcock told the audience, "The invention of televisions can be compared to the introduction of indoor plumbing. Fundamentally, it brought no change to the public's habits. It simply eliminated the necessity of leaving the house" [43].

Hitchcock's last great success was the movie *Frenzy* in 1972, leading *Time Magazine* to comment, "Hitchcock is still the master" [44]. He made one more movie in 1976 but then started to decline with increasing arthritis and anxiety. His last few months were marked by what appears to have been depression, with a loss of interest in the world and his refusing food and drink. Hitchcock died on April 29, 1980[45].

Immigrants have continued to come to the United States to work in all aspects of movies.

Haing Ngor was born in Cambodia in 1940. He became an obstetrician/gynecologist. Then, in 1975, the Khmer Rouge took control of Cambodia and began executing any educated citizen, including doctors. Ngor had to conceal his occupation but was sent along with hundreds of thousands of Cambodians to a labor camp. His wife died during childbirth when he was unable to use his skill to do a caesarian section because, as a doctor, he would be executed.

In 1979, when the Vietnamese overthrew the Khmer Rouge, he escaped to Thailand. After practicing medicine at a refugee camp in Thailand for 18 months, he immigrated to the United States in 1980. Unable to practice medicine, he was working as a social worker when he was invited to audition for the movie *The Killing Fields*, which told the story of two journalists during the Khmer Rouge's rule. For his role in the movie, playing the journalist Dith Pran, he won the Academy Award for Best Supporting Actor[46].

He continued his career in the movies while also raising money to fight poverty and disease in Cambodia. Then, on February 25, 1996, Haing Ngor was murdered outside his home in what was labeled a robbery gone wrong. Dith Pran said, "He is like a twin with me. He is like a co-messenger, and right now I am alone" [47].

Tyrus Wong was born in China in 1910. He arrived with his father in 1919, but due to the Chinese Exclusion Act, he could not become an American citizen until 1946. Wong left junior high in Pasadena for a scholarship at the Otis Art Institute. In 1938, Wong got a job working for Disney as an inspirational artist. He became the lead artist for the film *Bambi*. However, he was laid off as the result of an animator's strike. Wong was hired by Warner Brothers, where he worked for 25 years as a film production illustrator. Wong would illustrate greeting cards, paint murals, create ceramics, and make kites[48].

Wong won numerous awards. In 2015, *Tyrus*, a documentary about his life, was released. He died in 2016 at the age of 106.

There are many more immigrants who went on to become stars in movies and television, including Bob Hope (Great Britain), Michael J. Fox (Canada), Natalie Portman (Israel), Mila Kunis (Ukraine), Charlize Theron (South Africa), Jim Carrey (Canada), Salma Hayek (Mexico), Sofia Vergara (Columbia), and Arnold Schwarzenegger (Austria). The list goes on.

---

1 Carla Valderrama. *This was Hollywood: Forgotten Stars and Stories*, Running Press, Philadelphia, 2020, 2, 6.

2 Valderrama, 7.

3 Valderrama, 10.

4 Valderrama, 14.

5 Valderrama, 30.

6 Valderrama, 46.

7 Valderrama, 62.

8 Painter, 362.

9 Neal Gabler. *An Empire of Their Own*, Crown Publishers, New York, 1988, 15.

10 Gabler, 15-16.

11 Gabler, 32.

12 Gabler, 42.

13 Gabler, 42-3.

14 Gabler, 49-51.

15 Gabler, 54.

16 Gabler, 64.

17 Gabler, 68.

18 Gabler, 69.

19 Gabler, 71.

20 Gabler, 89.

21 Gabler, 119.

22 Gabler, 126.

23 Gabler, 131.

24 Gabler, 133.

25 Gabler, 142-3.

26 Gabler, 120.

27 Gabler, 195.

28 Gabler, 316.

29 Gabler, 343.

30 Gabler, 367.

31 Gabler, 429.

32 Beard, 264.

33 Beard, 265.

34 Aljean Harmetz. "Billy Wilder, Master of Caustic Films, Dies at 95," *The New York Times*, January 29, 2002.

35 Harmetz.

36 Harmetz.

37 Rachel Swaby. *Headstrong: 52 Women Who Changed Science—and the World*, Broadway Books, New York, 2018, 213.

38 Swaby, 214-5.

39 Swaby, 217.

40 Swaby, 218.

41 Peter Ackroyd. *Alfred Hitchcock*. Doubleday, New York, 2015, 20.

42 Ackroyd, 65.

43 Ackroyd, 233.

44 Ackroyd, 248.

45 Ackroyd, 260.

46 Veeda Bybee and Victo Ngai. *Shining a Light: Celebrating 40 Asian Americans and Pacific Islanders Who Changed the World*. Versify, New York, 2023, 57.

47 Jim Hill. "Actor Haing Ngor found gunned down outside LA home," CNN, February 27, 1996.

48 Bybee, 27.

Irving Berlin

Yo-Yo Ma

CHAPTER 13

Entertainment and Culture

Immigrants have had a huge impact on other areas of entertainment and culture in the United States, so much so that what follows is a few highlights that barely scratch the surface.

Immigrants have shaped and continue to shape American music. As we have seen, German immigrants helped establish some of America's first symphonies and singing groups.

The field of classical music would continue to be heavily influenced by immigrants. Some of the more important influences came from Hungary in the 1920s, 1930s, and 1940s. Many of these were Hungarian Jews or other liberals fleeing a hostile government. Bela Bartok, one of the twentieth century's greatest composers, came to America. So did Fritz Reiner, George Szell, Eugene Ormandy, Antal Dorati, and George Solti, five men who became famous as conductors of American symphony orchestras[1].

One of the greatest songwriters of the early twentieth century was Irving Berlin. Born Israel Baline in Russia in 1988, Berlin, the youngest of eight children, immigrated with his family to New York City in 1893. After working as a newsboy at age eight, Berlin moved out of his family's crowded household at age 13 following his father's death. Berline later recalled, "I never felt poverty because I had never known anything else. We had an enormous family. Eight or nine in four rooms"[2].

Berlin started singing, first in saloons, then in a chorus, before, at age 14, getting hired as a "song plugger" at a salary of $5 a week. Berlin sang newly composed songs to help their sales. This was an age where the advent of pianos at home led to a huge demand for sheet music and for songwriters to create new songs. Berlin later stated, "I never wanted to be a songwriter. All I wanted in those days was a job in which I could earn $25 a week. That was my idea of heaven" [3].

Berlin published his first song on May 8, 1907, earning 75 cents in royalties that year and $1.20 the next year. In 1909, he came out with his first hit, selling 300,000 copies, which netted him a penny each for a respectable sum of $3,000. He used the money to move his mother and sister out of the Lower East Side to a nice apartment in the Bronx. In 1911, Berlin wrote "Alexander's Ragtime Band," a megahit that sold two million copies in its first year. *Variety* declared it "the musical sensation of the decade" [4].

In February 1912, Berlin married, but his wife succumbed to pneumonia a few months later. Berlin's next hit, "When I Lost You," sold millions of copies, first on song sheets and later on phonograph records. Berlin was invited to perform in England. Afterward, the *Daily Express* wrote, "Go where you will, you cannot escape from the mazes of music he had spun. In every London restaurant, park, and theatre, you hear his strains; Paris dances to it. Berlin sips golden beer to his melodies. Vienna had forgotten the waltz, Madrid flung away her castanets, and Venice had forgotten her barcarolles. Ragtime has swept like a whirlwind over the earth and set civilization humming. Mr. Berlin started it" [5].

Berlin became an American citizen in 1918, just in time to be drafted. In the Army, he won a promotion and was enlisted to put on a show featuring the other recruits. A reviewer wrote, "As a show, it's a wonder. Here were 350 men, all from Camp Upton, giving a show that moved with the precision of a clock" [6].

In the 1920s, Berlin wrote songs for the Marx brothers' musical *Cocoanuts*. He married again in 1926 and continued to compose hits. In 1933, his musical *As Thousands Cheer* was a musical revue pretending to be a daily paper, with each song a news story. Berlin wrote the headline "Negro Lynched by Mob," which turned into a song sung by Ethel Waters. Waters was the first Black woman to star in a Broadway musical. Subsequently, Berlin spent most of his time in Hollywood, writing songs for movies.

In 1938, as war in Europe seemed imminent, Berlin wrote "God Bless America." Biographer James Kaplan wrote, " 'God Bless America' had become omnipresent ... thousands of ordinary Americans sang it every day, in schools and churches and all manner of public gatherings" [7].

The song engendered a backlash, with some attacking Berlin's presumption, as an immigrant and a Jew, in having written it. Still, it would be sung at both the Democratic and Republican conventions in 1940. Meanwhile, Berlin returned to Broadway.

When the United States entered WWII at the end of 1941, Berlin decided to do a new musical revue to help raise money for the Army Emergency Relief Fund. Berlin insisted on including two dozen Black soldiers in the performance, making the cast of *This is the Army* "the only integrated unit in the Armed Forces in World War II" [8]. The show was so successful that its eight-week run was extended to twelve and it would be made into a movie.

The same year, Berlin came out with White *Christmas*, which *Billboard* called "one of the most phenomenal hits in the history of the music business" [9]. Then Berlin and the cast of *This is the Army* went to England to perform a British version. The British loved it. After seeing it, Queen Elizabeth went backstage to meet Berlin, telling him, "I've never seen anything like it. 'My British Buddy' brought tears to my eyes" [10]. Berlin answered, "Thank you, Ma'am. I wrote the song in the bathtub" [11].

This is the Army would be performed by Berlin and the cast in other theaters of the war, from Italy to New Guinea. At the war's end, Berlin would be awarded the Medal of Merit, the nation's highest civilian honor.

Berlin worked frenetically in the next few years, producing multiple hits for Broadway and Hollywood. By the early 1960s, the nation's taste in music had changed. Berlin admitted, "It was as if I owned a store and people no longer wanted to buy what I had to sell. Everything changed. The world was a different place ... Music changed too. The Beatles and other groups reached audiences I couldn't" [12].

On Berlin's eightieth birthday, Ed Sullivan hosted a musical tribute. A reviewer commented, "Mr. Berlin has written more than 3,000 songs over the years, and 90 minutes could entertain younger viewers with only a sampling of them" [13]. Irving Berlin died on September 21, 1989, at the age of 101.

Yo-Yo Ma started impressing people as a young child. Born in Paris to Chinese parents on October 7, 1955, the family moved to the United States when Yo-Yo was seven. At age four, he started playing the cello. By age five, he was playing before audiences. At age seven, he performed at the Kennedy Center for President John F. Kennedy and former President Dwight D. Eisenhower. In 1964, he performed with his sister on the *Johnny Carson Show* [14].

After graduating high school at age 15, he attended the Julliard School of Music and graduated with a degree in anthropology from Harvard in 1976.

Yo-Yo continued to perform throughout this time, both as a solo cellist and as part of orchestras. He was featured in the soundtracks of several movies. As of now, he has released over one hundred albums and won 18 Grammy Awards. President Obama awarded him the Presidential Medal of Freedom in 2011 [15].

Another immigrant musician was the Russian-born Jascha Heifetz, regarded as one of the greatest violinists of all time.

Following his death, *The New York Times* music critic Harold Schonberg commented, "He set all standards for twentieth-century violin playing ... everything about him conspired to create a sense of awe" [16].

Born in Poland, Arthur Rubenstein was regarded as one of the greatest pianists in history. The German-born Bruno Walter is considered one of the greatest conductors of the twentieth century, as was the Italian immigrant Arturo Toscanini.

Enrico Caruso, born in Naples, Italy, in 1873, was considered one of the world's greatest tenors. Despite dying at the age of only 48, he was one of the nation's first musical celebrities.

I will just give inadequate mention to a few of the other musicians who immigrated to the United States, including Gloria Estefan (Cuba), Joni Mitchell (Canada), Eddie Van Halen (Netherlands), Carlos Santana (Mexico), and Wyclef Jean (Haiti).

Immigrants would help develop and enrich multiple other areas of American culture. Louis Agassiz, born in Switzerland, would become famous for his work in natural history in Europe. He immigrated to the United States in 1847, where he took a variety of teaching positions. Agassiz developed the theory that the earth had suffered through different ice ages. He published widely in both geology and zoology and would train a cohort of prominent American scientists who followed in his wake. A strong supporter of the Union in the Civil War, he also helped the foundation of the National Academy of Sciences. Agassiz wrote, "I feel I have a debt to pay to my adopted country, and all I can now do is to contribute my share toward maintaining the scientific activity which has been awakened during the last few years" [17].

Augustus St. Gaudens was born in Ireland in 1848 but was taken by his family to the United States the same year. He would grow up to be one of America's greatest sculptors. He was noted for his sculptures of Civil War heroes of the Union, including those of Admiral Farragut, General Sherman, and

President Lincoln. Historian Annie Beard wrote, "No native-born sculptor was ever more American than he" [18].

Walter Gropius was already a renowned architect by the time he moved to the United States. Born in Germany in 1883, Gropius was one of the founders of the "International Style" of design. After WWI, Gropius became head of the Bauhaus, a school of architecture and design. Beard wrote, "Under Gropius' direction, the Bauhaus was a tremendous success, attracting the foremost artists and the best craftsmen of the time" [19].

Gropius left Germany in 1934 after the Nazi takeover. In 1937, Gropius joined the Harvard faculty as a member of the architecture department and became chairman the following year. Harvard became one of the leading architectural centers in the nation. Gropius retired from Harvard in 1953 but continued to design buildings. Gropius died in 1969.

George Grosz was another German who was already famous when he immigrated to America. Grosz gained fame for his caricatures and satirical drawings that attacked the rich and the powerful in German society. His drawings brought fierce resentment from those he had mocked. Three times, he was attacked with knives and guns. Grosz fled Germany in 1932, just before Hitler's takeover. Hitler labeled him "Cultural Bolshevist No. 1" [20].

Grosz flourished in the United States, producing hundreds of drawings and paintings that filled American museums. Grosz became an American citizen in 1938, proclaiming, "It is the fulfillment of a wish dream; I had it since I was nine" [21]. George Grosz died in 1959.

Raymond Loewy was born in France in 1893. He studied engineering and was decorated seven times for bravery as a French officer in WWI. He followed a brother in immigrating to the United States after the war. He changed career paths, first to fashion design and then to industrial design. In 1926, he redesigned a printer, simplifying it and making it easier to repair. His first big success came in redesigning a refrigerator for Sears. He moved into redesigning trains, buses, trucks, and airplanes. He was so successful in redesigning a multitude of products that his company, Raymond Loewy Associates, soon netted over $3 million annually, a sum equal to far more in today's prices. Loewy was featured on the cover of *Time Magazine* in 1949 and was called the "Father of Industrial Design," which he described as combining "the functions of the artist, engineer, and silent salesman" [22]. From 1967–73, he helped design the Skylab space station for NASA. Loewy died in 1986.

In truth, the number of immigrants who contributed to American culture is so large that mentioning those found in this chapter while leaving out the others seems almost sacrilegious.

1 Daniels, 235.

2 James Kaplan. *Irving Berlin: New York Genius, Yale* University Press, New Haven, 2019, 7.

3 Kaplan, *Berlin*, 18.

4 Kaplan, *Berlin*, 42.

5 Kaplan, *Berlin*, 58-59.

6 Kaplan, *Berlin*, 83.

7 Kaplan, *Berlin*, 182.

8 Kaplan, *Berlin*, 204.

9 Kaplan, *Berlin*, 212.

10 Kaplan, *Berlin*, 221.

11 Kaplan, *Berlin*, 221.

12 Kaplan, *Berlin*, 319.

13 Kaplan, *Berlin*, 316.

14 Bybee, 61.

15 Bybee, 61.

16 Harold Schonberg. "Critic's Notebook: Repertory of Legends Immortalizes Jascha Heifetz," *The New York Times*, December 28, 1987.

17 Beard, 17.

18 Beard, 71.

19 Beard, 171.

20 Beard, 243.

21 Beard, 235.

22 Beard. 247.

Albert Einstein and Robert Oppenheimer

Physicists Working on the Chicago Reactor

CHAPTER 14

The Manhattan Project

America was the first nation to create the atomic bomb. A more accurate statement might be that the first atomic bomb was largely a product of American immigrants.

The theoretical basis for nuclear weapons was laid by one of the most famous immigrants, Albert Einstein. Einstein was born in Germany on March 14, 1879. Einstein was an indifferent student, doing well only in mathematics and literature. He dropped out of high school at a boarding school, frustrated with the school's resistance to new ideas. During this time, his family had moved to Milan, Italy. He stayed with them for a while until he decided he wanted to try going to college.

Einstein failed the entrance exam at the Swiss Federal Polytechnic School in Zurich. He did not solve the math problems on the test, instead doing more complicated ones of his devising. He was advised to take a year of high school review, after which he passed the entrance exam.

Einstein did not make much of an impression on anyone at the university. Upon graduation in 1902, having become a Swiss citizen, he took a job at the Swiss patent office. During his spare time, Einstein started to write articles on mathematics and physics, which were published in the German *Annals of Physics*. He noted that this job, with its light schedule, "is where I hatched my most beautiful ideas" [1]. The articles won him international fame, particularly his writing on "Theory of

Relativity." Three papers published in 1905 would revolutionize physics. First, Einstein showed that light is not only a wave but also a particle. In the second, Einstein noted the existence of measurable tiny particles. The third paper, on "special relativity," showed that time and space were elastic rather than fixed and that energy and matter were two forms of the same thing. Einstein gave a formula for calculating them: Energy (E)= Mass (m) times (x) the speed of light squared (c^2), $E=mc^2$.

Einstein had a series of university teaching jobs before he joined the faculty at the University of Berlin in 1913. He continued to write and publish, winning ever-increasing fame. Einstein now postulated his "General Theory of Relativity." He calculated how light would be bent by gravity while also concluding that the universe was expanding. In 1919, the first proof of Einstein's theory was announced by scientists studying a solar eclipse. In 1922, Einstein was awarded the Nobel Prize in Physics[2].

Einstein was asked to explain relativity. He answered, "When a man sits with a pretty girl for an hour, it seems to him a minute. But let him sit on a hot stove for only a minute—and it's longer than an hour. That's relativity" [3].

His life would be changed by the Nazi takeover of Germany in 1933. The Nazis burned all of Einstein's writings, including the old *Annals of Physics* articles, and seized his house and bank account. Fortunately, Einstein was abroad at this time.

In 1933, Einstein moved to the United States, where he joined the Institute for Advanced Study in Princeton, New Jersey. In 1939, Leo Szilard, a fellow German physicist who had fled to the United States, and Eugene Wigner, a refugee physicist and future Nobel laureate, told Einstein that Germany was, based on Einstein's theories, trying to build a super-powerful bomb. Szilard suggested that Einstein alert President Franklin Delano Roosevelt to the threat. Einstein answered, "Would it do any good for me to write to President Roosevelt? We have never met. He does not know me" [4]. Nevertheless, Einstein wrote a letter to the president.

On August 2, 1939, in a letter to President Roosevelt, Einstein wrote, "In the course of the last four months, it has been made probable ... that it may be possible to set up a nuclear chain reaction in a large mass of uranium ... this new phenomenon would lead to the construction of bombs ... A single bomb of this type ... exploded in a port might well destroy the whole port together with some of the surrounding territory" [5]. Einstein warned that the Germans might be working on building such a bomb.

Szilard passed on Einstein's letter to Alexander Sachs, an immigrant from Russia who had worked at the National Recovery Administration and wrote text for Roosevelt's speeches. On October 11, 1941, Sachs visited with President Roosevelt to pass on Einstein's concerns. Fortunately, Einstein's message was heeded. This set in motion the "Manhattan Project," the code name for America's effort to build an atomic bomb.

Einstein was horrified by the use of the bomb at Hiroshima and Nagasaki, as well as by news of the Holocaust. Einstein began campaigning for nuclear disarmament and civil rights and against racism and poverty. Einstein said, "There is no higher religion than human service. To work for the common good is the greatest creed" [6]. Albert Einstein died on April 18, 1955, at the age of seventy-six.

The development of the atomic bomb would be greatly aided by refugees from Hungary who fled the fascist-governed country in the 1920s–30s. Starting in 1920 anti-Semitic laws limited university entrance for Jews. The 15,000 Hungarian immigrants included scientists such as Leo Szilard, who persuaded Einstein to write to Roosevelt. Hungarian, usually Jewish, immigrants who would play an important role in the development of nuclear weapons included physicists such as Eugene Wigner, George de Hevsey, and Edward Teller and mathematician John von Neumann[7]. Wigner and de Hevsey would win Nobel Prizes for their work.

In fact, Germany seemed to be more likely to win the race to develop an atomic bomb than the United States. Historian Richard Rhodes, in his Pulitzer-winning book *The Making of the Atomic Bomb*, commented, "Germany had access to the world's only heavy-water factory and thousands of tons of uranium ore in Belgium and the Belgian Congo. It had chemical plants second to none and competent physicists, chemists, and engineers" [8].

In the first 32 years of Nobel Prizes (1901–32), Germans won 33 out of one hundred prizes in science, compared to 18 by British scientists and six by Americans. About a quarter of the German laureates were of Jewish descent [9].

When the Nazis came to power in Germany, German science was second to none. In April 1933, when the Nazis passed laws dismissing any non-Aryan from government employment, including the universities, which were state institutions. The law defined non-Aryan as anyone with a Jewish parent or grandparent. Rhodes wrote, "The new law abruptly stripped a quarter of the physicists of Germany, including eleven who had earned or would earn Nobel prizes, of their positions and livelihood ... to survive, they would have to emigrate" [10].

The dismissals totaled over eight hundred faculty in medicine and other sciences. The University of Berlin and the University of Frankfurt each lost a third of their faculty [11].

Historian Walter Isaacson wrote, "Fittingly, such refugees from fascism who left Germany or the other countries it came to dominate—Einstein, Edward Teller, Victor Weisskopf, Hans Bethe, Lisa Meitner, Niels Bohr, Enrico Fermi, Otto Stern, Eugene Wigner, Leo Szilard, and others—helped to assure that the Allies rather than the Nazis first developed the atom bomb" [12].

Hans Bethe was born in Germany in 1906 and was on the faculty at Tübingen in physics when he was dismissed. After time in England and Denmark, he moved to the United States in 1935 to become a faculty member at Cornell University. He became an American citizen in 1941. The next year, Robert Oppenheimer recruited Bethe, then a respected professor in physics, to help with the design of the atomic bomb. Bethe, as head of the Theoretical Division at Los Alamos, would be heavily involved in the development of the atomic bomb. Bethe would later win the 1967 Nobel Prize in Physics for his research during the 1930s.

Enrico Fermi was born in Italy in 1901. He excelled in school, telling a tutor, "I studied mathematics with passion because I considered it necessary for the study of physics, to which I want to dedicate myself exclusively" [13]. He graduated early and went on to the University of Pisa. By 1920, he had exceeded his teachers, writing, "In the physics department, I am slowly becoming the most influential authority" [14]. At age 26, Fermi became a professor of theoretical physics at the University of Rome. By 1933, Fermi had made major discoveries in the field of nuclear forces and decay.

In 1938, Mussolini promulgated the first anti-Semitic laws in Italy. Fermi's wife, Laura, was Jewish. The Fermis decided to move to America, with Fermi accepting a professorship at Columbia. Before they left, he would win the Nobel Prize for Physics in 1938. By 1939, the possibility that atoms could be split to release large amounts of energy had been established. In 1942, Fermi directed the building of the first full-scale reactor that would allow for a chain reaction of nuclear fission. It had been decided to locate the project in Chicago, so it ended up being built below the vacant football stadium of the University of Chicago. The "pile" contained over 90,000 pounds of uranium and over 700,000 pounds of graphite. On December 2, 1942, Fermi demonstrated the first energy-producing nuclear chain reaction[15].

Fermi and Bethe, along with a host of other physicists, would move to Los Alamos, where they designed and successfully tested the atomic bomb. There, John von Neumann would develop a method of creating implosions to trigger the bomb. George Kistiakowsky was born in the Ukraine, but prior to bomb development, he worked in chemistry at Harvard. Kistiakowsky would design and manufacture the explosive detonator for the bomb. Emilio Segre was born in Italy but, as a Jew, fled Italy due to the anti-Semitic laws. He was working at Berkley before moving to Los Alamos. There, he calculated fission rates for uranium and plutonium, allowing the bomb to be assembled quicker by needing less highly purified uranium-235.

Hungarian-born physicist Eugene Wigner had been one of the first to raise the alarm about the possibility of Germany developing atomic bombs. Wigner would also design the plutonium reactors necessary to create this crucial component of the bomb. Wigner would also win the Nobel Prize in Physics.

Edward Teller, born in Hungary, and Stanford Ulam, from Poland, would both work at Los Alamos as well. However, their greatest contribution would come later. After the Soviet Union exploded an atomic bomb in 1949, the United States decided to develop the more powerful hydrogen bomb. Ulam would produce the design for the bomb, while Teller converted it to a technically usable form. Bethe joked, "I used to say that Ulam was the father of the hydrogen bomb and Edward [Teller] was the mother" [16].

Another contributor to the Manhattan Project and future Nobel Laureate was Victor Weisskopf. Weisskopf was born in Austria to a Jewish family. In the 1920s, he studied physics at several of the major centers in Europe. With the rise of the Nazis, he initially moved to Copenhagen, where he was given refuge by Niels Bohr. In 1937, Bohr found Weisskopf a job at the University of Rochester. Weisskopf noted that immigrant scientists in America were often paid less than the native-born.

In 1943, having become an American citizen, Weisskopf was invited to Los Alamos to work on the development of the atomic bomb. In 1945, Weisskopf was awarded the Nobel

Prize in Physics. After the war, Weisskopf became a professor at MIT. He later became the president of the American Academy of Arts and Sciences[17].

Perhaps no one contributed to scientific progress in so many ways as John von Neumann, born in Hungary in 1903. As a child, he learned French, German, English, ancient Greek, and Latin, as well as his native Hungarian. He published his first work in mathematics at age 17. His father, explaining that "mathematics does not make money," talked him into pursuing degrees and then doctorates in math and chemical engineering at the same time[18].

Von Neumann earned both his doctorates by age 26. The early 1920s saw two scientists, Heisenberg and Schrodinger, each proposing their own theories to explain quantum physics. In 1925, the 22-year-old von Neumann showed that the theories were essentially the same. In 1932, von Neumann published his *Mathematical Foundations of Quantum Mechanics*, winning acclaim from physicists on different sides of the question[19].

Von Neumann also pioneered the field of game theory, writing *On the Theory of Parlor Games* in 1928. In the 1940s, he would return to the subject, publishing, along with economist Oskar Morgenstern, *Theory of Games and Economic Behavior* in 1944. Von Neumann biographer Ananyo Bhattacharya called it "the book that would forever change the social sciences and profoundly influence economic and political decision-making from the 1950s to the present day" [20]. Multiple economists would apply game theory to win Nobel Prizes over the next half-century.

Yet the above achievements were not related to von Neumann's contributions to the development of the atomic bomb. In 1930, von Neumann moved to the United States to take a position at Princeton's Institute of Advanced Studies with Albert Einstein and other eminent scientists. As the 1930s progressed, von Neumann foresaw the advent of a new European war. In

1935, he wrote to a friend, "There will be a war in Europe in the next decade," predicting that America would enter the war "if England is in trouble" [21]. Von Neumann began to work on calculating trajectories of artillery and the shock waves of bombs for the American military in the early 1930s, getting an official position at the military's Aberdeen Proving Ground in 1937. He would be awarded the Medal for Merit by President Truman for his research on the "effective use of high explosives, which resulted in the discovery of a new ordnance principle for offensive action" [22].

Von Neumann would be called away from work for the military in July 1944 when he received a letter from the Manhattan Project's scientific director, Robert Oppenheimer, saying, "We are in what can only be described as a desperate need of your help" [23]. Von Neumann arrived at Los Alamos, where he showed that the proposed trigger for the bomb would not work. He suggested a better design for an implosion device that would trigger the bomb.

Yet the military argued that von Neumann's work on ballistics and shock waves was too important to be neglected. Bhattacharya wrote that Von Neumann would be "the only scientist with full knowledge of the [Manhattan] Project who was allowed to come and go from Los Alamos as he pleased" [24]. By the summer of 1945, the bomb had been finished, leading to a successful test on July 16. In August, the dropping of the two bombs on Japan would bring its surrender and the end of WWII.

Following the end of WWII, the immigrant physicists dispersed to positions at universities throughout America. Bethe went back to Columbia and Wigner to Princeton, while Fermi and Teller joined the University of Chicago. Segre returned to the University of California at Berkley, where he would later win a Nobel Prize in 1959 for discovering two new elements and the antiproton. The contributions of all these immigrants to American science would continue.

Von Neumann, after returning to Princeton, would play a critical role in the development of the computer, the subject of Chapter 18 of this book.

Maria Goeppert Mayer was another German-born physicist, the seventh generation of professors in her family[25]. She studied physics at the University of Göttingen. There, she met Joseph Mayer, an American Rockefeller fellow who had boarded with Goeppert's family. After their marriage in 1930, the couple moved to the United States. Her husband was hired by John Hopkins. Although never paid, Maria was eventually able to teach and continue research. In 1938, when her husband was fired, they received jobs at Columbia University. Maria became friends with Enrico Fermi. In 1942, she became part of the Manhattan Project, supervising a team of chemists trying to separate out uranium isotopes. In 1945, the Mayers moved to Chicago, where Maria obtained a position in nuclear physics at the Argonne National Laboratory. During her years in Chicago, she developed a mathematical model explaining the structure of the shell of the nucleus and why some isotopes were more stable than others. She described the paths of the nuclear structure, using the analogy of the waltz, noting, "Think of a room full of waltzers. Suppose they round in circles, each circle enclosed within another. Then imagine that in each circle, you can fit twice as many dancers by having one pair go clockwise, and another pair go counterclockwise"[26]. In 1963, Maria Goeppert Mayer shared the Nobel Prize in Physics for discoveries related to nuclear shell structure. Three years earlier, she had accepted a full professorship in physics at the University of California at San Diego. Maria Goeppert Mayer died in 1972.

America's gain in scientific talent was Germany's loss. After winning 33 Nobel Prizes in Science in the 27 years before 1932, Germans would win only eight in the next 27 years[27]. Economist Fabian Waldinger wrote, "Calculations suggest that the dismissal of scientists in Nazi Germany contributed about nine times more to the decline of German science than the physical destruction during WWII[28].

1 Milton Meltzer. *Albert Einstein: A Biography*, Holiday House, New York, 2008, 12.

2 Bailey, 240.

3 Meltzer, 22.

4 Elma E. Levinger. *Albert Einstein*, Julian Messner, Inc. New York, 1949, 158.

5 Meltzer, 25.

6 Meltzer, 27.

7 Daniels, 235.

8 Richard Rhodes. *The Making of the Atomic Bomb*, Simon and Schuster, New York, 1986, 343-4

9 Jean Medawar and David Pyke, *Hitler's Gift: The True Story of the Scientists Expelled by the Nazi Regime.* Arcade Publishing, New York, 2000, 3.

10 Rhodes, 185.

11 Rhodes, 188.

12 Walter Isaacson. *Einstein: His Life and Universe*, Simon and Schuster, New York, 2008, 407.

13 Rhodes, 205.

14 Rhodes, 206.

15 Rhodes, 440.

16 Rhodes, 773.

17 Medawar, 141-2.

18 Ananyo Bhattacharya. *The Man from the Future: The Visionary Life of John von Neumann*, W.W. Norton and Company, New York, 2021, 21.

19 Bhattacharya, 41.

20 Bhattacharya, 151.

21 Bhattacharya, 70.

22 Bhattacharya, 83.

23 Bhattacharya, 82.

24 Bhattacharya, 84.

25 Swaby, 135.

26 Joan Dash. *A Life of One's Own: Three Gifted Women and the Men They Married,* Harpers and Row, New York, 1973, 316.

27 Medawar, 235.

28 Bhattacharya, 53.

Isidor Rabi

Chien-Shiung Wu

CHAPTER 15

American Science II

Immigrants continued to make major contributions to American science beyond the atomic bomb. The years after WWII saw American science rise to be the envy of the world.

A key ingredient was the hundreds of German scientists forced into exile by the Nazis for being Jewish or having Jewish blood, i.e., ancestors who were Jewish. Medawar and Pyke wrote, "The main effect of the Nazi persecution of the Jewish scientists was not so much in the expulsion of the famous but in the expulsion of the younger men—such as Krebs, Perutz, and Chain—who themselves grew up to be great" [1].

In the United States, the Emergency Committee for Aid to Displaced German Scholars helped to assist about half of the 1,700 academic refugees in the United States. Not everyone was eager to welcome these scientists. Journalist Ed Murrow noted "the general indifference of the [American] university world" [2].

A leading role in the rescue of the scientists was played by the great Danish scientist and Nobel laureate Niels Bohr. Bohr sheltered many refugee scientists in his Institute of Physics in Copenhagen and found them, and others, academic jobs else-wher [3].

Other immigrant scientists came from other countries. One contributor brought a most unlikely resume. Alexander Poniatoff was born in Russia in 1892. He would earn an advanced degree in engineering in Berlin. He returned to Russia, where he became a pilot in the Imperial Russian Navy in WWI and then for the White Russian forces in the subsequent Russian civil war. He left Russia following the Bolshevik victory to work for the Shanghai Power Company in China. He then moved to the United States. In 1932, he became an American citizen. Working as an engineer in the early years of the war, Poniatoff helped perfect motors and generators for airborne radar systems[4].

In 1944, Poniatoff founded his own company, Ampex. He was ready then when he learned of Magnetophon, a magnetic recording device built in Germany. The Magnetophon had been captured in the last days of WWII by a US Army engineer, Major Jack Mullin. Mullin shared the technology for free, feeling that he didn't really have ownership over it. Mullin and Poniatoff took the German machine apart, then built their own prototype[5].

Earlier magnetic tape had suffered a lot of interference. The new machine, the Ampex Model 200 A, was much improved. Mullin took the device to Bing Crosby at ABC. Crosby was doing two live shows a week on the radio but realized that the device would allow him to reduce this to one by taping it and using it again. Crosby immediately ordered twenty of the recording machines. This allowed Ampex to grow from a seven-person company to one employing 13,000 people within 15 years[6].

Poniatoff's company moved on to develop multiple track tapes for use in movies and in the space program, as well as small tape recorders for personal use. They subsequently moved on to develop video recording, allowing for the advent of prerecorded television[7].

An immigrant would prove central in the American development of the magnetic resonance imaging machine (MRI) that would greatly aid in the diagnosis of illness. Isidor Rabi was born in a small village in Galicia and brought by his family to the United States at age three. He grew up in a slum section of New York. Rabi earned a chemistry degree at Cornell and became the first Jewish professor in the sciences at Columbia. Rabi and his team would make, in the words of historian Peter Baker, "a breakthrough that determined how a bombardment of electromagnetic waves could reveal the chemical composition of nuclei" [8]. Rabi won the 1944 Nobel Prize in Physics for his discovery of nuclear magnetic resonance.

While Rabi's discovery would have implications in a whole number of scientific fields, it was Raymond Damadian, the son of Armenian immigrants, who took it further in medical diagnosis by using this knowledge to build the first MRI. The first actual MRI scan took place on July 3, 1977[9].

When Dr. Rabi had to get an MRI near the end of his life in 1988, he remarked, "I saw myself in that machine. I never thought my work would come to this" [10].

Today, millions of people will play video games on their television or computer. The first video game for home entertainment would be the invention of a refugee from Nazi Germany. Raph Baer was forced to leave his public school at age 11 when Hitler banned Jews from going to school with other Germans. Five years later, his family moved to the United States. Baer went to work at age 16 at a factory in the Bronx. He learned to repair radios through a correspondence course and then became a US Army intelligence officer in WWII. He returned to the United States after the war, using the GI Bill to get a degree in the new field of television engineering[11].

While designing a television in 1951, Baer suggested adding a game-playing feature. Baer was told, "Forget it. Just build the damn TV set; you're behind schedule as it is" [12]. Fifteen years later, Baer had the idea of building a "game box" that could be attached to any television. His employer at that time proved more open to the idea. Baer, along with engineers Bill Harrison and Bill Rusch, built a prototype that would allow a game called "Ping Pong" to be played on televisions. When Baer brought the prototype to the US Patent Office, he recalled,

"Within 15 minutes, every examiner on the floor of that building was in that office wanting to play that game" [13]. From this game would come a host of increasingly sophisticated other video games. Baker concluded, "From the mind of the 11-year boy the Nazis didn't want in school would flow Xbox, PlayStation, Wii, and doubtless many games yet to come" [14].

Chien-Shiung Wu was born in China in 1912. With schools for girls almost non-existent, her father opened the first school for girls in their area. She then went to a boarding school and a university where she studied physics. At age 24, she immigrated to the United States to be able to pursue her physics research. She settled at the University of California at Berkley. She struggled to overcome discrimination against women and Asians, as well as her limited English[15].

Then, in 1940, Wu was invited to work on the Manhattan Project, where she focused on processes to enrich uranium. Following the war, Wu stayed at Columbia, where she continued her work in nuclear physics. Two other physicists asked her to help them test whether a physics law called the principle of conservation parity might not always apply.

Wu succeeded in showing the law was not always true, leading *The New York Times* to declare the "shattering of a fundamental concept of nuclear physics" [16]. The other two scientists involved would win the Nobel Prize for the discovery, but Wu was only awarded the Wolf Prize in Physics, the second-highest award. After the experiment's success, Wu would comment, "There are moments of exaltation and ecstasy. A glimpse of this wonder can be the reward of a lifetime" [17]. Wu would continue her research for the rest of her life, passing away in 1997.

Peter Debye was born In Holland. He had become an experimental physicist. He was appointed director of the Kaiser Wilhelm Institute for Physics in Berlin. When Germany invaded the Netherlands, Debye left with the excuse of going on a lecture tour, but instead of returning to Germany, he traveled to the United States. He became a Professor of Physics at Cornell. In 1946, Debye won the Nobel Prize in Chemistry for his work on X-ray diffraction in gases. He commented, "Our science is essentially an art which could not live without the occasional flash of genius in the mind of some sensitive man, who, alive to the smallest of indications, knows the truth before he has the proof" [18].

Max Delbruck was trained as a physicist but won fame in biology. Delbruck was born in Germany in 1906. He became a nuclear physicist, but in 1937, he won a Rockefeller Fellowship to work in genetic research with one of the world's experts, T.H. Morgan, at the California Institute of Technology. There, Delbruck learned about bacteriophages, viruses that entered and destroyed bacterial cells. Delbruck moved to Vanderbilt University. He collaborated with Salvador Luria, an Italian refugee and another recent immigrant, and the two discovered that bacteria could develop resistance to the viruses via genetic mutation. Debruck and Luria, along with Alfred Hershey, would win the Nobel Prize in Medicine in 1969 "for their discoveries concerning the replication mechanism and the genetic structure of viruses."

Delbruck moved back to Caltech, where he led research on molecular biology. He was known for his openness, commenting, "The first principle had to be openness. That you tell each other what you are doing and thinking. And you don't care who has the priority" [19].

Austrian physiologist Otto Loewi was in his sixties when he was forced to flee when Hitler invaded Austria in 1938. Two years earlier, he had shared the 1936 Nobel Prize in Medicine for his work on how nerves transferred messages through the body. When the Germans moved into Austria, they arrested Loewi at gunpoint for being Jewish while keeping his family under house arrest. He would only be released when members of the International Physiology Congress threatened the Germans that they would cease all contact unless Loewi was freed. Loewi was freed but forced to transfer his Nobel Prize money to Germany. Loewi left Austria on September 28, 1938, but his wife would not escape until 1941. Loewi accepted a professorship at the College of Medicine at New York University, where he taught for the next 15 years. Grateful at becoming an American, Loewi wrote, "I am happy and deeply grateful to the fate that transported me to this country—where I continue to enjoy the stimulating, almost rejuvenating effect of new friendships and the wealth of new impressions and experiences"[20].

Rita Levi-Montalcini was born in Italy in 1909. She was barred from university research during WWII due to being Jewish. She moved to St. Louis in 1947 to take a faculty position at Washington University. She shared the 1986 Nobel Prize in Medicine for her work on increasing understanding of cell division and multiplication.

Albert Claude was born in Belgium in 1898. In 1928, he received his medical degree and moved to New York City to work at the Rockefeller Institute. By developing techniques to allow visualization of different parts of the cell, he is viewed as starting the field of cell biology[21]. Claude won the Nobel Prize in Medicine in 1974.

Elizabeth Stern was born in Canada in 1915. After becoming a doctor, she immigrated to the United States, where she became a citizen in 1943. Stern was the first to show the link between a virus and a cancer when she described the link between human papillomavirus (HPV) and cervical cancer[22].

American science would continue to be enriched by the contributions of immigrants, some others of whom are mentioned in later chapters.

---

1 Medawar, 46.

2 Medawar, 62.

3 Medawar, 64.

4 Baker, 78.

5 Baker, 79.

6 Baker, 79.

7 Baker, 79.

8 Baker, 197.

9 Baker, 199.

10 Baker, 199.

11 Baker, 247-8.

12 Baker, 248.

13 Baker, 248.

14 Baker, 248.

15 Schwartz, 90.

16 Schwartz, 92-3.

17 Swaby, 146.

18 Medawar, 153.

19 Medawar, 144.

20 Medawar, 147.

21 Mindy Weisberger. "Eleven Immigrant Scientists Who Made Great Contributions to America," LiveScience, February 7, 2017.

President Johnson Signing 1965 Immigration Reform at Statue of Liberty

CHAPTER 16

Reopening the Golden Gate

The 1924 law kept immigration at a low level compared to historical norms. President Truman tried to change the law but was unsuccessful in eliminating the discriminatory quotas that made immigration from all but a few favored nations almost impossible.

Another quarter-century would pass till the laws really would be changed. Truman set the groundwork when, in his last months in office, he created a commission to make recommendations on immigration. He named figures sympathetic to reform to the commission. Thus, on January 1, 1953, the Commission on Immigration recommended eliminating the national origins quota system. The Commission recommended that immigration visas be allocated "without regard to national origin, race, creed, or color," being instead based on the right of asylum, family reunification, and national needs[1].

Nevertheless, opposition in Congress blocked even milder proposals from President Eisenhower from being enacted. Eisenhower's successor, President John F. Kennedy, had built a reputation of being in favor of immigration reform. Yet it would not be until July 1963 that Kennedy sent a message to Congress urging a revised law. In the proposals, the quotas would be reduced by 20% annually until they disappeared. Priority would be given to those "with the greatest ability to aid the national welfare," followed by the reunification of families[2]. Yet, this proposal, like many of those of the Kennedy administration, made no progress in Congress. Then, on November 23, 1963, Kennedy was assassinated, making Vice President Lyndon Johnson, former Senate majority leader, the new President. The arch-conservative chair of the Senate Judiciary Committee, James Eastland, had blocked most of Kennedy's proposals on civil rights and immigration reform. Eastland, hearing the news, exclaimed, "Good God, Lyndon's president. He's going to pass a lot of this damm fool stuff"[3].

Johnson later commented, "There is but one way for a president to deal with the Congress, and that is continuously, incessantly and without interruption ... He's got to know them better than they know themselves. And then, on the basis of this knowledge, he's got to build a system that stretches from the cradle to the grave, from the moment a bill is introduced to the moment it is officially enrolled as the law of the land"[4].

Johnson introduced a new immigration proposal that was almost identical to Kennedy's. Initially, the same conservatives who dominated the relevant committees and subcommittees blocked any progress. Finally, Congressman Michael Feighen (D-OH), the chair of the House Judiciary Committee, agreed to hold hearings. Proponents of the reform emphasized its symbolic value. Secretary of State Dean Rusk talked about how the quotas interfered with the nation's foreign policy goals by giving nations the idea that the United States thought negatively about them. Rusk estimated that if the quotas were eliminated, only another 14,000–15,000 immigrants would enter[5].

In 1924, the American Federation of Labor supported the restrictive law. Now, the new AFL-CIO supported abolishing the quota system. In October 1964, President Kennedy's book *A Nation of Immigrants* would be published posthumously. Still, the immigration bill did not progress.

Then, in 1964, Johnson won a landslide reelection, sweeping in the most liberal Congress since the height of the New

Deal in 1936. Meeting with his staff in February 1965, Johnson told them, "I want you to work for my legislative program and get much passed in the next 90 days and in 1965 as is humanly possible" [6].

Johnson pushed ahead on immigration. Conservatives now said that in exchange for eliminating quotas, they wanted, for the first time, a limitation on immigration from the rest of the Western Hemisphere, for the cutoff on Asian immigration in the late 1800s had made employers turn to Mexican immigrants to build the railroads and harvest the crops in the Southwest.

Prejudice against Mexican immigrants was not new. In the 1920s, Texas Representative John C. Box warned that allowing continued Mexican immigration could result in increased racial mixing due to their more casual attitude to interracial union[7]. Nevertheless, the Johnson-Reed bill did not place any limits on immigration from the Western Hemisphere.

It was with difficulty that this proposed limitation on immigration from Mexico and the rest of the Americas was defeated. Finally, on July 22, 1965, the immigration subcommittee passed a new bill. Quotas would be phased out in three years, with immigration capped at 330,000 with unlimited immigration allowed from the Western Hemisphere and for family unification. Family unification would take the highest priority, followed by accepting those with the desired skills[8].

Few expected a surge in immigration as a result of the bill. Attorney General Robert F. Kennedy told a House subcommittee, "I would say [the number of immigrants] to be expected for the Asia-Pacific Triangle ... would be approximately 5,000, Mr. Chairman, after which immigration from that source would virtually disappear" [9]. Another administration official, Nicholas Katzenbach, testified, "If you look at the present immigration figures from the Western Hemisphere countries, there is not much pressure to come to the United States" [10]. Immigration historian Nathan Glazer wrote, "Among the other things that the Act of 1965 did not expect and did not take into account was the grim possibility of mass refugee movements and mass expulsions" [11].

The House passed the bill on August 25, 1965, by a vote of 318 to 95, with most opponents being conservative Southern Democrats. House Judiciary Chairman Emmanual Celler had been the only member of the House who had been in Congress in 1924, when he had strongly opposed the Johnson-Reed immigration bill. Celler commented, "I made a speech then against this theory. I am glad ... that we are now to obliterate and nullify and cancel out this abomination called the national theory of immigration" [12].

In the Senate, James Eastland agreed not to oppose the measure in exchange for picking a judge in Mississippi. Still, conservatives demanded a limit on immigration from the Western Hemisphere.

The final Hart-Celler Act abolished the quota system based on national origins and put family reunification and job skills as the new main criteria for immigration[13]. The bill set a limit of 170,000 immigration visas for the Eastern Hemisphere and 120,000 for the Western. Three-quarters of the visas would be reserved for family reunification, although spouses, children, and parents of American citizens would be exempt from the cap[14]. Family reunification, in fact, took precedence over a preference for immigrants with needed skills. Congress passed the bill on September 30. 1965

President Johnson announced that the signing ceremony would be three days later at the Statue of Liberty. At the signing ceremony, Johnson declared, "Our beautiful America was built by a nation of strangers. From a hundred different places or more, they have poured forth into an empty land, joining and blending in one mighty and irresistible tide" [15].

The Act would be one of the least well-known and yet one of the most important reforms of Lyndon Johnson's Great Society. It would set forth a huge new wave of immigration.

The new immigrants would come to a large degree from the Spanish-speaking nations of the Americas and from Asia. An estimated 30 million immigrants would arrive in the last 35 years of the twentieth century. In 2000, an estimated six million were in the nation illegally. The immigrants would make up an estimated 12% of the workforce then[16].

The emphasis on family reunification helped drive the great increase, for, just as in the years before 1924, when one family member came to America, he would bring his family with him. As a citizen, the new immigrant could bring in his siblings and their spouses and children. Historian Roger Daniels noted, "Since the 1965 Act went into effect, the preponderance of all non-refugee migration has been the chain migration of relatives" [17].

In contrast, those admitted with needed professions and skills, the alternative preference to family reunification, has amounted to less than 4% of immigrants[18].

Other immigrants would be refugees fleeing one dictatorship or national disaster after another. The Refugee Act of 1980 attempted to solve the question of admitting refugees. The Act allowed for the admission of 50,000 refugees each year. However, the president could raise that number after consultation with Congress. The Act also created a new class, asylees, refugees already in the United States who appealed for asylum. The Act set the total in this category at five thousand, although it soon increased[19].

Statistics revealed an increase in immigrants in each decade since the 1930s for most of the rest of the century. There were one million in the '40s, 2.5 million in the '50s, 3.3 million in the '60s, 4.5 million in the '70s, and 6 million in the 1980s[20]. The number of immigrants living in the United States quadrupled from 9.6 million in 1970 to 44.4 million in 2017, increasing the percentage of the country's foreign-born to the highest ratio since 1910[21].

Illegal immigration in the United States only became a

phenomenon with the passage of laws limiting immigration. Thus, the first large group of illegal immigrants were from Asia, as a result of the Chinese Exclusion Act and other measures barring their legal entry. Historian Erika Lee commented, "The effort to exclude Asian immigration from the United States contrasted too sharply with the demand for immigrant labor and immigrants' intense need and desire to seek entry" [22].

A large industry arose to smuggle Asian immigrants into the United States. The enormous American borders with Canada and Mexico were initially almost unpatrolled. In 1902, there would be only 66 American border inspectors, most on the Canadian border. By 1909, the number had increased to three hundred. The US Border Patrol was formally established in 1924, but there were still far too few border officials to effectively block immigration[23].

The limits on European immigration resulted in Europeans trying to enter illegally as well. The US government unofficially conceded the difficulty of preventing illegal immigration. In 1927, Secretary of Labor James Davis commented that even if the US Army were placed on the border, "We couldn't stop them. If we had the Navy on the waterfront, we couldn't stop them. Not even a Chinese wall nine thousand miles in length and built over rivers and deserts and mountains and along the seashores would seem to permit a permanent solution" [24].

There would be no illegal Mexican or Central American immigrants until 1965, for there had been no limits on their immigration. Unfortunately, the new restriction on the number of immigrants from the Western Hemisphere created a new problem, for the numbers wanting to enter from Mexico and Central and South America far exceeded their allowed quota, leading to a large spike in the number of immigrants illegally in the nation.

Immigrants helped meet the otherwise unmet needs of

American society. For example, a survey in 1972 reported that 46% of all licensed physicians in the United States were foreign-born[25].

In 1980, the Refugee Act of 1980 tried to better define the status of refugees while setting a limit on the numbers allowed to immigrate. Congressman Peter Rodino called it "one of the most important pieces of humanitarian legislation ever enacted by a US Congress" [26].

The next major overhaul of immigration laws came in 1986 when Republican President Ronald Reagan gave amnesty to millions of undocumented immigrants while increasing enforcement at the borders and making it illegal for employers to knowingly hire undocumented immigrants[27].

In 1990, another immigration law was passed under President George H.W. Bush. This law doubled the number of green cards for legal immigrants while setting the annual visa number at 675,000. The law also created the H1-B visa for high-skill temporary workers and the diversity lottery, setting aside 50,000 visas[28]. The lottery was initially for residents of "adversely affected areas," countries that had previously supplied large numbers of immigrants. Initially, 40% of the slots were reserved for the Irish[29]. The lottery rules were subsequently changed to widen the nations from which immigrants could apply to come and to eliminate the preference for the Irish. Some 10 to 20 million people apply every year for the 50,000 spots in the diversity lottery.

---

1 Yang, 192.

2 Yang, 224.

3 Yang, 229.

4 Yang, 233.

5 Yang, 238.

6 Yang, 245.

7 Gregory Rodriguez. In *Reinventing the Melting Pot: The New Immigrants and What It Means to be American,* ed. Tamar Jacoby, Basic Books, New York, 2004, 132.

8 Yang, 254.

9 Nathan Glazer. "Introduction," in *Clamor at the Gates,* ed. Nathan Glazer, Institute for Contemporary Studies, San Francisco, 1985, 7.

10 Glazer, "Introduction," 7.

11 Glazer, "Introduction," 10.

12 Yang, 256.

13 Meltzer, *Bound for America,* 96.

14 Yang, 259.

15 Yang, 263.

16 Meltzer, *Bound for America,* 99-100.

17 Daniels, 343.

18 Daniels, 343-344.

19 Daniels, 345-6.

20 Daniels, 344.

21 Yang, 266.

22 Lee, 192.

23 Lee, 200.

24 Lee, 204.

25 Joshua Zeitz. *Building the Great Society: Inside Lyndon Johnson's White House,* Viking, New York, 2018, 196.

26 Lee, 341-2.

27 Yang, 268-9.

28 Kane, 197.

29 Ungar, 336.

I.M. Pei

Albert Pujols

CHAPTER 17

Immigrants: New Origins

Immigration from outside Europe was, for many years, a small part of the picture. In the hundred years from 1820–1920, only 1.3 million immigrants in total came to the United States from the Western Hemisphere excluding Canada. Of these, approximately 750,000 were from Mexico, 425,000 from the West Indies, 113,000 from South America, and a mere 43,000 from Central America[1].

The Mexican-American War ended in 1848, with Mexico ceding the area that encompasses the current states of California, Arizona, and New Mexico. With the transfer of this territory, some 116,000 Mexicans became residents of the United States, (this number is not included in the totals above)[2].

The cutoff in European immigration during WWI and then after 1924 created an increased need for workers. Between 1900–1930, over a million Mexicans, a tenth of Mexico's population, would immigrate to the United States[3]. In the 1920s, some 500,000 Mexicans would immigrate to the United States. About 85% of Mexican immigrants lived in the Southwest, with the majority in California and Texas[4].

Many of the Mexican immigrants would be brought in by American businesses looking for workers. The Santa Fe and Southern Pacific Railroad would hire 16,000 Mexicans in 1908 to work on the railroad. Bethlehem brought in a thousand workers in 1923 to work in its Pennsylvania steel mills, while the Great Western Sugar Beet Company would bring in over

30,000 Mexicans to work in its Colorado beet fields in the 1920s and '30s[5].

The 1930s saw an effective hiatus in Mexican immigration, while "repatriation" programs forced many Mexicans to return to Mexico. With the outbreak of WWII, labor shortages in the United States led to the creation of the bracero program, bringing about 100,000 Mexican workers into the United States annually on a temporary basis. By now, many of the Mexican Americans were second-generation citizens born in the country. Some 375,000 Mexican American men would serve in the American armed forces in WWII[6].

Mexican immigration would increase with each subsequent decade: 60,000 in the 1940s, 275,000 in the 1950s, 440,000 in the 1960s, and 640,000 in the 1970s[7].

Prior to the passage of the 1965 Immigration Act, which for the first time set quotas on immigration from the Western Hemisphere, there were no "illegal" Mexican immigrants. Subsequently, with immigration from the Western Hemisphere capped, a percentage of Mexican immigrants to the United States would be in the country illegally. The estimated number of illegal immigrants varied widely, with the Immigration and Naturalization Service estimating one million in 1972 but changing that estimate to the wildly different number of 4 to 12 million in their 1974 report[8].

As noted, a portion of the Mexican community in the United States, such as in Texas, New Mexico, and California, preceded the addition of these states to the United States. However, in the 1980 Census, 57.8% of Mexican Americans reported that they had immigrated since 1970[9]. While Mexican Americans are more likely to be farm workers than the rest of the population, by the 1970s, some 85% of Mexicans lived in cities[10].

Overall, in the years 1820–2008, some 7.4 million legal Mexican immigrants moved to the United States, making Mexico the biggest source of legal immigrants in that time period[11].

Mexican immigration tended to come in waves. There was a large surge at the beginning of the twentieth century, caused in part by population growth in Mexico and in part by civil war that broke out there. The Mexican immigrants, who clustered in a few Southwestern states, more than doubled in number from 1900–1910 and doubled again in the next decade to some 400,000. The vast majority were employed on the railroads, in mining, and in agriculture[12].

This wave of immigration ended with the Great Depression, which saw mass deportations of Mexicans, including some American citizens. The labor shortage in WWII reopened the faucet, but the early 1950s saw deportations resume. Throughout all of this history, there were significant movements of Mexicans into the United States and others returning to Mexico.

The next wave of Mexican immigration into the United States started in the 1960s, when some 440,000 Mexicans legally immigrated to the United States[13].

Mexican immigrants faced discrimination for much of their time in the United States. This began to change in the 1960s when the Civil Rights Movement led to increased political power for Mexican Americans, particularly in areas where they were a dominant portion of the population, such as in South Texas. The increasing number of Americans of Mexican descent led to more and more of these individuals being elected to prominent positions, particularly in the American Southwest.

Puerto Rico had been acquired by the United States in the 1898 Spanish-American War, so Puerto Ricans cannot be considered, in a strict sense, as immigrants. Puerto Ricans had been gradually migrating to the mainland before WWII, with some 135,000 living there by the war's end. The next decade and a half would see a rapid acceleration of Puerto Rican migration to the rest of the United States. By 1960, some one million Puerto Ricans lived in the nation (outside of Puerto Rico itself)[14].

Puerto Rican migration would be marked by large numbers moving to the continental United States and large numbers returning to the island. Notable success stories of those born in Puerto Rico included actors such as Mel Ferrar, Rita Moreno, and Benicio del Toro; baseball stars Roberto Clemente and Orlando Cepeda; singer Ricky Martin; and boxer Felix Trinidad.

The largest motivating factor in the move was economics, for the 1930s saw harsh economic conditions on the island, particularly for the rural poor. The majority of Puerto Rican migrants settled in New York City.

Before 1900, immigrants from the Caribbean were a tiny percentage of the American population. Emancipation of slaves in the West Indies occurred on August 1, 1838, more than two decades before the United States, but immigration to the United States would not really take off until the twentieth century. Most of the West Indian immigrants were Black, mostly from cities. About 30,000 arrived from 1900–1910, almost double that in the next decade and then another 40,000 in the 1920s. By 1930, they were about 1% of the Black population. West Indian immigrants had lower crime rates than either Black or White Americans. Over time, West Indians have had incomes higher than the average of the population and lower rates of unemployment[15].

In the 1950s, economic and political disturbances led about 80,000 Cubans to settle in the United States. The takeover of power by Fidel Castro on January 1, 1959, led to an acceleration of Cuban immigration in the next three years. The Cuban Missile Crisis of October 1962 largely shut off this migration, as only 30,000 Cubans immigrated until 1965, when the Johnson administration made an agreement with Castro to allow additional immigration. In total, some 800,000 Cubans have entered the United States since 1960[16]. The Cuban immigrant community is largely clustered in Florida, particularly in the city of Miami. At the turn of the twenty-first century,

20% of Cubans lived outside Cuba, with at least half in Miami[17].

The Cuban refugees of the 1960s and 1970s included a large number of well-educated people with needed technical skills. While only 4% of the total Cuban population had reached twelfth grade, some 36% of these immigrants had gone to college[18]. In the 1966 Cuban Adjustment Act, Cuban immigrants received a host of benefits not provided to other immigrants, including eligibility for public assistance, Medicaid, food stamps, and low-interest college loans. The state of Florida provided direct cash payments to Cuban families.

As a result of these factors, Cubans proved very successful in general. By 1987, there were 61,000 Hispanic-owned firms in Miami, most of them Cuban, with gross receipts of $3.8 billion, topping any other city in the United States[19].

One Cuban immigrant whose story combined both triumph and tragedy was Orlando Padron. Padron was born in 1926 and grew up on his family's tobacco farm. In the 1950s, he fought alongside Castro against the Baptista dictatorship. However, disenchanted by Castro's rule, in 1961, he immigrated to the United States. Largely penniless on arrival, he opened Padron Cigars in 1964. The business became very successful, winning awards multiple times for the best cigar of the year[20]. Bandleader Mitch Miller, comedian Carl Reiner, and Polish President Lech Wałęsa all gave testimonials to their quality.

In the 1970s, Padron became an advocate for dialogue with Castro. In 1978, Padron traveled to Cuba, where he won freedom for family members, friends, and more than three thousand prisoners. Padron said, "Fidel treated me with respect ... When he asked what I thought of the new Cuba, I would say, 'This is not what I had in mind. This is not what I fought for.' " [21].

However, right-wing members of the Cuban exile community attacked Padron on his return, focusing on a picture of him giving a cigar to Castro. He was accused of selling out to communism. His company headquarters was bombed. Padron withdrew from public view for many years, although his company flourished. On his death in 2017, it was noted, "No other cigar company has received as many accolades from *Cigar Aficionado* as Padron" [22].

Large numbers of immigrants would come from certain other countries, largely driven by economic factors. From 1960–1986, over 400,000 people would legally immigrate to the United States from the Dominican Republic. By 1990, some 300,000 Dominicans lived in New York City[23]. The Dominican exodus largely began after a pro-democracy movement was suppressed in 1965 with the assistance of American troops. The Dominican immigrants in the next two decades were often fleeing the oppressive right-wing government of Joaquin Balaguer. The Dominican immigrants of these years were also disproportionately educated and politically active. They would launch a host of successful businesses in New York City while enrolling in large numbers in the public university system [24].

Dominican immigrants would succeed in a wide variety of fields. Dominican-born designer Oscar de la Renta would win numerous awards, as has writer Junot Diaz in literature. It is baseball where Dominican immigrants make up a disproportionate percentage of great players. Perhaps the greatest is Albert Pujols. Born in the Dominican Republic in 1980, he moved to the United States at age 16. In his 22 years in major league baseball, he was named the most valuable player three times. At his retirement at the end of 2022, he had become the second player in baseball history to have amassed over seven hundred home runs, over three thousand hits, and 2,200 runs batted in.

Central American immigration largely began in the 1980s, driven by poor governance, instability, and economic conditions. The most important factor was the lengthy, bloody civil wars in El Salvador, Nicaragua, and Guatemala. At the time of the 1986 amnesty law, about 138,000 Salvadorans, 51,000

Guatemalans, and 1,500 Nicaraguans applied for amnesty[25].

The 1980 census showed 94,000 Salvadorans in the nation. By 1990, there were over 700,000. By 2011, there would be 1.2 million, a number equal to 20% of El Salvador's population at that time. A high percentage was from cities, and many had previously worked as migrant workers in Honduras[26].

In Guatemala, the CIA aided the overthrow of the liberal president, Jacobo Arbenz, in 1954, setting the stage for the start of a decades-long civil war. By 1989, some 140,000 Guatemalans had been killed, most at the hands of the army. Others fled, pushing the Guatemalan population in the United States from 71,000 in 1980 to 226,00 in 1990[27]. The Guatemalan immigrants, mainly poorly educated peasants, would enter disproportionately into agriculture.

Nicaraguan immigrants increased from 25,000 in 1980 to 125,000 in 1990. Since they were fleeing a left-wing rather than a right-wing government, almost ten times as many Nicaraguans received refugee status compared to the Salvadorans and Guatemalans[28].

The Central American immigrants would share a strong work ethic. The labor force participation rate of Salvadorans and Guatemalans was among the highest of any ethnic group[29].

Central American immigration has only accelerated in the last three decades.

Yet another civil war, this time in Colombia, would produce another large group of immigrants. Conflict started in 1948. In the nine-year-long civil war, an estimated 200,000 Colombians died. There were only a few years of peace before a new war started between a variety of guerrilla groups and the government. The killings in this 35-year-long civil war were exacerbated by bloody battles between rival drug cartels starting in the 1970s. As a result, over 70,000 Colombians immigrated to the United States in the 1960s, an equal number in the 1970s, and 122,00 in the 1980s. Others arrived on tourist visas and overstayed the allotted time. A high percentage were skilled middle-class workers[30].

Following multiple murders of political figures in Colombia, the government cracked down on the cartels in 1989. The unfortunate side effect was that many criminals hid among the Colombian immigrant communities in the United States. The drug gangs blatantly murdered two of the leading figures among the immigrants, a businessman and a journalist. The solving of one murder and a crackdown on gang leaders would reduce the efforts of the drug lords to terrorize and control the Colombian immigrants[31].

Along with the huge growth in Hispanic immigrants, the biggest change has been the rapidly increasing number of Asian immigrants. 1952–1969 saw some 45,000 Japanese immigrants, 85% women, most married to non-Japanese American veterans. There was a brief uptick in immigration in the 1960s, but the improved economic conditions and lack of major population growth have reduced Japanese immigration, resulting in the dropping of Japanese Americans from the largest Asian community in the United States in 1970 to perhaps the sixth-largest by 2000[32]. Around 1980, the number of Americans of Japanese descent numbered roughly 600,000, with a third in Hawaii, a third in California, and the rest in other states[33].

In contrast, the Chinese American community has grown rapidly. The first surge included many Chinese who had moved to Hong Kong following the Communist takeover in 1949. The 1960s saw a doubling of the Chinese population in the United States, from 237,000 to 435,000[34].

Many immigrants from other Asian communities, such as the Vietnamese, were ethnic Chinese living abroad. While a portion of these immigrants were poor, others have found great success, such as the technology magnate An Wang and the architect I. M. Pei. Two Chinese American women, Maxine Hong Kingston and Jade Snow Wong, have become noted authors[35].

I. M. Pei was born in 1917 In China and grew up in Shanghai. In 1935, Pei immigrated to the United States, where he attended college first at the University of Pennsylvania and then at MIT, from which he received a degree in architecture in 1940. He went on to the Graduate School of Design at Harvard. During WWII, Pei became an expert on fusing bombs as part of the National Defense Research Committee. After the war, Pei returned to Harvard as an assistant professor of design.

In 1948, Pei joined an architectural firm. Pei won increased recognition for his designs, eventually forming his own firm. Pei designed hotels, concert halls, and museums all over the United States and then the world. Among the projects he designed were the John F. Kennedy Presidential Library, the East Building of the National Gallery of Art, the Meyerson Symphony Center in Dallas, and the Louvre Museum in Paris. In 1983, Pei won the Pritzker Prize, the highest honor for architects. Pei passed away in 2019[36].

By 2010, the Census Bureau recorded 3.3 million adult Chinese Americans, making up the largest group of Asians, with three-quarters being foreign-born[37]. Chinese immigration increased rapidly after the 1989 Tiananmen Square massacre. While there is a portion of these immigrants who are poor and unskilled, a high proportion are well-educated professionals, particularly in information technology, engineering, and science. Over half the Chinese immigrants had bachelor's degrees, compared to 28% of the total American population[38].

Since the Philippines were under American rule from 1898 until after WWII, Filipinos began coming to the United States early in the nineteenth century. By 1930, some 100,000 Filipinos had settled in the United States, mainly in Hawaii and California. With the increasing population came an increased backlash. In 1928, the national convention of the American Federation of Labor resolved, "Whereas, there are a sufficient number of Filipinos ready and willing to come to the United States to create a race problem ... we urge exclusion of the Filipino race" [39]. Filipinos remained ineligible for citizenship at that time.

World War II improved the image of the Filipinos, who came to be seen as loyal allies against the Japanese. In 1946, Filipinos were made eligible for citizenship. Far more immigrated than their nominal quota of one hundred. The Filipinos who served in the American armed forces were automatically eligible, along with their families, to immigrate. Post-1965, Filipinos were the largest or second-largest group of immigrants. By 1980, there were an estimated 1.4 million Filipinos in America. A large proportion of recent immigrants have been nurses or employed in other medical fields[40]. Almost half of Filipino immigrants would settle in California, with Hawaii and New York being the next most popular destinations[41]. By 2010, there were 2.55 million Filipino Americans[42]. Filipinos are second only to Mexicans in serving in the American military and are the largest supplier of healthcare staff, such as nurses, from any foreign country[43].

The earliest immigrants from the Indian subcontinent were Sikhs, who found employment on western railroads and lumber mills at the start of the twentieth century. They would face persistent discrimination, being called "Hindoos" or "Ragheads," for the turbans the Sikh religion prescribes. Of the 10,000 early immigrants, perhaps half stayed in the United States[44].

Another seven thousand Indians would come between 1948–65. The most prominent of the early Indian immigrants was Dalip Singh Saund. Shocked by the massacre of a crowd in Amritsar in 1919 by the British Army, he decided to leave India for the United States. There, he added three more degrees to his mathematics degree, including a Ph.D. in mathematics at the University of California at Berkley. He became a rancher and businessman. Soon after becoming a citizen, he was elected to a judgeship. In 1956, Saund was elected to Congress, becoming the first Asian American elected and the first member of Congress who was born in Asia. He would serve three terms before being disabled by a stroke[45].

The 1965 Immigration Act spurred large-scale Indian immigration to the United States. By 1990, there were over 815,000 immigrants from the Indian subcontinent in the nation. The vast majority were well-educated, with many succeeding as professionals or entrepreneurs[46]. Indian American immigrants would contribute a quartet of Nobel Prize winners: Har Gobind Khorana (Medicine, 1968), Subrahmanyan Chandrasekhar (Physics, 1983), Venkatraman Ramakrishnan (Chemistry, 2009) and Abhijit Banerjee (Economics, 2019).

In 2012, some 15% of all startup businesses were founded by Indian immigrants. Eighty-one percent of recent Indian immigrants have a college degree, far higher than the general population. However, there is another group of Indian immigrants, more working-class than those with degrees. It is estimated that Indian Americans, most from the Western Indian state of Gujarat, own half of all motels in the United States[47].

Korean immigration began to accelerate after the Korean War, starting with the brides of US service members. The numbers increased greatly after the 1965 law was passed. By 1990, there were an estimated 800,000 Korean Americans, although this total includes descendants of immigrants, born in the United States. The majority lived in the West and achieved high levels of education[48]. Koreans were notable for their entrepreneurship at this point in the nation's history. In 1982, Koreans, who made up less than 1% of the population in Los Angeles County, owned and operated 5% of retail businesses[49]. The 2010 census showed 1.26 million Korean Americans, of whom 80% were born abroad, while 67% of the total had become US citizens[50].

Los Angeles, which now has the largest concentration of Koreans outside Asia, is a city that has been transformed by immigrants from many nations. While in 1960, only 9% of the people in Los Angeles County had been born abroad, by 1990, the percentage had risen to nearly a third of residents[51].

Two of the most successful Korean immigrants were a

husband and wife, Do Won Chang and Jin Sook Chang, who immigrated to the United States in 1981. In 1984, they opened a clothing store in the largely Korean American neighborhood of Highland Park in Los Angeles. The business, renamed Forever 21, rapidly expanded. By 2013, Forever 21 boasted 480 stores worldwide. In 2020, the couple sold Forever 21 for $81 million[52].

Almost all of the Vietnamese immigration occurred after the Vietnam War. The 1980 census reported 245,000 Vietnamese. A 1985 estimate reported another 218,000 Laotians and 160,000 Cambodians, although other estimates report fewer of these immigrants. Unlike many of the other Asian immigrants, many were from rural areas and not well prepared for life in the United States[53]. Many of the immigrants, particularly from Laos, were ethnic Hmong, largely a rural minority, which had been allied with the United States during the Vietnam War. The Vietnamese settled most often in California. Eventually, some 1.2 million immigrants would come to the United States from Vietnam, Cambodia, and Laos[54].

While many Vietnamese fled immediately after the end of the war, there would be a second wave starting in 1978. In March 1978, the Vietnamese government suddenly abolished all "bourgeois trade" in Ho Chi Minh City, closing small businesses and confiscating their assets. Some 80% of these businesses were owned by ethnic Chinese. Pressed to leave, the Chinese were forced to pay large fees to the government to secure boat transportation out of the country. Half a million people would leave, large numbers of which were taken in by the United States. The hard currency receipts from the refugees, as of June 1978, were estimated at $115 million a year, half of Vietnam's hard currency earnings that year and 2.5% of its GNP[55].

Andrew Ly and his family were "boat people" who would undergo repeated privation before achieving success in America. After fleeing Vietnam in 1978, their boat was raided by pirates who stole all the possessions of those aboard. The Ly family spent the next year in a refugee camp in Malaysia. Then, the Lys came to San Francisco, where the nine members of the family lived in a one-bedroom apartment. In 1984, the family pooled their savings to open a donut shop, the Sugar Bowl Bakery. Andrew Ly, who had trained as an accountant, took charge[56].

The Sugar Bowl Bakery expanded to five more neighborhood bakeries and then eventually became one of the biggest food production companies in the Bay Area. Andrew Ly commented, "We came here as boat people, so we don't take things for granted. Success is a journey, not a destination" [57].

In 2007, the *San Francisco Business Times* named Ly "The Most Admired CEO in the Bay Area." In 2008, Sugar Bowl Bakery sold its retail stores to focus on food production. By 2015, the company had sales of $100 million[58]. Ly retired as CEO in January 2023.

Barone wrote, "Overall, Asian immigration since the 1965 immigration act opened the doors has slowly changed from being a movement of people with low levels of education and high levels of aspiration ... into [a] movement of people with increasingly high levels of education and very high levels of competence, concentrated in the most innovative and high-skill centers of American society" [59].

Few images of immigrants have changed as much of that as Asians. Professor Peter Rose explained, "No longer viewed as kowtowing inferiors ... inscrutable heathens, Mongolians, scabs, or untrustworthy neighbors loyal only to their motherlands, they are now seen by many as members of 'model minorities' ... the pariahs have become paragons, lauded for their ingenuity and industry" [60].

While these stereotypes are not always accurate, there are ways in which different immigrant groups stand out. In 1971, William Petersen reported, "Of all types of crime, delinquency, dependency, or social disorganization about which we have usable statistics, the incidence is lower for Japanese than for any other ethnic group in the American population, including native-born Whites of native-born parents. That remarkable record remains" [61]. Rose noted, "Recently arrived Indians constitute a uniquely high-status group of immigrants. According to several reliable sources, 93 % were already either "professional/technical workers" or "spouses and children of professional/technical workers" when they arrived" [62].

Three other groups contributed large numbers of the new immigrants. Many Jews pushed to leave the Soviet Union. With the initial warming of relations followed by the collapse of the Soviet Union, some 100,000 would immigrate to the United States. The largest concentration of these immigrants would be found in Brooklyn[63].

Another group that came in large numbers was the Irish, many of whom were here illegally, often overstaying their visas. Most of these came after the 1982 amnesty. In 2000, there were an estimated 150,000 illegal Irish immigrants, mainly clustered in the Northeastern corridor from Boston to Philadelphia[64].

A third group of new immigrants were people from sub-Saharan Africa. A mere 130,000 in the 1980 census, their numbers had increased to 691,000 by 2000 and then, after a million more immigrants in the last two decades, up to two million[65].

The list of immigrant success stories goes on and on. Hamdi Ulukaya was born in Turkey, where his family had a dairy farm. After living in the United States for several years, he founded Chobani, a company that produced yogurt. It sold its first yogurt in 2007. By 2021, Chobani sold over 20% of the yogurt in the United States[66].

Lowell Hawthorne had learned baking growing up in Jamaica. He immigrated to the United States in 1981 and, in 1989, with the help of family, launched the Golden Krust chain of bakeries/restaurants. It has grown to over 125 franchises with sales of over $100 million. Sadly, Hawthorne committed suicide in 2017.

Indra Nooyi, almost destitute at the time, immigrated from India and became a very successful CEO of PepsiCo. Shahid Khan arrived in the United States from Pakistan at age 16. He went to work for and eventually bought Flex-N-Gate, one of the largest auto parts suppliers in the nation. He now owns the Jacksonville Jaguars of the NFL and is a billionaire. Khan became an American citizen in 1991[67].

While there is a perception among some that the nation is overrun by immigrants, the percentage of the population born abroad, at least in 2000, remained below the level that existed from the Civil War to 1924. Some seven million immigrants would arrive in the 1980s and close to ten million in the 1990s[68].

Statistics showed the rate of immigrants becoming citizens also increased. This would have increased further except for bureaucratic delays from the Immigration and Naturalization Service[69].

The new immigration would show up in statistics. In 2010, 53% of all foreign-born people in the United States were from Latin America and another 28% from Asia[70].

Despite the successes of immigrants, there was still large opposition to more immigrants in the late twentieth century. Polls consistently showed majorities wanting fewer immigrants[71]. The increased backlash led to the Immigration Reform Act of 1986. The Act contained four major provisions: amnesty for immigrants currently in the country illegally, requirements that employers verify that employees were not in the country illegally, stiff penalties for employers hiring illegal immigrants, and a provision allowing foreign agricultural workers to work on a temporary basis. Some 3.1 million immigrants would receive amnesty. Seventy percent were from Mexico and another 20% from other parts of the Western Hemisphere[72].

However, the Act was less successful in preventing the hiring of illegal immigrants. Moreover, the idea of "controlling the borders" was a near impossibility given the thousands of miles of the United States that border Canada and Mexico.

1 Daniels, 307.

2 Juan Gonzalez. *Harvest of Empire: A History of Latinos in America,* Penguin Books, New York, 2011, 47.

3 Gonzalez, 77.

4 Daniels, 310.

5 Gonzales, 77.

6 Gonzalez, 103.

7 Daniels, 311.

8 Daniels, 311.

9 Daniels. 311.

10 Daniels, 318.

11 Gonzalez, 97.

12 Sowell, 248-9.

13 Sowell, 256.

14 Gonzalez, 81.

15 Sowell, 219-220.

16 Daniels, 373-4.

17 Ungar, 196.

18 Gonzalez, 111.

19 Gonzalez, 112.

20 David Savona. "Death of a Master: Jose Orlando Padron," *Cigar Aficionado,* December 5, 2017.

21 Ungar, 215.

22 Savona.

23 Gonzalez, 117.

24 Gonzalez, 118.

25 Daniels, 382.

26 Gonzalez, 129.

27 Gonzalez, 130.

28 Gonzalez, 129.

29 Gonzalez, 146.

30 Gonzalez, 149.

31 Gonzalez, 162.

32 Daniels, 352-3.

33 Sowell, 177.

34 Sowell, 148.

35 Daniels, 355.

36 Bybee, 37.

37 Lee, 288.

38 Lee, 289.

39 Daniels, 357.

40 Daniels, 359.

41 Barone, 243.

42 Lee, 293.

43 Lee, 294.

44 Ungar, 277.

45 Daniels, 362.

46 Daniels, 362.

47 Lee, 296-7.

48 Daniels, 363.

49 Ivan Light. "Immigrant Entrepreneurs in America: Koreans in Los Angeles," in *Clamor at the Gates*, ed. Nathan Glazer, Institute for Contemporary Studies, San Francisco, 1985, 162.

50 Lee, 299.

51 Daniels, 367.

52 Gunderson, 48-9.

53 Daniels, 368.

54 Lee, 334.

55 Peter I. Rose. "Asian Americans: From Pariahs to Paragons," in *Clamor at the Gates*, ed. Nathan Glazer, Institute for Contemporary Studies, San Francisco, 1985, 182.

56 Gunderson, 53.

57 Gunderson, 54.

58 Dinah Eng. "How A Family of Refugees Turned a Bakery into a Desert Powerhouse," *Fortune*, May 24, 2015.

59 Rose, 193.

60 Rose, 197.

61 Michael S. Teitelbaum. "Forced Migration: The Tragedy of Mass Expulsion," in *Clamor at the Gates*, ed. Nathan Glazer, institute for Contemporary Studies, San Francisco, 1985, 206-8.

62 Barone, 247.

63 Daniels, 385.

64 Daniels, 401.

65 Kane, 223.

66 Michelle Cheng. "How Chobani swallowed 20% of the US yogurt market," *Quartz*, November 19, 2021.

67 Tania Ganguli. "Shahid Khan has true rags to riches American story," *Florida Times-Union*, December 3, 2011.

68 Daniels, 409.

69 Daniels, 430.

70 Lee, 286.

71 Daniels, 438.

72 Daniels, 393.

Isaac Bashevis Singer

Salman Rushdie

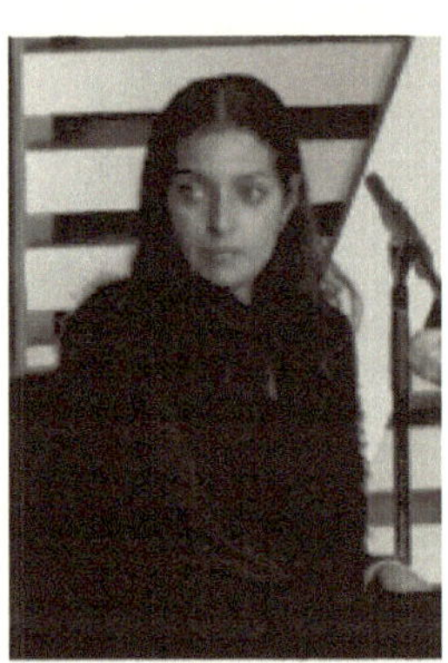

Jhumpa Lahiri

CHAPTER 18

The Writers

The United States has been impossibly enriched by the writings of immigrants. With a list that would require a book of its own, I will just mention a few names.

O.E. Rolvaag was born in Norway in 1876 and immigrated to the United States in 1896. He would attend and then teach at St. Olaf's College in Minnesota. His book *Giants in the Earth* tells the story of a Norwegian immigrant family in the Dakota Territory.

Vladimir Nabokov was born in Russia in 1899. He lived for over a decade in Germany but made his way to the United States in the 1940s, fleeing the Nazi invasion of France. He became a US citizen in 1845. His books *Lolita* and *Pale Fire* are considered two of the greatest novels of the twentieth century. The *Christian Science Monitor* commented, "The list of authors influenced by Nabokov's work is longer than one of his books" [1].

W. H. Auden was born in 1907 in England. At the time he immigrated to the United States in 1939, he was considered "the most famous living English poet" [2]. Auden became an American citizen in 1946.

Christopher Isherwood, born in England, immigrated to America on the same ship as Auden. Isherwood became a successful author, playwright, and screenwriter.

Ayn Rand was born in Russia in 1905 and immigrated to the United States in 1926. Her books *The Fountainhead* and

Atlas Shrugged sold over thirty million copies. She developed a philosophy that she called Objectivism that has served as an inspiration for libertarians.

Isaac Bashevis Singer was born in Poland in 1904. He immigrated to the United States in 1935. After writing for the Yiddish newspaper *The Forward,* he began writing fiction in Yiddish, which he then translated into English. Singer won the Nobel Prize for Literature in 1978.

Thomas Mann was born in 1875 in Germany. His books won him the Nobel Prize in Literature in 1929. He left Germany upon the rise of the Nazis. He arrived in the United States in 1939 and became a citizen in 1945. When he was invited to post-war Germany, he wrote back, "Today I am an American citizen, and long before Germany's frightful defeat, I publicly and privately declared that I had no intention of ever again turning my back on America" [3].

Czeslaw Milosz, born in Poland in 1911, served in the Polish resistance against the Germans and went into exile after Soviet control of his country began. He moved to the United States in 1960, taking a job teaching at Berkley. His poetry won him the Nobel Prize in Literature in 1980.

Isaac Asimov was born in Russia in 1920. His family moved to the United States in 1923. During WWII, he worked at the Philadelphia Navy Yard with L. Sprague de Camp and Robert Heinlein. All three became famed writers of science fiction. Asimov would write or edit over five hundred books in his lifetime, most famously in science fiction but also in many other fields. He died in 1992.

Denise Levertov was born in England in 1923 but moved to the United States in 1948 after marrying an American. She became a US citizen in 1955. She won the Lannan Award for poetry. She would publish 24 books of poetry.

Eli Wiesel was born in Romania in 1928. During WWII, he survived the Auschwitz and Buchenwald concentration camps. He moved to the United States in 1955. He wrote for over 40 years, particularly about the Holocaust, and campaigned for human rights. In 1986, he was awarded the Nobel Peace Prize, with the Award noting, "Wiesel is a messenger to mankind. His message is one of peace, atonement, and human dignity" [4].

Art Spiegelman was born in Sweden in 1948 to Polish Jewish parents. They moved to the United States in 1951. He began writing comics that culminated in his serial comic about the Holocaust, *Maus*. Critics noted that "*Maus* became one of the first comic books ever studied seriously as literature," winning Spiegelman a special Pulitzer Prize in 1992[5].

Jhumpa Lahiri was born to Indian parents in England in 1967. The family moved to the United States three years later. Lahiri has written multiple award-winning books. Her work *The Interpreter of Maladies* won the Pulitzer Prize for Fiction.

Ha Jin was born in China in 1956. He was studying in the United States when the Tiananmen Square massacre convinced him to stay in America. His novel *Waiting* won a National Book Award. He noted that he was disliked by the Chinese government, stating, "I came to America. I don't serve the party's cause. To them, I'm a very negative example" [6].

Khaled Hosseini was born in Afghanistan in 1965. Following the 1980 Soviet invasion, his family sought asylum in the United States. Hosseini became an American citizen and a physician. He practiced for ten years before his bestselling novel *The Kite Runner* was published in 2003.

Azar Nafisi was born In Iran in 1948. She was a professor of literature before she fled the oppression of the theocratic government to immigrate to the United States in 1997. *The New York Times* said of her book *Reading Lolita in Tehran*, "Resonant and deeply affecting ... an eloquent brief on the transformative power of fiction" [7].

Christina Garcia was born in 1958, one year before her family fled Cuba for the United States. She became a successful journalist. Her book *Dreaming in Cuban* was published in 1992.

Joseph Brodsky was born in the Soviet Union in 1940. His

poetry was accused of being anti-Soviet. At a 1964 trial, the judge sneered, "Who has enrolled you in the ranks of poets?" to which Brodsky answered, "No one. Who enrolled me in the human race?" [8]. Brodsky was expelled from the Soviet Union in 1972. He immigrated to America. Brodsky won the Nobel Prize in Literature for his poetry in 1987 and was named Poet Laureate of the United States in 1991.

Colum McCann was born in Ireland in 1965 but decided to immigrate to the United States in 1986. He has written multiple books. His book *Let the Great World Spin* won the National Book Award in 2009.

Jamaica Kinkaid was born in Antigua in 1949. In 1966, she came to the United States to work as an au pair. She started taking evening classes at a community college at the same time. She has been a teacher, journalist, and author. In 2022, the Paris Review awarded her its lifetime achievement award.

Salman Rushdie was born in India in 1947. He moved to Britain. He would win the Booker Prize in 1981 for his book *Midnight's Children*. In 1988, Iran claimed that his book *The Satanic Verses* was blasphemous and offered to pay for his assassination. After a number of years in hiding, Rushdie moved to the United States in 2000 and became a citizen in 2016. He continues his prolific writing and is thought to be a strong candidate for the Nobel Prize in Literature.

Abraham Verghese was born in 1955 in Ethiopia to Indian parents. The family moved to the United States after a military coup. Verghese had started medical training in Ethiopia but would complete it in India and the United States. He is now a professor of medicine at Stanford. He has written two memoirs and two novels so far, including his bestselling novel *Cutting for Stone.*

Junot Diaz was born in the Dominican Republic in 1968. His family moved to America when he was six. His book *The Brief Wondrous Life of Oscar Wao* won the 2008 Pulitzer Prize in Fiction. In 2015, a poll of American book critics declared the book the "21st century's best novel so far" [9].

Kiran Desai was born in India in 1971 and later moved to the United States. She was the youngest woman to win the Booker Prize, which she did in 2006 for her work *The Inheritance of Loss*.

Li-Young Lee was born in Indonesia in 1957 to Chinese parents. The family immigrated to the United States in 1964. He has won multiple awards for his poetry.

In looking at these writers and others, we see a variety of human experiences. Some writers were already famous for their writing before they came to the United States, while others started writing in the United States. Some grew up here from childhood, while others were already middle-aged upon arrival.

Other immigrants became journalists. News anchors Robert McNeill at PBS and Peter Jennings at ABC were both born in Canada. So were Morley Safer and David Brooks. Jorge Ramos, long-time news anchor at Univision, was born in Mexico. Fareed Zakaria was born in 1964 in India. He has excelled in both print and television journalism, as well as authoring multiple books.

What is indisputable is that American literature and journalism are much richer as a result of immigrants' contributions.

---

1 Ben Frederick. "10 Influential Authors Who Came to the US as Immigrants," *Christian Science Monitor*, March 29, 2013.

2 Ilan Stavans, ed. *Becoming Americans: Four Centuries of Immigrant Writing*, Library Classics, New York, 2009, 302.

3 Thomas Mann. In *Becoming Americans: Four Centuries of Immigrant Writing*, ed. Ilan Stavans, 338-9.

4 Joseph Berger. "Elie Wiesel, Auschwitz Survivor and Nobel Peace Prize Winner, Dies at 87," *The New York Times*, July 2, 2016.

5 Frederick.

6 Sarah Fay. "Ha Jin, The Art of Fiction No. 202," *The Paris Review*, Issue 191, Winter, 2009.

7 Michiko Kakutani. "Books of the Times: Book Study as Insubordination Under the Mullahs,"

8 *The New York Times*, April 15, 2003.

9 Robert Dennis McFadden. "Joseph Brodsky, Exiled Poet Who Won Nobel, Dies at 55," *The New York Times*, January 29, 1996.

10 Allison Flood. "The Brief Wondrous Life of Oscar Wao was declared the 21st century's best novel so far," *The Guardian*, January 20, 2015.

John von Neumann

Andy Grove and colleagues at Intel

CHAPTER 19

The Information Revolution

The invention of the computer, the Internet, and all the other features of the new digital age have changed America. As with almost everything else, immigrants have contributed to the development and use of the new technology.

Perhaps the first contribution came from Kurt Godel. Godel was born in a Czech portion of the Austrian Empire in 1906. In 1924, he moved to Vienna to attend the famous University of Vienna. He changed from an early interest in physics to mathematics. Five years later, he received his doctorate. At age 24, he provided answers to two key questions about the systems of mathematics that would prove important in the design of computers. Godel's "incompleteness theorem" demonstrated that there were statements that could be neither proved nor disproved[1]. Godel's analysis would have other important implications.

Bhattacharya wrote, "In 1930, Godel had written a computer program long before any machine capable of running it would exist. He had dissolved in one fell swoop the rigid distinction between syntax and data. He had shown that it is possible to devise a rigorous system in which logical statements [that were very much like computer commands] could be rendered as numbers" [2].

The rise of Nazism and fascism led Godel, who was not

Jewish, to decide to immigrate to America. Godel wrote a friend, American mathematician Oswald Veblen, saying, "The situation at the university [of Vienna] is as unpleasant as possible. While I don't believe that Austria has more than 45% Nazis, the percentage at the university is certainly 75%" [3]. Godel took a position at the newly formed Princeton's Institute for Advanced Study alongside two other immigrants, Albert Einstein and John von Neumann.

Godel would be recognized as one of the century's leading logicians, or developers of logical thinking. His close friend Einstein called him "the greatest logician since Aristotle" [4].

Against anti-Semitic warnings about too many foreign mathematicians, the Institute's founder, Abraham Flexner, wrote, "I will undertake to get a position within a reasonable time for any really first-rate American mathematician, and I will also undertake to do the same for any first-rate foreign mathematician whom Hitler may dismiss. The more the merrier" [5].

Godel, along with his brilliance, began to display evidence of obsessive-compulsive disorder and paranoid mental illness in the late 1930s, leading to hospitalization for four months in early 1936. He had returned to Austria to marry when Germany annexed the country. It was thanks to John von Neumann, who wrote, "Godel is absolutely irreplaceable ... Salvaging him from the wreck of Europe is one of the greatest single contributions anyone could make," that Godel received a rare visa that allowed him to return to Princeton in 1940[6].

Godel would continue working on mathematical ideas for the next thirty years. However, the death of Einstein and other of his closest friends over the years contributed to his worsening mental health. With his own physical health deteriorating, the last straw was when his wife was hospitalized and had to go to a nursing home. Godel stopped eating and essentially starved to death. Biographer Stephen Budiansky wrote, "Godel's public renown continued to grow after his death ... the general idea that there are truths that cannot be proved had an irresistible appeal" [7].

The next contributor was John von Neumann. Born in Hungary, von Neumann was recognized in childhood as brilliant. Edward Teller commented, "If a mentally superhuman race ever develops, its members will resemble Johnny von Neumann" [8]. Von Neumann left Hungary in 1919 after a brief interval in which the Communists seized power. He studied chemistry and mathematics in Zurich, Berlin, and Budapest, earning a doctorate at age 23. In 1930, he moved to the United States, taking a position at Princeton, teaching quantum physics.

After moving to the Institute for Advanced Study, von Neumann developed ways to model shock waves mathematically. Von Neumann thus became part of the Manhattan Project in 1943, where he also focused on developing an explosive lens to generate a plutonium implosion. This development would require the solution of a host of equations to calculate the effect of the atomic bomb[9].

Von Neumann studied George Stibitz's Complex Number Calculator, an early form of computer, and Howard Aiken's Mark I, another stage in the development of computers that used electromechanical relays to transfer information. Von Neumann found that the Mark I was so slow that his atomic bomb calculations would take months. Historian Walter Isaacson wrote, "Von Neumann became convinced that the only solution was to build a computer that worked at electronic speeds and could store and modify programs in an internal memory" [10].

It is here that the logical analyses of Godel and British mathematician Alan Turing would play a role in the development of the computer. Bhattacharya wrote, "The formalisms of the two logicians would help von Neumann crystallize the structure of the modern computer" [11].

By chance, von Neumann met, on a train, a member of the team developing the ENIAC computer at the University of Pennsylvania. ENIAC could solve a differential equation in a fraction of the time of the Mark I, but each new question required slow, laborious reprogramming. Von Neumann helped develop a set of instruction codes that were part of storing the programs in the same computer as the data. ENIAC team member Jean Jennings commented, "The thing von Neumann had, which I noticed that other geniuses have, is the ability to pick out, in a particular problem, the one crucial thing that is important" [12].

Von Neumann would summarize the developments in a letter to a colleague, who distributed it as "First Draft of a Report on the EDVAC by John von Neumann." Von Neumann described for the first time the structure of a stored-program computer, consisting of five components: a central arithmetic unit for performing mathematical operations, a central control unit to ensure that instructions were done in the proper order, a memory unit that would store both computer code and numbers, and input and output units to transfer information into and out of the machine [13].

Von Neumann believed in the free dissemination of knowledge, but the document aggravated members of the ENIAC team who had hoped to patent some of the new developments [14]. Von Neumann later wrote, "I certainly intend to do my part to keep as much of this field 'in the public domain' [from the patent point of view] as I can" [15]. Isaacson wrote that the "Draft Report" would guide the development of subsequent computers for at least a decade" [16].

Von Neumann pushed back on criticisms of computer development by Princeton colleagues, arguing, "I think it is soberly true to say that the existence of such a computer would open up to mathematicians, physicians, and other scholars areas of knowledge in the same remarkable way that the two-hundred-inch telescope promises to bring under observation universes which are at present entirely outside the range of any instrument now existing" [17].

Von Neumann continued his work on computer development at Princeton but left there in 1952 to join the Atomic

Energy Commission. He would return to Princeton to work on the development of artificial intelligence shortly before his death in 1957. Von Neumann would die of bone and pancreatic cancer, which may have been related to radiation exposure from nuclear testing[18].

The next immigrant to play a key role was Andy Grove. Born Andras Grof to a Jewish family in Hungary, he was eight when the Nazis took over. While his father was sent to a concentration camp, he and his mother assumed false identities. Reunited with his family after the war, he would leave Hungary when the Russians crushed the Hungarian revolt against Communism in 1956. He wrote in his memoirs, "By the time I was twenty, I had lived through a Hungarian Fascist dictatorship, German military occupation, the Nazi's Final Solution, the siege of Budapest by the Soviet Red Army, a period of chaotic democracy in the years immediately after the war, a variety of repressive Communist governments, and a popular uprising that was put down at gunpoint" [19].

Grove arrived in the United States in 1957. He taught himself English and then graduated first in his class at City College of New York. *The New York Times* noted, "A Hungarian refugee who three years ago didn't know horizontal from vertical—in English, today [is] at the head of the class of engineering students" [20]. After getting a Ph. D in chemical engineering at Berkley, he joined Fairchild Semiconductor. Journalist David Kaplan wrote that Grove "was to earn the reputation that would follow him for the next thirty-five years: aggressive, disciplined, tactless, unyielding, combustible—and gifted at getting things done" [21].

When Gordon Moore and Robert Noyce left to found Intel, Grove came along as the director of engineering. The three would share the management of Intel, with Grove bringing in toughness in management. Personnel director Ann Bowers, who married Noyce, said, "Andy was the guy who made sure the trains all ran on time" [22].

Journalist Michael Malone, in his book *The Intel Trinity*, wrote, "Without Grove, Intel would probably have grown into a middling company, famed for its innovative products, but not much more ... With Grove, Intel beat or destroyed them all" [23].

Intel pioneered the microprocessor, essentially a computer on a chip, which would be used in hundreds of devices, most notably the personal computer. Isaacson wrote, "The microprocessor spawned hundreds of new companies making hardware and software for personal computers" [24]. Malone noted that after Intel introduced its microprocessor in March 1974, "Intel had taken market leadership. And over the next forty years as the microprocessor became the 'brains' of thousands of products throughout scores of major industries and against seemingly endless challenges from the cleverest competitors, Intel would never give up that leadership" [25].

After 1975, when Intel, for the first time, had to lay off many employees due to financial losses, Andy Grove became chief operating officer at Intel. By the end of the decade, Noyce had retired as chairman of the board, and Gordon Moore had left most of the decision-making to Grove. Malone wrote, "For Intel, and by extension the world economy, the eighties and nineties belonged to Andy Grove. And happily, Grove would prove to be the greatest businessman of the age" [26].

Along the way, Grove would write textbooks on engineering and management and his bestselling book on business, *Only the Paranoid Survive*. In 1997, Grove was named *Times* Man of the Year. In 1998, Grove retired as CEO of Intel. Two years later, he was diagnosed with Parkinson's disease. Andy Grove would die in 2016.

The advent of microchips and personal computers brought the need for accompanying software. The stories of Bill Gates and Steve Jobs in this regard are well known. Less well-known is the role of Linus Torvalds.

Torvalds was born in and grew up in Finland. He became

interested in computers as a child when his grandfather bought him one of the first personal computers. Torvalds graduated from the University of Helsinki with a master's in computer science in 1996. Several years earlier, he had wanted to install the program UNIX on his home computer, but it was too expensive. Torvalds bought an abbreviated copy of UNIX called MINIX that had been used for teaching purposes. He set out to rewrite and expand it in 1991. By the fall of 1991, he had a basic system that he called Linux. Rather than marketing it, he offered it free to the public. He explained, "I suppose I would have approached it differently if I had not been raised in Finland, where anyone exhibiting the slightest sign of greediness is viewed with suspicion, if not envy. And yes, I undoubtedly would have approached the whole no-money thing a lot differently if I had not been brought up under the influence of a diehard academic grandfather and a diehard communist father" [27].

Torvalds correctly surmised that having operators around the world have the code for free would lead to them improving it in a collaborative effort. Within a year after its release, the Linux user group would have thousands of members.

In 1997, Torvalds took a job in California, where he worked for the next six years. In 2003, Torvalds and his family moved to Oregon to be near the Open Source Development Labs. As part of this group, which later became the Linux Foundation, Torvalds continued to work on developing open-source, i.e., freely shared, software. Torvalds became an American citizen in 2010.

The tens of thousands of Linux users would add continual improvements. Torvalds commented, "Money is not the greatest of motivators. Folks do their best work when they are driven by passion ... Hackers are also motivated, in large part, by the esteem they gain in the eyes of their peers by making solid contributions" [28].

Others recognized what had happened. Open-software theorist Eric S. Raymond concluded, "Who would have thought that a world-class operating system could coalesce as if by magic out of part-time hacking by several thousand developers scattered all over the planet, connected only by the tenuous strands of the Internet?" [29].

"High tech" would become the nation's fastest-growing economic sector in the last quarter of the twentieth century. Playing a key role in the formation of many new technology companies was another immigrant.

Eugene Kleiner was born in Vienna, Austria, in 1923. His family fled in 1938 with the Nazi takeover, settling in New York City in 1940. He got a degree in mechanical engineering at Polytechnic University of New York and a master's in industrial engineering at NYU. He left Western Electric in 1956 to work for William Shockley. Kleiner was one of the "traitorous eight," along with Robert Noyce and Gordon Moore, who left the harsh working conditions under Shockley to found Fairchild Semiconductor. After six years at Fairchild, during which he ran a host of departments, Kleiner opened his own tech company, Edex. He sold that company to Raytheon for $5 million. Kleiner decided to get in the business of helping new companies develop, commenting, "I liked the work. It was fun being involved in starting companies—the variety, not being tied down to a job that would become routine" [30].

In 1972, he joined with engineer-businessman Tom Perkins to found Kleiner and Perkins (KP). Now Kleiner Perkins Caulfield and Byers, the firm would raise some $1.4 billion in capital from 1972–1999 and fund more than three hundred companies. By 1997, these companies were worth $125 billion, a number that would grow much larger as time went on[31]. One of the first successes was Genentech, which pioneered the commercial use of gene-splicing. In 1980, KP's initial $200,000 investment in Genentech would be worth $160 million[32]. In the 1980s, KP helped fund Sun, Compaq Computers, Symantec, Quantum, Cypress Semiconductor, and Lotus. KP would go on to fund Amazon, AOL, Google, and Netscape.

Kleiner would be known for his pithy guidelines for KP investments, such as, "When the money's available, take it," and "There is a time when panic is the correct response," which meant to get out of bad deals quickly[33]. Kleiner gave up most responsibilities at the firm by the end of the 1980s. He passed away in 2003.

The development of the Internet led to further developments in the software revolution. In January 1994, there were only seven hundred websites in the world. By the end of the year, there were 10,000, and by the end of 1995, 100,000[34]. The number would continue to proliferate. A new problem arose, which was how to navigate through the thousands of sites to find relevant information and connections.

In the spring of 1994, two Stanford graduate students, Jerry Yang and David Filo, created a directory of their favorite websites originally called "Jerry's Fast Track to Mosaic," later renamed "Jerry and David's Guide to the World Wide Web." Jerry Yang was born in 1968 in Taiwan. His family moved to San Jose, California, when he was ten. He got a bachelor's and master's in electrical engineering from Stanford. In 1989, he met a fellow student, David Filo. The two would spend six months in an exchange program in Japan in 1992, where Yang met his future wife.

As their directory grew, the pair renamed it Yahoo! They created a search engine to help users find the sites they were looking for. By late 1994, Yahoo! had passed 100,000 "page views" a day. In 1995, there would be a million, and by 1998, 167 million daily views[35]. In 1995, Yahoo! received venture capital funding, with its business model predicated on the selling of ads on the site. Thirteen months later, Yahoo! made an initial stock offering that went for unheard-of amounts of money, making Yang and Filo millionaires. Yahoo added a free e-mail service and pushed its brand and image. Despite relatively modest revenues ($50 million in 1998), the market valued Yahoo! at $44 billion in January 1999[36].

Yahoo!'s value would plummet when the dot-com bubble burst. Jerry Yang would remain a billionaire. He stayed at Yahoo! through 2012, serving as CEO in 2007–9. Subsequently, he started his own venture capital firm. He has been a major philanthropist, giving tens of millions to Stanford and to the Asian Art Museum of San Francisco.

The advent of the Internet saw two other men meet at graduate school at Stanford and create another world-changing company. Larry Page was the son of a computer science professor at the University of Michigan. At an orientation program, Page met a second-year student named Sergey Brin.

Brin was born in Moscow, where his parents were mathematicians. As Jews, his parents' careers would face strong obstacles of prejudice. Then, when his father applied to emigrate, both of his parents lost their jobs. In 1979, when Sergey was five, the family received exit visas. They moved to the United States.

Brin graduated from high school in three years and from the University of Maryland at age 19 with degrees in computer science and math. Brin and Page became friends and intellectual partners. The outgoing Brin complimented the more reserved Page. For his dissertation project, Page wanted to assess the importance of different sites based on the number of links to the site. His scheme involved following all the links on all the sites. Brin joined him on the project, later noting, "This was the most exciting project, both because it tackled the Web, which represents human knowledge, and because I like Larry" [37].

First, the pair developed a web "crawler" named Backrub to explore sites. They also created an algorithm named PageRank to analyze the links and rank web pages based on their connections. Whereas prior search engines had listed sites based on keywords, the new design was able to prioritize the most important sites. Meanwhile, the World Wide Web continued to expand at an astonishing rate. The number of sites would triple in size from 1996 to 1997[38].

By 1998, Page and Brin's database included some 518 million hyperlinks. As they were both still in graduate school, they decided to sell the database and finish their degrees. They tried to market the concept to other tech companies, who were not interested in paying for it, concluding, as Page remembered, "Search is not that important" [39]. The big search engines instead wanted to bring users to their sites and keep them there with a variety of features, allowing them to sell more ads to bring in revenue.

Brin and Page decided to start their own company, which they named Google. They quickly incorporated and were able to raise money from venture capitalists. After they received the first investment of $100,000, the pair went out to Burger King to celebrate.

The Google World Headquarters started in the garage of Susan Wojcicki, from whom Brin and Page also rented two bedrooms for a total of $1,700 in monthly rent. What Google was doing became more and more known, being named by *PC Magazine* in December 1998 as one of the one hundred best websites. Google's mission statement explains its goal, "To organize the world's information and make it universally accessible and useful" [40].

The number of daily searches on Google rose from 100,000 a day in early 1999 to over 500,000 by the end of the year. Two years after its founding, Google became the number one search engine in the world, handling fifteen million daily searches by the end of 2000[41].

To bring in revenue, Google sold ads that were targeted to the subject of searches. In 2002, Google made a profit of $100 million[42].

Isaacson wrote, "Google became the culmination of a sixty-year process to create a world in which humans, computers, and networks were intimately linked. Anyone could share with people anywhere and ... enquire within upon everything" [43].

The success of Google made both Page and Brin billionaires. They continued to innovate new products, from Google Translate, which allows people to understand other languages, to Google Earth, allowing people to visualize places anywhere in the world.

In 2005, three friends built a website where people could upload videos and share them with others. They called it YouTube. Two of the three were immigrants. Born in 1978, Steve Chen immigrated to the United States with his family at age eight. After school, he took a job at PayPal, which helped people buy and sell things online. There, he met Chad Hurley and Jawed Karim. Karim was born in East Germany in 1979. His family immigrated to the United States when he was 13. After college, he took a job at PayPal, where he met Hurley and Chen. YouTube became available to the public in a test form in May 2005. The site became so popular that the trio could sell it to Google the next year for $1.65 billion[44].

Jan Koum grew up in the Ukraine. At age 16, his family immigrated to the United States. Koum worked for Yahoo! for nine years, then quit traveling. He realized that messaging friends around the world required hefty international texting fees. Koum and his partner Brian Acton produced an app to allow texting without these fees, which the pair named WhatsApp. Within two years, WhatsApp was in the top twenty of US apps. Three years later, Koum sold WhatsApp to Facebook for $19 billion[45].

Not everyone in information technology is an immigrant, but it is astonishing how many immigrants have made and are making amazing contributions.

---

1 Walter Isaacson. *The Innovators: How a Group of Hackers, Geniuses and Geeks Created the Digital Revolution*, Simon and Schuster, New York, 2014, 43.

2 Bhattacharya, 115-6.

3 Stephen Budiansky. *Journey to the Edge of Reason*, W.W. Norton and Company, New York, 2021, 144.

4 Budiansky, 1.

5 Budiansky, 156.

6 Budiansky, 201.

7 Budiansky, 277.

8 Isaacson, *Innovators*, 102.

9 Isaacson, *Innovators*, 104.

10 Isaacson, *Innovators*, 105.

11 Bhattacharya, 111.

12 Bhattacharya, 123.

13 Isaacson, *Innovators*, 107.

14 Isaacson, *Innovators*, 111.

15 Bhattacharya, 127.

16 Isaacson, *Innovators*, 111.

17 Bhattacharya, 129-130.

18 Isaacson, *Innovators*, 105.

19 Andrew Grove. *Swimming Across*, Grand Central, 2001, 2.

20 David A. Kaplan. *The Silicon Boys and Their Valley of Dreams*, William Morrow and Company, New York, 1999, 63.

21 Kaplan, 63.

22 Isaacson, *Innovators*, 195.

23 Michael S. Malone. *The Intel Trinity*, HarperCollins Publishers, New York, 2014, 115-6.

24 Isaacson, *Innovators*, 198.

25 Malone, 195.

26 Malone, 289.

27 Isaacson, *Innovators*, 377.

28 Isaacson, *Innovators*, 378.

29 Eric S. Raymond. *The Cathedral and the Bazaar*, O'Reilly Media, 1999.

30 Kaplan, 167.

31 Kaplan, 157.

32 Kaplan, 179.

33 Kaplan, 176.

34 Isaacson, *Innovators*, 446.

35 Kaplan, 307.

36 Kaplan, 318.

37 Isaacson, *Innovators*, 458.

38 Anna Crowley Redding. *Google It: A History of Google*, Feiwel and Friends, New York, 2018, 32.

39 Isaacson, *Innovators*, 462.

40 Crowley, 53.

41 Crowley, 72.

42 Crowley, 97.

43 Isaacson, *Innovators*, 465.

44 Gunderson, 9-10.

45 Gunderson, 17.

Immigrants Becoming US Citizens

March Supporting Immigration and America

CHAPTER 20

Immigration: Escaping the Demographic Trap

The most advanced nations in the world share a major demographic problem. In Europe, Russia, China, Japan, and others, the number of children born is not keeping pace with deaths. The inevitable result will be a declining and aging population in each of these nations.

The fertility rate in the United States has fallen as well, leading to an aging population. The median age among White Americans rose from 34.0 years in 1992 to 41.1 in 2008[1]. Yet the American population, almost unique among developed nations, has continued to grow. The difference is immigration.

Economist Vernon Briggs noted, "Though the 1970s and early 1980s, the United States has legally admitted twice as many immigrants and refugees for permanent settlement as the remaining nations of the world combined" [2]. More than fifty years ago, in 1981, demographer Leon Bovier observed, "Immigration now appears to be almost as important as fertility insofar as US population growth is concerned" [3]. Subsequently, as the fertility rate fell in the United States, our population increase was increasingly due to immigration.

For example, *The Wall Street Journal* reported in 2019 that the share of US population growth attributable to immigrants was 48%, up from 35% at the start of the decade[4]. The article noted that the fertility rate for American women ages 15–44 had fallen to 60.2 births per thousand women in 2017, the lowest since such measurements started being recorded over one hundred years earlier. Economist Aparna Mathur commented, "We have a situation where U.S. fertility rates are really low and we're not actively adding to the workforce through natural increase. We cannot afford to talk about immigrants as bad for the U.S. economy" [5].

The impact of the Covid pandemic helped make 2021 the year with the slowest population growth in US history[6]. Both birth rates and immigration fell, leaving population growth at a rate of .1%. Contrary to some accepted wisdom, the largest portion of the foreign-born were in the middle-age range, with 20% of those 40–64 having been born overseas. More than two-thirds of immigrants had been in the United States for over a decade[7].

The New York Times noted that the slowdown in immigration had contributed to the shortage of workers. Pia Orrenius, an economist at the Federal Reserve Bank of Dallas, commented, "The pandemic offers a little taste of what we may be facing if demand is robust and we don't have workers" [8]. Other economists commented that if immigration had continued at a pre-pandemic pace, the economy would have had two million additional foreign-born workers[9].

In the last half a century, the new immigrants have overwhelmingly been from Asia and Latin America. It is likely that the percentage from Asia may fall in the future as many, although not all, Asian nations face aging and declining populations.

In contrast, while population growth has slowed in Latin America, the economic problems have not disappeared. The population of Latin America and the Caribbean increased from 167 million in 1950 to 556 million in 2005. Yet economic growth has not kept pace. In the "lost decade" of the 1980s, the region's per capita gross national product (GNP) declined[10].

Many nations in Latin America increasingly depend on

the money sent home by their citizens working in the United States. As much as 20% of the gross domestic product (GDP) for several Central American nations is supplied by remittances from workers in the United States. Since incomes remain so much higher in the United States than in most of Latin America, there is likely to be a continued flow of workers to the north.

Meanwhile, even in the absence of civil wars, the harsh economic conditions and endemic violence in many Latin American countries act as a continued motivation for people to immigrate to the United States.

The new immigrants differ from some other immigrants. For many years, most, although not all, Mexican immigrants were single male workers who sought employment and, in many cases, would eventually return to their home villages. In contrast, the Central American immigrants are predominantly made up of entire families[11].

Contrary to those who argue that we are overrun with immigrants, the number of immigrants admitted each year per one thousand Americans from 1983–92 was 3.7. This is far less than the 11.1 immigrants admitted each year per one thousand Americans from 1904–14[12]. The immigrant percentage of the population is certainly not more than in the past.

In time, the number of immigrants from Central America may join that of other historical sources of immigrants in declining. The last sixty years have seen a large drop in the fertility rate, the number of live births per woman, even in the poorest countries in the region. In Honduras, the rate dropped from 7.5 in 1960 to 2.5 in 2018; in El Salvador, it went from 6.7 to 2.0 in the same period[13]. A fertility rate of 2.1 is considered necessary to keep a population stable in the absence of immigration.

We need to return to the general link between population and national power. Economist Tim Kane wrote, "For most of human history, population was synonymous with power"[14].

Over time, and especially after the Industrial Revolution, a nation's level of technology became another crucial factor in its strength. A sense of national purpose is another key factor. Yet the importance of population cannot be overstated.

Historians generally agree that the decreasing population was a major factor in the decline of the Roman Empire. Drops in population due to famine or war would weaken other nations throughout history. Thus, the size of the American population is important.

Even while much of America's influence comes from culture and wealth, a dropping population would certainly weaken the nation. Kane postulated an alternative history in which anti-immigrant sentiment cut immigration in half after 1820 (the start of accurate data on immigration in the United States). Instead of a population of 331 million in 2020, there would be 242 million. If there had been no immigration after 1820, our population would have been 146 million[15].

Under this second scenario, the United States in 1940 would have been smaller than Nazi Germany, with a commensurate smaller economy. The outcome of WWII might have been vastly different.

Alternatively, if restrictions on immigration of Asians starting in the 1880s and of Southern and Eastern Europeans in the 1920s had not occurred, our current population might be 453 million, with an economy 40–50% large[16]. It is hard to argue that this would have had no impact. Even if this had occurred, the population density in the United States would still be far below that of most developed nations.

It is worth considering what might have happened if the United States had banned large-scale immigration after gaining independence. We easily might be a divided nation following the South's victory in the Civil War or a subject nation following the German victory in WWII.

It is quite likely that we would have never had the Erie Canal or the transcontinental railroad. We would not have been the first nation to have the atomic bomb or land a man on the moon. Our science would be middling. The lack of labor would have prevented the American economy from becoming the largest in the world. We would not have Hollywood, and it is unlikely that our culture would have such influence around the world. Much of what we consider American food, from hamburgers to pizza to bagels to tacos, would not exist here. A host of American presidents, from Eisenhower to Biden, would not have been elected if their ancestors had not migrated here.

We would be a respectable power, given our natural resources and size, but not a superpower, perhaps more resembling Australia, another nation formed by British immigrants that differed from us in largely restricting immigration until very recently.

For many years, immigration has been frowned upon by those worrying about overpopulation.

There has been a gradually abating worry about overpopulation potentially resulting in corrective starvation. Such Malthusian prophecies have proved incorrect except in occasional nations where a combination of war, poor government, and a poor harvest has resulted in widespread suffering.

There would be those who argue that American power, starting after WWII, has not been an unmixed blessing. Our hubris led us into costly conflicts in Vietnam and Iraq. The role of American corporations abroad, particularly in Latin America, has often been very destructive and reinforced the social and political problems of many smaller nations.

However, I would argue that American influence has also resulted in a better world. The repetitive European wars of so many centuries have been nearly non-existent in recent years. Our example, admittedly flawed at times, has encouraged the spread of democracy. The rules-based world order that America established after WWII has resulted in a general drop in violence and poverty compared to the years before.

I think few would believe the world would have been better

off if it were instead dominated by a few dictator-run nations.

The United States, with all its myriad problems, still looms as the favored destination of the world. A 2018 poll found that 15% of the world's population wanted to migrate. The preferred destination of one of five of them, some 158 million people, is the United States. No other location comes close[17].

Joseph Nye, former dean of the Kennedy School of Government, made a compelling case that a nation's influence is also based on its "soft power," its ability to get the outcomes it desires without force or money but simply by persuasion. Among America's sources of soft power is the central role of immigration. Nye, noting that the United States has attracted six times as many immigrants as the next most desired destination, argued that this appeal has secondary benefits[18]. Nye wrote, "Several characteristics of the United States make it a center of globalization. America has always been a land of immigration, and its culture and multiethnic society reflect many different parts of the world. America has borrowed freely from a variety of traditions, and immigration keeps it open to the rest of the world"[19].

America's "soft power" retains its attraction even after the 9/11 attacks brought forth more suspicion of foreigners. Nye concluded, "People want to come to America, and they often do well here ... Foreigners can envisage themselves as Americans, and many successful Americans 'look like' them. Moreover, connections of individuals in the diasporas, such as the Indian and Chinese, with their countries of origin help to convey accurate and positive information about the United States"[20].

Ironically, our soft power helps increase our attraction to immigrants. Ungar noted, "We sell our country hard—through Hollywood movies, television programs, music, clothing styles, soft drinks, and fast food that we export ... every day, we send out the message, none too subtly, that anyone in the world in his or her right mind would want to live in America. It is hardly surprising, then, that so many people seek to come" [21].

Those opposed to immigration often postulate that the new immigrants will not fit in. Tamar Jacoby wrote, "Today, as before in our history when the immigrant tide was rising, nativists peddle a frightening array of grim scenarios: balkanization, civil strife, economic ruin, and worse. Very few of these nightmare scenarios are based in fact, and all are unlikely. Indeed ... the nation is steadily absorbing millions of newcomers: people of all ages and backgrounds, who are finding work, learning English, making their way through school and up into more comfortable circumstances than they knew at home" [22].

Americans sometimes go from believing that we are the greatest country to the belief that we are a fatally flawed society. Immigrants belie the latter belief. Ungar wrote, "America still feels like the most open place on earth, where anything is possible. It is more than ever a magnet for those who seek to improve themselves economically" [23].

Our success in incorporating immigrants is the exception, not the norm. Political scientist Peter Salins noted, "One of the most important things that sets the United States apart from other nations in the post-Cold War era is its unique success as a multiethnic society ... the United States has forged one of the world's most unified and prosperous societies from a blend of peoples differing sharply in national ancestry, language, race, and religion" [24]. Salins explained the reasons for this success, stating, "From the very beginning, the Founders proposed to resolve the potential problems created by ethnic diversity by decisively repudiating both repression and ethnic federalism. Instead, the American model is grounded not only in a conception of individual liberty but also in constitutional protections and a fundamental respect for individual achievement rather than group membership" [25].

As an aside, those stressing group identity ignore how much this has led to ethnic and religious conflict in so much of the world. Tamar Jacoby wrote, "American identity leaves ample room for all kinds of ethnicity: for communal enclaves and all that goes on there. What it does not do—or did not do in the past—was allow those divisions to play any official role in the public life of the nation as a whole" [26].

Some argued that the racial differences of the new immigrants when compared to the White majority would make the assimilation of immigrants much harder. The evidence instead suggests that "the new immigrants are not only assimilating but are doing so at an even faster rate than did earlier immigrants from Europe" [27].

Salins noted that in contrast to many societies, "Americans never asked immigrants to shed their distinctive ethnic, cultural or religious identities ... Americans have been remarkably indifferent to the surface trapping of cultural assimilation ... Immigrants were expected only to abide by the basic tenets of an unspoken assimilation contract: allegiance to the nation's democratic principles, respect for individualism and hard work, and—yes—willingness to learn English and use it outside their homes ... Sealing the immigration contract, America has always made it easy for immigrants to become citizens ... Even today, a majority of nations give immigrants only residency privileges, not full citizenship—if they allow immigration at all" [28].

The above principles hold for both legal and illegal immigrants, although the latter are blocked from achieving citizenship.

Writer Gary Shteyngart, who immigrated to the United States in 1979, wrote, "Our nation's success is built squarely on its continued ability to compete favorably with the other industrialized democracies for the labor pool of talented immigrants ... Immigrants have helped make America the world's leading economy, while America has offered them an escape from some of the world's most stifling plutocracies and theocracies" [29].

"Illegal" immigrants contribute greatly to the American economy. Most have a fervent desire to become Americans. Journalist Jose Antonio Vargas won a Pulitzer Prize while at *The Washington Post*, but later, in 2011, admitted that he was an undocumented immigrant. Testifying before the Senate in 2013, Vargas said, "I come to you as one of our country's 11 million undocumented immigrants, many of us Americans at heart, but without the right papers to show for it ... We dream of contributing to the country we call our home" [30].

Moreover, our efforts to stop illegal immigration have been dismal failures. Writing in *The New York Times*, Marcela Valdes noted, "The three most recent presidents have tried and failed to fix the problem of mass unauthorized migration into the United States ... Unauthorized migration, for all the obstacles America throws at it, remains a boon for US employers and a reasonable bet for migrants in search of a better life" [31].

Ironically, the difficulty of being able to immigrate legally has greatly contributed to illegal immigration. David J. Bier, Associate Director of Immigration Studies at the Cato Institute, observing that only 3% of people who try to immigrate were able to do so legally, commented, "Legal immigration is less like waiting in line and more like winning the lottery. It happens, but it is so rare that it is irrational to expect it in any individual case" [32]. Valdes concluded, "Illegal immigration is the natural consequence of the conflict between America's thirst for foreign labor and its strict immigration laws" [33].

Sowell noted that each group of immigrants had, over time, risen economically both in absolute terms and relative to the rest of the American population. Sowell remarked, "Progress is so generally taken for granted in the United States that it is necessary to realize that it is not automatic. In many parts of the world, people still live at economic levels not much above their ancestors ... There are wide variations in the rates of progress among American ethnic groups, but progress itself is pervasive" [34].

Far from too many immigrants, evidence suggests that we

are letting in too few. Bier wrote, "America desperately needs immigrants. Population growth is the lowest in American history. We have averaged nearly ten million job openings over the last two years. Our worker-to-retiree ratio continues to fall. We need more workers, taxpayers, and contributors. The president should embrace—not stop—immigration" [35].

Legal immigration is hampered both by immigration law restrictions and bureaucratic delays. In the spring of 2023, the US Citizenship and Immigration Services, the agency that handles the requests, had a backlog of 8.9 million pending applications[36]. The process is hampered by inadequate staff and archaic processes. On the legal side, the number of legal immigrants has not been raised while the economy has doubled. The requirement that no more than 7% of the visas go to citizens of any nation has also hampered immigration, particularly from India.

One hopeful note is a US population growth of 1.6 million in 2023, two-thirds of it attributable to immigration along with a decreased death rate from Covid. *The Washington Post* reported, "Without immigration, the US population is projected to decline as deaths are forecast to outnumber births by the late 2030s" [37].

Immigrant and journalist Fareed Zakaria summed it up well: "The United States has one crucial advantage over Europe and most of the developed world. The United States is demographically vibrant, with a growing population [powered by immigration]" [38]. Zakaria concludes, "For advanced industrial countries which are already comfortable, satisfied, and less prone to work hard—bad demographics are a killer disease" [39].

Immigration is one of the key factors of American strength and success.

---

1 Gonzalez, 223.

2 Vernon M. Briggs, Jr. "Employment Trends and Contemporary Immigration Policy," in *Clamor at the Gates*, ed. Nathan Glazer, Institute for Contemporary Studies, San Francisco, 1985, 135.

3 Briggs, 136.

4 Janet Adamy and Paul Overberg. "Immigration's impact on Nation Grows—U.S. is relying more on newcomers who now propel population gains in 10% of countries, *The Wall Street Journal*, April 18, 2019.

5 Adamy.

6 Miriam Jordan and Bobert Gebeloff. "Amid Slowdown, Immigration is Driving U.S. Population Growth," *The New York Times*, February 2, 2022.

7 Jordan.

8 Jordan.

9 Jordan.

10 Tim Kane. *The Immigrant Superpower: How Brains, Brawn and Bravery Make America Stronger*, Oxford University Press, New York, 2022, 134.

11 Kane, 38.

12 Ungar, 100.

13 Kane, 134.

14 Kane, 124.

15 Kane, 128.

16 Kane, 130.

17 Kane, 136.

18 Joseph S. Nye, Jr. *Soft Power: The Means to Success in World Politics*, Public Affairs, New York, 2004, 33.

19 Nye, 41.

20 Nye, 58.

21 Ungar, 366-7.

22 Tamar Jacoby. *Reinventing the Melting Pot: The New Immigrants and What it Means to be American*, Basic Books, New York, 2004, 8.

23 Ungar, 23.

24 Peter D. Salins. In *Reinventing the Melting Pot: The New Immigrants and What it Means to be American*, ed. Tamar Jacoby, Basic Books, New York, 2004, 99.

25 Salins, 100.

26 Jacoby, 311.

27 Stephen Steinberg. In *Reinventing the Melting Pot: The New Immigrants and What it Means to Be American*, ed. Tamar Jacoby, Basic Books, New York, 2004, 240.

28 Salins, 102.

29 Gary Shteyngart. In *Reinventing the Melting Pot: The New Immigrants and What it Means to Be American*, ed. Tamar Jacoby, Basic Books, New York, 2004, 290-1.

30 Lee, 399.

31 Marcela Valdes. "Why Can't We Stop Unauthorized Immigration? Because it Works," *The New York Times*, October 1, 2023.

32 Valdes.

33 Valdes.

34 Sowell, 275.

35 David J. Bier. "Biden Can't Stop Immigration. Time to embrace It," *The New York Times*, November 3, 2023.

36 Lisa Rein. "A Broken Immigration System Keeps Workers Out of Jobs the US Needs to Fill," *The Washington Post*, December 21, 2023.

37 Mike Schneider. "Immigration Fuels Uptick in US Population Growth," *The Washington Post*, December 19, 2023.

38 Fareed Zakaria. *The Post-American World*. W.W. Norton and Company, New York, 2008, 196.

39 Zakaria, 198.

Immigrant US Navy Sailors Becoming Citizens

Italian Immigrant Michael Valente receiving the Congressional Medal of Honor

CHAPTER 21

Immigration: Making America Great

This book has attempted to chronicle the role and contributions of immigrants to the United States. This final chapter will attempt to assess the overall impact of immigration.

There are multiple ways in which immigration has improved our nation and made it stronger.

As outlined in the prior chapter, the United States would have been far weaker and perhaps not even a superpower were it not for the economic and military strength of the increased population. Most nations' populations have increased through an excess of births over deaths. This was, in fact, the major factor in population growth in colonial times and the first decades of the United States. While this natural increase always played a role in our population growth, the impact of immigration was far more important to the United States than all but a handful of countries.

Second, immigration has contributed to the wealth and prosperity of the United States. Kane argued, "Being a nation of immigrants is a fundamental cause of the extraordinary prosperity and military power for the United States" [1]. Kane noted that the facts of the United States being the richest nation in the world and the one that annually accepts the greatest number of new immigrants are very much related.

One little-known fact is the role of immigrants in the

military. Earlier sections discussed immigrants' roles in the American Revolution and in the Civil War. Immigrants volunteer for the military to a greater degree than native-born Americans in times of war, and relative to the size of the population, immigrants have won twice as many Congressional Medals of Honor, the military's highest honor, than native-born Americans[2]. Of the 1,522 Medals of Honor given in the Civil War, 369 went to immigrants, a proportion far higher than the immigrants' proportion of the population[3].

One of the arguments against immigration prior to WWI was the canard that they would not fight for the nation in times of war. In *The Passing of the Great Race*, Madison Grant wrote, "When the test of actual battle comes, it will, of course, be the native-born (White) American who will do the fighting and suffer the losses"[4].

In fact, some 800,000 immigrants from 46 different nations would fight in the American military during WW1.

Immigrants made up 18% of the American forces while comprising only 14% of the total US population[5].

The ratio of Jewish soldiers in combat units has far exceeded their proportion of the overall population. One of the most famous was Samuel Dreben, who won the nickname the "Fighting Jew."

Drebben had immigrated to the United States at age 20 in 1898 and, six months later, enlisted in the US Army. He served for many years, but soon after retiring, he reenlisted as a private at age 40 to be able to fight in WW1. Dreben was soon promoted to first sergeant of his regiment, won the Distinguished Service Cross for his leadership in battle, and was invited by General Pershing, the commander of the American forces in France, to be his guest at headquarters. Pershing announced that Dreben was "the finest soldier and one of the bravest men I ever knew"[6]. When Drebben encountered Grand Duke Nikolai Nikolaevich, former commander in chief of the Russian army, in a Paris restaurant, Drebben punched him in the nose to protest years of anti-Jewish pogroms. Returning home to El Paso, Drebben had one more battle to fight. When the Klu Klux Klan tried to take over the local American Legion post in El Paso, Drebben proposed a resolution barring Klansman from holding leadership positions. The resolution passed. Drebben died in 1925 at age 47 as a result of a medical error[7].

Another immigrant soldier was born in Slovakia. Matej Kocak arrived in the United States in 1906. He enlisted in the Marines in 1907 and reenlisted in 2015. Kocak would fight in all the major battles of American troops in the war. On July 18, 1918, Kocak single-handedly took out two German machine gun positions. He later would be awarded the nation's highest award, the Congressional Medal of Honor, for this feat. On October 4, 1918, Kocak would be one of 292 Marines killed in the attack at Blanc Mont[8].

Michele Valente, from a small village in Southern Italy, had arrived in the United States in 1914. Three years later, Valente enlisted in the New York National Guard. Valente was a soldier in the 27th Infantry Division when his unit attacked the fortified Hindenburg Line in September 1918. When his company was pinned down by machine gun fire, Valente and his buddy Joseph Mastine attacked the German machine guns on their own initiative. Before the fight was over, Valente had taken two machine gun nests, killed at least five Germans, and captured 21. Wounded during the fight, Valente was evacuated to a hospital in the rear. Valente later commented, "Of course I should have asked permission of my commanding officer to do the job. I was crazy then[9].

Eleven years later, Valente was awarded the Congressional Medal of Honor by President Hoover. Valente said, "I did not forget, while the president of the republic was conferring the Congressional Medal, that he had decorated an American of Italian origin. [I'm] proud of these origins, happy that through him honor can come to the entire mass of Italians who immigrated here, of which I am a humble part" [10]. Valente died in

1976 at age 80. Italian Americans would total 10% of American casualties in WWI despite being only 4% of the population[11].

Bhagat Singh Thind was the first soldier in the US Army to wear a turban. Born in India in 1892, he arrived in the United States at age 21. While a college student, he joined the US Army in WWI in July 1918. He earned a promotion to sergeant. Thind was granted US citizenship on December 9, 1918, only to have it revoked four days later since he was not a White man. He applied again and won citizenship in 1919, only to have it be taken away again. Thind took his case to the Supreme Court, which ruled against Thind in 1923 since, as an Asian, he was not eligible for citizenship[12].

Meanwhile, Thind earned a Ph.D. in theology and literature from the University of California at Berkley. He remained in the United States, writing and lecturing. Finally, in 1936, he gained US citizenship through a New York law granting it to WWI veterans regardless of race. Thind authored many books, principally on religion. He passed away in 1967[13].

The number of immigrants fighting in the American Army may have been a factor in persuading Congress to pass a law in May 1918 that granted immediate citizenship to American immigrant soldiers.

The cutoff of immigration in 1924 meant that immigrants played a smaller, but not absent, role in WWII, the Korean War, and the Vietnam War.

Macario Garcia was born in Mexico in 1920. His family moved to the United States in 1923. In 1942, Garcia, a farmworker, was drafted. He won a Purple Heart during the landing in Normandy. By November 1944, he was leading his squad when they were pinned down by German machine guns. Although wounded, Garcia went on ahead to destroy two machine gun positions and capture four prisoners. His company commander called him the best soldier in the army. In August 1945, Garcia was awarded the Congressional Medal Of Honor. One month later, he was denied service at a Texas restaurant as a Mexican. He was beaten with a baseball bat and then arrested. The resulting outcry led to the dismissal of the charges. Garcia became a citizen in 1947 and died in a car crash in 1972[14].

Another immigrant arrived in the United States in 1938 at the age of fifteen with his family fleeing the Nazi regime in Germany. Five years later, he was drafted, serving in the American forces in Europe. His German fluency led to a transfer to counterintelligence and a promotion to sergeant. Less than thirty years later, Henry Kissinger became first National Security Adviser and then became Secretary of State. He was a controversial co-winner of the Nobel Peace Prize.

The relaxation of immigration restrictions in 1965 resulted in some 760,000 immigrants enlisting in the armed forces and becoming American citizens. Of these, 100,000 have served since the 9/11 attack[15]. As of 2011, 5% of the troops serving in the American armed forces were born overseas. A spokesman for the Department of Homeland Security said that the foreign-born soldiers "identify with the ideals of the United States, and they are willing to fight and protect these ideals, even before they've secured all the liberties of citizenship" [16].

Another canard about immigrants is that they contribute to crime. A literature review instead found that "immigrants are less likely to commit serious crimes or be behind bars than the native-born, and high rates of immigration are associated with lower rates of violent crime and property crime" [17]. Kane wrote, "Half as many young immigrant males are incarcerated than young native-born males ... if you only consider young males ages 19–39 with a low level of education, native[-born people] are three or four times more likely to be in jail" [18].

As earlier chapters demonstrate, immigrants have made major contributions to American science. Since WWII, America has dominated the Nobel Prize awards in science. This dominance is increasing. In 2014, four of the nine American Nobel Prize laureates were immigrants; in 2016, it was six of seven[19].

The National Foundation for American Policy reported that "between 1901 and 1959, [American] immigrants won 21 Nobel Prizes in Chemistry, Medicine, and Physics but won 84 Prizes in these fields—four times as many—between 1960 and 2019" [20].

Foreign students are studying in large numbers at American universities. Some 20% of all students studying abroad are in the United States. Two-thirds of all foreign graduate students are in the United States, while foreigners account for some 50% of Ph.D. candidates in America in the fields of science, technology, engineering, and math (STEM)[21].

Historically, many of these students stay in the United States as immigrants following their education. One study reported that of students receiving a science or technology Ph.D. in 2002 in the United States, some 92% of the Chinese and 81% of the Indians were still in the United States in 2007[22].

Immigrant and journalist Fareed Zakaria noted, "America's edge in innovation is overwhelmingly a product of immigration. Foreign students and immigrants account for 50% of the science researchers in the country" [23].

Foreign nations have made progress in efforts to lure graduates back home, but the bigger problem are the obstacles the United States throws up to prevent these students from staying. Writing in *The New York Times* in 2022, Allison and Schmidt noted that "the current backlog of green cards—which entitles their holders to permanent residency and unrestricted work—is well over million for highly skilled immigrants," with the process taking an average of six years[24].

The United States cannot assume that it will always have a technological edge. Each year, China produces four times as many students with undergraduate degrees and twice as many graduate students in STEM when compared to the United States. Chinese leader Xi Jinping said in 2021, "Technological innovation has become the main battleground of the global playing field" [25].

The main hope of competing for the United States lies

in attracting immigrants. Allison and Schmidt wrote, "China's great weakness is its spectacular inability to attract talent from other countries ... China naturalizes fewer than 100 citizens each year while the United States naturalizes nearly 1 million people annually" [26].

Zakaria concluded, "America's potential new burst of productivity, its edge in nanotechnology, biotechnology, its ability to invent the future—all rest on its immigration policies. If America can keep the people it educates in the country, the innovation will happen here. If they go back home, the innovation will travel with them" [27].

Immigrants also play an outsized role in business entrepreneurship. Immigrants make up 13% of the population but start 30% of new companies. Half of Silicon Valley startups were founded or co-founded by immigrants[28]. Since 2000, half of all US unicorns—startups valued at $1 billion or more—have been founded or co-founded by immigrants[29]. Ivan Light, remarking on immigrants' willingness to take the risk of starting a new business, noted, "Koreans are not the only entrepreneurially inclined new immigrants. Immigrants have been more frequently self-employed than native[-born] Whites in every decennial census since 1880" [30].

Recent immigration has accentuated this difference. Light noted, "With the exception of Mexican and some Latin American immigrants, the general level of socioeconomic status among new immigrants surpasses that of the American common man ... US immigration laws have awarded priority to ... persons prepared to invest in a business they own and manage. When unable to find suitable employment in the general labor market, educated immigrants have the motive and resources to start their own small business enterprises" [31].

A National Academy of Sciences study reported that as of 2012, 53% of immigrants had at least some college, with 16% having a further graduate education[32].

Historically, besides bigotry, one of the strongest arguments against immigration is its purported effect on jobs and wages. Professor George Borjas, an expert on immigration and labor economics, wrote that immigration depressed "the economic opportunities faced by the least skilled workers" [33]. He noted that an increased supply of workers in a field would lower the wages employers would need to pay.

At times, surveys have shown that at least half of Americans believe that undocumented immigrants are taking jobs from Americans[34]. Yet the reality is that many of these are low-income jobs few Americans want, such as picking fruit. Indeed, statistics showed that 80% of American farmhands are foreign-born. On the other hand, 26% of patents are held by foreign-born. Jacoby suggests that current immigrants are clustered at the bottom and the top of the job ladder, reflecting their level of education before they immigrated[35].

Yet, the overall economy benefits, and there is no decrease in the average worker's wages due to the growth of the economy. Kane noted that states with the fastest immigration growth also experienced the fastest growth in gross domestic product (GDP)[36]. Economist Gregory de Freitas noted, "The question always seems to be phrased in terms of immigrants taking jobs away from Americans, when lots of Americans have jobs because of the impact of immigrants on the economy" [37].

Chiswick found that "At the aggregate level, income of native-born households rises as a result of an immigration inflow" [38]. Thomas Muller commented, "The argument is seldom, if ever, made that the millions of native-born Americans who moved from northern industrial states to the South and West during the 1970s took jobs from the native-born residents of these regions ... From an economic perspective, however, one can expect the local private sector to be stimulated by population growth that results in a productive labor force, regardless of its origin" [39].

Another canard about immigrants is their cost to society and government. First, data shows that immigrants are healthier overall. A 2009 study found, "Immigrants' per-person unadjusted medical expenditures were approximately one-half to two-thirds as high as expenditures for the US-born ... Recent immigrants were responsible for only about 1% of public medical expenditures even though they constituted 5% of the population" [40].

Immigrants also contribute significantly more to the government than they cost. Even legal immigrants cannot participate in food stamps or Medicaid for at least five years and not in Social Security until they work for at least ten years. Undocumented immigrants, who are not eligible for any of these programs, still contribute billions of dollars in taxes[41]. Economist Julian Simon showed that while "illegal immigrants" almost never receive Social Security, 77% pay Social Security taxes and 73% have federal income tax withheld from their paychecks[42].

Kane reported that a 2016 study showed that the average existing immigrant in the United States would add $58,000 more in taxes than they would cost in services, while the average new immigrant would add $259,000 more in revenues than they would cost[43].

A Harvard Medical School study showed that immigrants generated surpluses in the Medicare hospital trust fund of $115 billion dollars from 2002–9, while the American-born population incurred a deficit of $28 billion in the same period[44]. Leah Zallman, the lead author, commented that this result "pokes a hole in the widespread assumption that immigrants drain health care spending dollars" [45].

A parallel analysis was made for Social Security. Stephen C. Gross, the chief actuary of the Social Security Administration, estimated that immigrants in 2010 generated a surplus of $12 billion for the Social Security Trust Fund[46].

While immigrants generate money for Federal programs, they can be an added cost for state and local governments who pay for schools. Another report concluded that immigrants help the financing of the federal government but don't pay enough state and local taxes to cover the cost of services at this level of government. Study author Stephen Moore commented, "The problem is that most of the taxes go to Washington, D.C." [47].

Immigrant children, on the other hand, do well in American schools. A ten-year study in San Diego and Miami "found that whatever country they come from, across the board, immigrant children work harder than their native-born classmates ... they aspire to greater achievement, get better grades and drop out fare less often—between a third and half as often" [48].

A later study by the National Academy of Sciences concluded that immigration could burden local governments, particularly for the costs of schools. The study concluded that over an extended period, the fiscal impacts of immigrants "are generally positive at the federal level and negative at the state and local levels" [49]. The obvious solution would be for the federal government to share some of the extra revenues with state and local governments.

Thus, while immigrants can have a negative economic impact on particular individuals and perhaps on particular individual local governments, on the whole, they are a tremendously positive economic factor. The issue, then, is one of distribution. Those hurt could be compensated while still leaving a substantial surplus.

Overall, the National Academy concluded, "Immigration enlarges the economy while leaving the native[-born] population slightly better off on average ... The prospects for long-run economic growth in the United States would be considerably dimmed without the contributions of high-skilled immigrants" [50].

Another anti-immigrant slur is that immigrants come here to get on welfare. The reality is that the nation could use more of the immigrant work ethic.

Simon's data showed that "immigrants work harder than native[-born people], save more of what they earn and are more inclined to start small businesses ... they are less likely than the general population to commit crimes or be unemployed" [51].

Immigrants are also more likely to work than native-born. Briggs wrote, "It seems certain that the labor force participation rate of all immigrants since 1965 is considerably higher than that of the labor force as a whole" [52].

Jacoby noted, "While most brand-new arrivals make less than the native-born, by the time they have been in the United States for ten or fifteen years, they are usually making more ... by the time they have been in the country for fifteen to twenty years, immigrants are also less likely than the native-born to be living in poverty" [53]. By the time immigrants have been here for 25 years, significantly more own their homes compared to the native-born [54].

Those complaining about inflation and immigration fail to realize that immigrant labor reduces prices for Americans. A 2015 Texas A&M study of the dairy industry found that if immigrant labor were eliminated, the retail prices of milk would nearly double [55]. Indeed, the resumption of immigration following the Covid epidemic has contributed to a reduction in price inflation.

Another slur on immigrants is that they won't learn English. Jacoby answered, "True, the first generation often had trouble with English. This was true in 1900, and it's true today ... what really matters is the second generation; the linguistic future lies with those who come of age in the United States. And the fact is ... virtually everyone who grows up in America today eventually learns English. This is true for every national group and at every socioeconomic level, and it happens no matter what language your parents or grandparents speak at home" [56].

A study showed that while 72% of foreign-born Hispanics spoke Spanish as their main language, by the second generation, this fell to 7% and by the third generation to zero [57].

Immigrants are also often more positive about the United States. A poll of immigrants asked if they would still come if they could decide again. Eighty percent said yes, while a similar 80% said that the United States is a "unique country" that "stands for something special in the world" [58].

Stanford Ungar concluded, "Immigration is still an extraordinary positive feature of American life-immigrants invariably contribute at least as much as they take; they help the United States maintain its place as an international leader by changing, evolving, and adapting" [59].

The contributions of immigrants are, if anything, becoming greater over time. Two of America's great tech companies, Microsoft and Google, currently have CEOs who are immigrants. Elon Musk, an immigrant from South Africa, essentially started the electric car industry and the private space industry in the United States. Dr. Katalin Kariko, a Hungarian immigrant, shared the 2023 Nobel Prize in Medicine with her colleague Dr. Drew Weissman for their work with m-RNA that made the vaccines against Covid possible.

Yet anti-immigrant hysteria has not abated. *The New York Times* reported that, if elected in 2024, Trump "plans to scour the country for unauthorized immigrants and deport people by the millions per year ... millions of undocumented immigrants would be barred from the country or uprooted from it years or even decades after settling here ... Numerous people who have been allowed to live in this country temporarily for humanitarian reasons would also lose that status" [60].

It is hard to imagine actions that would be more damaging for the United States than this. Let's leave out the heartlessness of it. For such mass deportations would tarnish the reputation of the United States, dealing a tremendous blow to our "soft power." Second, the insanity of doing this at a time of nearly the lowest unemployment in the last 50 years is hard to believe. When businesses have trouble finding workers today, eliminating hundreds of thousands of workers by deporting them would be catastrophic for the economy. There is not a huge mass of Americans willing to work in nursing homes, hospitals, and farms that would take the place of the deported immigrants. Third, such an action will be devastating in the cost of lost revenues for the government and reduced workers to contribute to Social Security and Medicare. Fourth, this action when American birth rates are below replacement would put us in the same demographic trap that leads to a decline as seen in Europe and Japan. No Russian or Iranian agent could hope to do as much damage to the United States as this plan would do.

Rational thought would realize how much immigrants have contributed and are still contributing to the United States throughout our history. A rational strategy would be to raise the level of legal immigration. Illegal immigration, after all, is a construct of the last hundred years, for previously, the United States would welcome almost anyone who sought a new life here. In addition, the federal government could institute a revenue-sharing program to distribute some of the increased federal largesse to those state and local governments that have increased costs as a result of immigration.

Moreover, despite how many billions we spend, it will be impossible to eliminate illegal immigration no matter how many walls we build. At least half of illegal immigrants come to the country legally but then overstay their legal time[61].

As long as jobs are plentiful in the United States for wages that far exceed those in the immigrants' country of origin, people will try to come here. It makes more sense to take advantage of the gift of the additional labor and brainpower that we gain from immigration rather than spending billions trying unsuccessfully to close off our borders.

Zakaria notably pointed out, "Immigration also gives America a quality rare for a rich country—hunger and energy. As countries become wealthy, the drive to move up and succeed weakens. But America has found a way to keep itself constantly revitalized by streams of people who are looking to make a new life in a new world" [62].

The recent improvement in the economy owes much to the recent increase in immigration. Congressional Budget Office Director Phil Swagel recently wrote that as a result of these immigration-driven revisions to the size of the labor force, "we estimate that, from 2023–2024, GDP will be greater by about $7 trillion and revenues will be greater by about $1 trillion than they would have been otherwise" [63].

Federal Reserve Chairman Jerome Powell commented, "The US economy has benefited from immigration. And frankly, just in the last year, a big part of the labor market coming back into better balance is immigration returning to levels that were more typical of the pre-pandemic era" [64].

Immigration is crucial to who we are. Our welcome mat is one of the best parts of us. George Washington said, "The bosom of America is open to receive not only the opulent and respectable stranger, but the oppressed and persecuted of all nations and religions, whom we shall welcome to a participation of all our rights and privileges" [65].

Thus, from purely a question of humanity, extending a welcome to immigrants is an honorable decision. Yet even thinking from a purely selfish position, immigrants are a great gift to the United States, more than hope expected or national merit deserved.

Immigrants benefit rather than hurt the nation. Immigrants have helped make America great, contributing immensely to the success of the United States throughout our history. Indeed, they are not our curse but our salvation.

---

1 Kane, 7.

2 Kane, 11.

3 Kane, 141.

4 Kane, 143.

5 Kane, 143.

6 Kane, 145.

7 Laskin, 334-336.

8 Laskin, 280.

9 Laskin, 267.

10 Laskin, 326.

11 Sowell, 129.

12 Bybee, 11.

13 Bybee, 11.

14 Mike Glenn. "Medal of Honor Recipient wasn't always Celebrated," *Houston Chronicle*, August 9, 2016.

15 Kane, 147.

16 Laskin, xxi.

17 Kane, 23.

18 Kane, 23.

19 Kane, 165.

20 National Foundation for American Policy. "Immigrants and Nobel Prizes 1901–2019," NFAP Policy Brief, October 2019.

21 Ben Wildavsky. *The Great Brain Race: How the Global Universities are Reshaping the World*, Princeton University Press, Princeton, NJ, 2011, 15.

22 Kane, 168.

23 Zakaria, 198.

24 Graham Allison and Eric Schmidt, "The United States Needs Million Talents Program to Retain Technology Leadership," *The New York Times*, July 16, 2022.

25 Allison.

26 Allison.

27 Zakaria, 198.

28 Kane, 170.

29 Allison.

30 Light, 168.

31 Light, 175.

32 Jeffrey Sparshott. "Immigration Study Sees More Pros than Cons." *Wall Street Journal*, September 23, 2016.

33 George Borjas. *Heaven's Door*, Princeton University Press, Princeton, NJ, 1999, 11.

34 Thomas Muller. "Economic effects of Immigration," in *Clamor at the Gates*, ed. Nathan Glazer, Institute for Contemporary Studies, San Francisco, 1985, 111.

35 Jacoby, 18.

36 Kane, 195.

37 Ungar, 367.

38 Muller, 112.

39 Muller, 122-123.

40 Leighton Ku. "Health Insurance Coverage and Medical Expenditures of Immigrants and Native-Born Citizens in the United States," *American Journal of Public Health*, 2009; 99(7), 1322-8.

41 United States Congressional Budget Office. "The Impact of Unauthorized Immigrants on the Budgets of State and Local Governments," December 2007.

42 Ungar, 96.

43 Kane, 201.

44 Sabrina Tavernise. "For Medicare, Immigrants Offer Surplus, Study Finds," *The New York Times*, May 20, 2013.

45 Tavernise.

46 Tavernise.

47 Karen Brandon. "Foreign-Born Help US Economy, Immigration Groups Study Says," *Chicago Tribune*, July 8, 1998.

48 Jacoby, 22.

49 Sparshott.

50 Sparshott.

51 Ungar, 96.

52 Briggs, 146.

53 Jacoby, 20.

54 Jacoby, 24.

55 Ungar, 24.

56 Valdes.

57 Jacoby, 23.

58 Stephen Thernstrom. In *Reinventing the Melting Pot: The New Immigrants and What It Means to Be American*, ed. Tamar Jacoby, Basic Books, 2004, 58.

59 Jacoby, 27.

60 Charlie Savage, Maggie Haberman, and Jonathan Swan. "Sweeping Raids, Giant Camps and Mass Deportations: Inside Trump's 2025 Immigration Plans," *The New York Times*, November 12, 2023.

61 Ungar, 369.

62 Zakaria, 198-9.

63 Catherine Rampell. "The surge in immigration is a $7 trillion gift to the economy," *The Washington Post*, February 13, 2024.

64 Rampell.

65 Kennedy, 51.

BIBLIOGRAPHY

Ackroyd, Peter. *Alfred Hitchcock*. Doubleday, New York, 2015.

Adamy, Janet and Paul Overberg. "Immigration's Impact on Nation Grows—U.S. is relying more on newcomers who no propel population gains in 10% of counties." *Wall Street Journal*, New York, April 18, 2019.

Alden, John Richard. *The American Revolution*. Harper Torch books, New York, NY, 1954.

Allison, Graham, and Eric Schmidt. "The United States Needs a Million Talents Program to Retain Technology Leadership," *The New York Times*, July 16, 2022.

Asimov, Isaac. *The Golden Door: The United States from 1865–1918*, Houghton Mifflin, Boston, 1977.

Atkinson, Rick. *The British Are Coming*. Henry Holt and Company. New York, 2019.

Bailey, Helen Miller. *Forty American Biographies*. California State Series, Sacramento, 1967.

Baker, Kevin. *America The Ingenious: How a Nation of Dreamers, Immigrants and Tinkerers Changed the World*. Workman Publishing Company, New York, 2016.

Barber, James G. *A Short History of the Civil War*. Smithsonian, Smithsonian-Penguin Random House, London, 2020.

Barone, Michael. *Shaping Our Nation: How Surges of Migration Transformed America and Its Politics*. Crown Forum, New York, 2013.

Beard, Annie E. S. *Our Foreign-Born Citizens*. Thomas Y. Crowell Company, New York, 1955.

Berger, Joseph. "Elie Wiesel, Auschwitz Survivor and Nobel Peace Prize Winner, Dies at 87," *The New York Times*, July 2, 2016.

Bhattacharya, Ananyo. *The Man from the Future: The Visionary Life of John von Neumann.* W.W. Norton and Company, New York, 2021.

Bier, David J. "Biden Can't Stop Immigration. Time to Embrace It," *The New York Times,* November 3, 2023.

Bigelow, John. *Retrospections on an Active Life, 1817–63.* Baker and Taylor, New York, 1909.

Birmingham, Stephen. *Our Crowd: The Great Jewish* Families *of New York.* Dell, New York, 1967.

Borjas, George. *Heaven's Door.* Princeton University Press, Princeton, NJ, 1999.

Brandon, Karen. "Foreign-Born Help US Economy, Immigration Groups Study Says," *Chicago Tribune.* July 8, 1998.

Briggs, Vernon M., Jr. "Employment Trends and Contemporary Immigration Policy," in *Clamor at the Gates,* ed. Nathan Glazer, Institute for Contemporary Studies, San Francisco, 1985.

Budiansky, Stephen. *Journey to the Edge of Reason.* W.W. Norton and Company, New York, 2021.

Burns, James MacGregor. *The Vineyard of Liberty.* Random House, New York, 1982.

Bybee, Veeda and Victo Ngai Nagai. *Shining a Light: Celebrating 40 Asian Americans and Pacific Islanders Who Changed the World.* Versify, New York, 2023.

Cavanagh, Michael. *Memoirs of Gen. Thomas Francis Meagher.* Messenger, Worchester, MA, 1892.

Charles River Editors. *Baron von* Steuben, Charles River Editors.

Cheney, Margaret. *Tesla: Man out of Time.* Touchstone, New York, 1981.

Cheng, Michelle. "How Chobani swallowed 20% of the US yogurt market," *Quartz,* November 19, 2021.

Chernow, Ron. *Alexander Hamilton,* Penguin Books, New York, 2004.

Cohen, Naomi W. *Jacob Schiff: A Study in American Jewish Leadership.* Brandeis University Press, Hanover, 1999.

Coodley, Gregg and David Sarasohn. *The Green Years: When Democrats and Republicans Untied to Repair the Earth.* University Press of Kansas, Lawrence, KS, 2021.

Coodley, Gregg and David Sarasohn. *Taming Infection: The American Response to Illness from Smallpox to Covid.* Atmosphere Press, 2022.

Creel, George. "A Way to Industrial Peace," *Century Magazine*, July 1915.

Daniels, Roger. *Coming to America: A History of Immigration and Ethnicity in American Life.* Second edition, Harper Perennial, New York, 2002.

Dash, Joan. *A Life of One's Own: Three Gifted Women and the Men They Married.* Harper and Row, New York, 1973.

Doyle, Don H. *The Cause of All Nations: An International History of the American Civil War*, Basic Books, 2015.

Egan, Timothy. *Immortal Irishman: The Irish Revolutionary Who Became an American Hero.* Houghton Mifflin Harcourt, New York, 2016.

Egan, Timothy. *A Fever in the Heartland.* Viking, New York, 2023.

Eng, Dinah. "How a Family of Refugees Turned a Bakery into a Desert Powerhouse," *Fortune*, May 24, 2015.

Evans, Harold. *They Made America.* Little, Brown and Company, New York, 2004.

Fast, Howard. *Citizen Tom Paine*, Grove Press, New York, 1943.

Fay, Sarah. "Ha Jin, The art of Fiction No. 202," *The Paris Review*, Issue 191, Winter 2009.

Flood, Allison. "The Brief Wondrous Life of Oscar Wao was declared 21st century's best novel so far," *The Guardian*, January 20, 2015.

Foner, Phillip. *Mother Jones Speaks.* Monad Press, New York, 1983.

Fraser, Steven. *Sidney Hillman, Labor's Machiavelli*, in *Labor Leaders in America.* University of Illinois Press, Urbana, IL, 1987.

Fraser, Steven. *Labor Will Rule: Sidney Hillman and the Rise of American Labor.* Free Press, New York, 1991.

Frederick, Ben. "10 Influential Americans Who Came to the US as Immigrants," *The Christian Science Monitor*, March 29, 2013.

French, Allen. Review of John McAuley Palmer's *General von Steuben. The American Historical Review.* 43(4). July 1938.

Gabler, Neal. *An Empire of Their Own.* Crown Publishers, New York, 1988.

Ganguli, Tania. "Shahid Khan has true rags to riches American story," *The Florida Times-Union*, December 3, 2011.

Gee, Emma. "Issei: The First Women." *Civil Rights Digest.* Spring, 1974.

Glazer, Nathan. "Introduction," in *Clamor at the Gates*, ed. Nathan Glazer, Institute for Contemporary Studies, San Francisco, 1985.

Glenn, Mike. "Medal Of Honor recipient wasn't always celebrated," *Houston Chronicle*, August 9, 2016.

Goldman, Emma. *Red Emma Speaks.* Third edition, Ed. Alix Kate Shulman, Humanity Books, Lanham, MD, 1995.

Golway, Terry. *The Organizer: Mary "Mother" Jones*, in *Nine Irish Lives: The Fighters, Thinkers, and Artists Who Helped Build America*, ed. Mark Bailey, Algonquin Books, Chapel Hill, 2018.

Gompers, Samuel. *Seventy Years of Life and Labor: An Autobiography.* E.F. Dutton and Company, Inc, New York, 1925.

Gonzalez, Juan. *Harvest of Empire: A History of Latinos in America.* Penguin Books, New York, 2011.

Gorn, Elliott J. *Mother Jones: The Most Dangerous Woman in America.* Hill and Wang, New York, 2001.

Gould, Benjamin Apthorp. *Investigations in the Military and Anthropological Statistics of American Soldiers.* Hurd and Houghton, New York,

1869.

Greeley, Horace. *An Overland Journey from New York to San Francisco in the Summer of 1859.* New York, 1860.

Greene, Meg. *Thaddeus Kosciuszko: Polish General and Patriot.* Chelsea House Publishers, Philadelphia. 2002.

Greenhouse, Steven. *Beaten Down, Worked Up: The Past, Present and Future of American Labor.* Alfred A. Knopf, New York, 2019.

Griffith, Willam. "Andrew Carnegie, Apostle of Peace," *The New York Times,* November 6, 1904.

Grove, Andrew. *Swimming Across.* Grand Central, 2001.

Gunderson, Jessica. *Immigrants Who Built an Empire.* Capstone Press, North Mankato, MN, 2021.

Handlin, Oscar. *The Uprooted.* Little, Brown, and Company. Boston. Second edition, 1979.

Harmetz, Aljean. "Billy Wilder, Master of Caustic Films, Dies at 95," *The New York Times,* March 29, 2002.

Heligman, Deborah. *Clara Lemlich.* Philomel Books, New York, 2021.

Hill, Jim. "Actor Haing Ngor found gunned down outside LA home." CNN, February 27, 1996.

Hochschild, Adam. *American Midnight: The Great War, A Violent Peace and Democracy's Forgotten Crisis,* Mariner Books, New York, 2022.

Housel, Debra J. *Famous Immigrants.* Teacher Created Materials. Huntington Beach, CA, 2008.

Hull, Michael D. *Peter Francisco: American Revolutionary War Hero.* www.historynet.com/peter-francisco-america-revolutionary-war-hero.

Isaacson, Walter. *Einstein: His Life and Universe.* Simon and Schuster, New York, 2008.

Isaacson, Walter. *The Innovators: How a Group of Hackers, Geniuses, and Geeks Created the Digital Revolution.* Simon and Schuster, New York,

2014.

Jacoby, Tamar, ed. *Reinventing the Melting Pot: The New Immigrants and What It Means to Be American*, Basic Books, New York, 2004.

Jayyusi, Salma Khadra. *Modern Arabic Poetry: An Anthology.* Columbia University Press, New York, 1987.

Jones, Mother. *The Autobiography of Mother Jones.* Ed. Mary Field Parton, Charles H. Kerr and Company, Chicago, 1925.

Jordan, Miriam and Robert Gebeloff. "Immigration is Driving U.S. Population Growth," *The New York Times*, February 5, 2022.

Josephson, Matthew. *The Robber Barons*, Harcourt, Brace, Jovanovich, Orlando, 1914.

Kakutani, Michiko. "Books of the Times: Book Study as Insubordination Under the Mullahs," *The New York Times*, April 15, 2003.

Kamphoefner, Walter D. and Wolfgang Johanne Helbich. *Germans in the Civil War: The Letters They Wrote Home.* University of North Carolina Press, Chapel Hill, 2006.

Kane, Tim. *The Immigrant Superpower: How Brains, Brawn and Bravery Make America Stronger.* Oxford University Press, New York, 2022.

Kaplan, David A. *The Silicon Boys and the Valley of Dreams.* William Morrow and Company, Inc, New York, 1999.

Kaplan, James. *Irving Berlin: New York Genius.* Yale University Press, New Haven, 2019.

Kennedy, John F. *A Nation of Immigrants*, Harper Perennial, New York, 2008.

Ku, Leighton. "Health Insurance Coverage and Medical Expenditures of Immigrants and Native-Born Citizens in the United States," *American Journal of Public Health*, 2009. 99(7), 1322.

Laskin, David. *The Long Way Home: An American Journey from Ellis Island to the Great War.* Harper Perennial, New York, 2010.

Laslett, John H. M. *Samuel Gompers and the Rise of American Business*

Unionism, in *Labor Leaders in America*, ed. Melvyn Dubofsky and Warren Van Tine, University of Illinois Press, Urbana, IL, 1987.

Lee, Erika. *The Making of Asian America.* Simon and Schuster, New York, 2015.

Levinger, Elma E. *Albert Einstein.* Julian Messner, Inc., New York, 1949.

Lewis, David Allen. *Forgotten Patriot: The Story of Haym Salomon,* Bridges for Peace, Jerusalem, 2007.

Light, Ivan. "Immigrant Entrepreneurs in America: Koreans in Los Angeles," in *Clamor at the Gates,* ed. Nathan Glazer, Institute for Contemporary Studies, San Francisco, 1985.

Livesay, Harold C. *Samuel Gompers and Organized Labor in America.* Little, Brown, and Company. Boston. 1978.

Malone, Michael S. *The Intel Trinity.* HarperCollins Publishers, New York, 2014.

Mann, Thomas. In *Becoming Americans: Four Centuries of Immigrant Writing,* ed. Ilan Stavans, Literary Classics, New York, 2009.

Marcus, Jacob Rader. *Early American Jewry: The Jews of Pennsylvania and the South 1655–1790.* Jewish Publication Society of America, Philadelphia, 1953.

Marrin, Albert. *Thomas Paine: Crusader for Liberty,* Alfred A. Knopf, New York, 2014.

May, Gregory. *Jefferson's Treasure: How Albert Gallatin Saved the New Nation from Debt.* Regnery History. Washington, DC, 2018.

McClellan, George B. *The Armies of Europe.* Lippincott, Philadelphia, 1861.

McCourt, Frank. "Scraps and Leftovers: A Meditation," in Michael Coffey and Terry Golway, eds., *The Irish in America,* Hyperion, New York, 1997, 41.

McCraw, Thomas K. *The Founders and Finance: How Hamilton, Gallatin and Other Immigrants Forged a New Economy,* Belknap Press, 2013.

McFadden, Robert Dennis. "Joseph Brodsky, Exiled Poet Who Won Nobel, Dies at 55," *The New York Times*, January 29, 1996.

Medawar, Jean and David Pyke. *Hitler's Gift: The True Story of the Scientists Expelled by the Nazi Regime.* Arcade Publishing, New York, 2000.

Meltzer, Milton. *Voices from the Civil War.* HarperCollins Publishers, New York, 1989.

Meltzer, Milton. *Albert Einstein: A Biography.* Holiday House. New York, 2008.

Meltzer, Milton. *Taking Root: Jewish Immigrants in America.* Farrar, Strauss and Giroux, New York, 1976.

Meltzer, Milton. *Bound for America: The Story of European Immigrants.* Benchmark Books, New York, 2002.

Middlekauff, Robert. *The Glorious Cause: The American Revolution 1763–1789.* Oxford University Press, New York, 2005.

Moore, Michael. *The Muckraker: Samuel S. McClure.* in *Nine Irish Lives: The Fighters, Thinkers and Artists Who Helped Build America,* ed. Mark Bailey, Algonquin Books, Chapel Hill, 2018.

Morrison, Samuel Elliot. *John Paul Jones.* Time Incorporated, New York, 1959.

Muir, John. "Yosemite Glaciers," *New York Herald Tribune.* December 5, 1871.

Muir, John. *Our National Parks.* (Houghton Mifflin, Boston, 1901), quoted in Benjamin Kline. *First Along the River: A Brief History of the US Environmental Movement.* (Acada Books, San Francisco, 1997).

Muller, Thomas. "Economic Effects of Immigration," in *Clamor at the Gates,* ed. Nathan Glazer, Institute for Contemporary Studies, San Francisco, 1985.

Nasaw, David. *Andrew Carnegie,* Penguin Press, New York, 2006.

National Foundation for American Policy. "Immigrants and Nobel Prizes 1901–2019." NFAP Policy Brief, October 2019.

Nelson, James L. *Reign of Iron*. HarperCollins. New York, 2004.

The New York Times. "Adopted Citizens and the War," August 12, 1861.

The New York Times. "Mother Jones Defiant" March 11, 1913.

Novic, Sara. *America is Immigrants*, Random House, New York, 2019.

Nye, Joseph S. Jr. *Soft Power: The Means to Success in World Politics*. Public Affairs, New York, 2004.

Okrent, Daniel. *The Guarded Gate*. Scribner, New York, 2019.

Olson, Lynne. *Last Hope Island*. Random House, New York, 2017.

Paine, Thomas. *Common Sense*, Civic Classics, New York, 2012.

Paine, Thomas. *The Collected Writings of Thomas Paine*. Ed. Philip S. Foner, Citadel Press, New York, 1945.

Paine, Thomas. "African Slavery in America." https://www.constitution.org/2-Authors/tp/afri.htm

Painter, Nell Irvin. *The History of White People*. W.W. Norton and Company, New York, 2010.

Petersen, Peter L. *Jacob a. Riis*, in *American Portraits: History Through Biography: Volume II from 1865*. Donald W. Whisenhunt, editor, Kendall Hunt, Dubuque, IA, 1993.

Phelan, Craig. *Samuel Gompers. American Portraits: History Through Biography, volume II from 1865*. Donald W. Whisenhunt, Editor, Kendall-Hunt Publishing, Dubuque, IA, 1993.

Rampell, Catherine. "The surge in immigration is a $7 trillion gift to the economy," *The Washington Post*, February 13, 2024.

Raymond, Eric S. *The Cathedral and the Bazaar*, O'Reilly Media, 1999.

Reagan, Ronald. Https://www.reaganlibrary.gov/archives/speech/remarks-presentation-ceremony-presidential-medal-freedom-5.

Redding, Anna Crowley. *Google It: A History of Google*. Feiwel and Friends, New York, 2018.

Rein, Lisa. "A broken immigration system keeps workers out of jobs the US needs to fill," *The Washington Post*, December 21, 2023.

Rhodes, Richard. *The Making of the Atomic Bomb.* Simon and Schuster, New York, 1986.

Rodriguez, Gregory. *Reinventing the Melting Pot: The New Immigrants and What It Means to Be an American,* ed. Tamar Jacoby, Basic Books, New York, 2004.

Rose, Peter I. "Asian Americans: From Pariahs to Paragons," in *Clamor at the Gates,* ed. Nathan Glazer, institute of Contemporary Studies, San Francisco, 1985.

Salins, Peter D. *Reinventing the Melting Pot: The New Immigrants and What It Means to Be American,* ed. Tamar Jacoby, Basic Books, New York, 2004.

Savage, Charlie, Maggie Haberman, and Jonathan Swan. "Sweeping Raids, Giant Camps and Mass Deportations: Inside Trump's 2025 Immigration Plans." *The New York Times,* July 12, 2023.

Savona, David. "Death of a Master: Jose Orlando Padron." *Cigar Aficionado.* December 5, 2017.

Scarpaci, Vincenza. *The Journey of the Italians in America.* Pelican Publishing, Gretna, LA, 2009.

Schatz, Ronald. *Phillip Murray and the Subordination of the Industrial Unions to the United States Government,* in *Labor Leaders in America,* ed. Melvyn Dubofsky and Warren Van Tine, University of Illinois Press, Urbana, IL, 1987.

Schneider, Mike. "Immigration Fuels Uptick in US Population Growth." *The Washington Post,* December 19, 2023.

Schonberg, Harold. "Critic's Notebook: Repertory of Legends Immortalizes Jascha Heifetz." *The New York Times,* December 28, 1987.

Schwartz, Ella. *Stolen Science.* Bloomsbury Children's Books, New York, 2021.

Sella, Andrea. "Kyrides' Seal," *Chemistry World,* July 30, 2021.

Shteyngart, Gary. *Reinventing the Melting Pot: The New Immigrants and What It Means to Be American,* ed. Tamar Jacoby, Basic Books, New York, 2004.

Stark, Peter. *Astoria.* HarperCollins, New York, 2015.

Stavans, Ilan, ed. *Becoming Americans: Four Centuries of Immigrant Writing,* Literary Classics, New York, 2009.

Steinberg, Stephen. *Reinventing the Melting Pot: The New Immigrants and What It Means to Be American,* ed. Tamar Jacoby, Basic Books, New York, 2004.

Seward, William. *Circular 19.* August 8, 1862. Foreign Relations of the United States 1861–65, University of Wisconsin Digital Collections. http://uwdc.library.wisc.edu/collections.FRUS

Sowell, Thomas. *Ethnic America: A History.* Basic Books, New York, 1981.

Sparshott, Jeffrey. "Immigration Study Sees More Pros Than Cons." *Wall Street Journal.* September 23, 2016.

Swaby, Rachel. *Headstrong: 52 Women Who Changed Science—and the World.* Broadway Books, New York, 2015.

Tavernise, Sabrina. "For Medicare, Immigrants Offer Surplus, Study Finds." *The New York Times.* May 30, 2013.

Teitelbaum, Michael S. "Forced Migration: The Tragedy of Mass Expulsions," in *Clamor at the Gates,* ed. Nathan Glazer, Institute for Contemporary Studies, San Francisco, 1985.

Thernstrom, Stephen. *Reinventing the Melting Pot: The New Immigrants and What It Means to Be American.* Ed. Tamar Jacoby, Basic Books, 2004.

Tuchman, Barbara. *The Proud Tower.* The MacMillan Company, New York, 1962.

Twain, Mark. *Roughing It.* New York, 1882.

Udall, Stewart. *The Quiet Crisis and the Next Generation.* Gibbs Smith, Layton, UT, 1988.

Ungar, Sanford J. *Fresh Blood: The New American Immigrants.* University of Illinois Press, Urbana, 1998.

United States Congressional Budget Office, "The Impact of Unauthorized Immigrants on the Budgets of State and Local Governments," December 2007

Valderrama, Carla. *This was Hollywood: Forgotten Stars and Stories.* Running Press, Philadelphia, 2020.

Valdes, Marcela, "Why Can't We Stop Unauthorized Immigration? Because It Works," *The New York Times,* October 1, 2023.

Weisberger, Mindy. "Eleven Immigrant Scientists Who Made Great Contributions to America," *LiveScience,* February 7, 2017.

Welsh, Peter. *Irish Green and Union Blue: The Civil War Letters of Peter Welsh, Color Sergeant, 28th Regiment, Massachusetts Volunteers.* Fordham University Press, New York, 1986.

White, Richard. *Railroaded: The Transcontinentals and the Making of Modern America.* W.W. Norton and Company, New York, 2011.

Wildavsky, Ben. *The Great Brain Race: How Global Universities are Reshaping the* World. Princeton University Press, Princeton, NJ, 2011.

Williams, John Hoyt. *A Great and Shining Road: The Epic Story of the Transcontinental Railroad.* University of Nebraska Press, Lincoln, 1988.

Yang, Jia Lynn. *One Mighty and Irresistible Tide.* W.W. Norton and Company, New York, 2020.

Zakaria, Fareed. *The Post-American World.* W.W. Norton and Company. New York. 2008.

Zeitz, Joshua. *Building the Great Society: Inside Lyndon Johnson's White House.* Viking, New York, 2018.

Index

About Atmosphere Press

Founded in 2015, Atmosphere Press was built on the principles of Honesty, Transparency, Professionalism, Kindness, and Making Your Book Awesome. As an ethical and author-friendly hybrid press, we stay true to that founding mission today.

If you're a reader, enter our giveaway for a free book here:

SCAN TO ENTER
BOOK GIVEAWAY

If you're a writer, submit your manuscript for consideration here:

SCAN TO SUBMIT
MANUSCRIPT

And always feel free to visit Atmosphere Press and our authors online at atmospherepress.com. See you there soon!

About the Author

GREGG COODLEY is a primary care doctor and director of the Fanno Creek Clinic. He is the author of five prior histories, most recently *Patients in Peril: The Demise of Primary Care in America*.